Praise for NOURISHMENT

"This extraordinarily well-written autobiography should be a 'must' read for all affected by Tourette and obsessive compulsive disorder as well as those involved in the care of such patients and involved in research into neurobehavioral disorders. The book not only provides personal insights into these disorders but also conveys hope to those touched by neurological and mental illness. Melissa's story is compelling and inspirational."

> —**Joseph Jankovic, M.D.**, Professor of Neurology and Director of
> Movement Disorders Clinic at Baylor College of Medicine

"*Nourishment* is a must read for everyone. This autobiography truly shows the power of one person's struggle to embrace these complex psychological and neurological disorders. Melissa writes with such passion that it was difficult putting this book down. I found myself moved by her ability to continue on despite all the setbacks and complications. This book truly inspired me and was at the same time a spiritual experience."

> —**Ira M. Sacker, M.D.**, Eating Disorders Specialist
> and Author of *Regaining Your Self* and *Dying to Be Thin*

"Melissa Binstock tells a complex story about the intersecting psychological and neurological problems she suffered as a child. I found her story so compelling that I used it in my course on pathography in a doctoral seminar. Parents, children, school teachers, psychologists, psychoanalysts, and professors of education will certainly be interested in the way that this extremely gifted young person worked through her issues."

> —**Dr. Marla Morris**, Associate Professor of
> Education at Georgia Southern University

"(*Nourishment*) had some elements of my own life, which both terrified me and gave me hope. . . . (My son) and I are still working on rebuilding a relationship. He saw me as the pill-pusher and also felt unloved and unworthy—especially since I always seemed to be sending him away somewhere. . . . As (the book) implies, the 'cure' is not so easily reached but is on-going and a matter of degrees. Hurrah on receiving your pretty package—life!"

—**Cindy Sacks**, Executive Assistant
for the Tourette Syndrome Association of Texas

"This world needs more real, authentic heroes. Melissa Binstock is one. In *Nourishment*, she shows all of us—regardless of our particular struggles in life—that hurdles are meant for overcoming and freedom can be chosen in each moment. Thanks, Melissa, for not giving up on yourself and for sharing your experience so that we might not quit either."

—**Jenni Schaefer**, Author of *Goodbye Ed,
Hello Me* and *Life Without Ed*

"I can truly relate to feeling worthless; feeling unloved by a parent and seeking love and acceptance from another; being tired of feeling sick and in pain; worrying about what others think of me while trying to fit in; experiencing side effects from various antidepressants; and many of the other experiences Melissa went through. Unlike some other books on eating disorders, *Nourishment* really touched my heart."

—**Tiffany Salinas,** Student

"Melissa Binstock takes us on a voyeuristic journey to expose the quiet, controlled silence of young women who suffer the stigma of neurological and psychiatric disorders. This is a gripping ride, and her life experiences illustrate our commonality; we are all forces of spirit, striving to glide over intense, complicated, painful barriers to gain the real prize—a joyful life. You will be inspired, changed, humbled, and all the wiser as you, too, come to realize that perfection isn't measured by caloric nourishment but by loving and being loved."

—**Elizabeth S. Dybell, Ph.D.**, Clinical Psychologist

NOURISHMENT

FEEDING MY STARVING SOUL WHEN

MY MIND AND BODY BETRAYED ME

MELISSA BINSTOCK

Health Communications, Inc.
Deerfield Beach, Florida

www.bcibooks.com

Library of Congress Cataloging-in-Publication Data

Binstock, Melissa.
  Nourishment : feeding my starving soul when my mind and body betrayed me/
Melissa Binstock.
     p. cm.
  ISBN-13: 978-0-7573-1542-8
  ISBN-10: 0-7573-1542-9
  1. Binstock, Melissa—Mental health. 2. Mentally ill—Biography. I. Title.
[DNLM: 1. Mentally Ill Persons—Personal Narratives. 2. Anorexia Nervosa—
Personal Narratives. 3. Attention Deficit Disorder with Hyperactivity—Personal
Narratives. 4. Learning Disorders—Personal Narratives. 5. Obsessive-
Compulsive Disorder—Personal Narratives. 6. Tourette Syndrome—Personal
Narratives. [WM 40]
  RC464.B56A3 2011
  362.196'890092—dc22
  [B]
                                                              2010039690

Publisher: Health Communications, Inc.
3201 S.W. 15th Street
Deerfield Beach, FL 33442-8190

Author photo by Mark Katz
Cover design by Lawna Patterson Oldfield
Inside book design and formatting by Dawn Von Strolley Grove

To my loving parents
Cathy and Bob Binstock:
Without your undying care and support,
I know I would not be here today.
Thank you for standing by me
through the years, thank you
for never giving up, and most of all,
thank you for loving me.

Contents

FOREWORD

As a psychiatrist, a parent, and someone who knows Melissa and her family, I found *Nourishment* fascinating on many levels. It is a story about the insidious onset of mental illness and the ebb and flow of that disease over time. It is a story about treatment, treatment facilities, and treatment professionals, both good and bad. It is a story about being different and how that differentness is viewed, tolerated, and often abused by others. It is a comment on tolerance; as a society, we often have trouble accepting, making adjustments for, and listening to someone who is a little different— even if, or maybe particularly when, that person is a child. It is about life, reality, dealing with the hand that one is dealt, and managing one's expectations—as a child, a parent, or a concerned outsider.

But mostly it is a story about love and hope. Even when Melissa's situation seems hopeless, her family's support never wavers—even when she shuns them, thinks their support is toxic, and eventually avoids them altogether as her disease progresses. As Melissa takes us along through her ups and downs and the fleeting moments of hope that come crashing down again and again, the reality of the interplay between psychic turmoil, physical illness, and real-life events becomes palpable.

Melissa details the development of her eating disorder from its beginning: a young girl's attempt to control *something* when she feels out of control and is slowly losing what little she has as the disease takes over. That she has been able to heal and write so movingly about that time is a tribute to the fortitude of her desire to move forward in her life and become content.

Melissa's story is also a comment on medicine, psychiatry, and the pharmaceutical industry. It is incredible that large pharmaceutical companies help us hope (if not believe) that medicine will fix everything, yet this adolescent patient attempted to identify the destructive effects of many of the medications she was given and no one would listen to her because of her youth. Sadly, Melissa also experienced the "art" in psychiatry—there is not just one recommended treatment for a problem—and her story reflects the lack of accountability that often occurs in all branches of medicine. Therapists, for example, often cannot keep their own agendas and baggage out of their work, and as Melissa details, this negatively affects the weak, needy, and vulnerable who are under their care. That Melissa was able to persist through this process, recognize what did and did not work for her, and then move on is a tribute to her inner strength.

Finally, and most important, this is a story about a family's unwavering love and support, even when they didn't always know what to do. Today it appears that their persistence and tenacity have paid off. While some of Melissa's early hopes and dreams (specifically, to become an Olympic equestrian) did not work out, she has written a book of Olympian proportions about her struggles and challenges. Melissa's journey to make sense out of what was happening to her and about her attempt to extricate herself from it (or at least make the pain seem meaningful) is an incredible one.

—**George S. Glass, M.D.**, Clinical Associate Professor of
Psychiatry at the Baylor College of Medicine in Houston
and the University of Texas Medical School in Houston.

PROLOGUE

By the time I was eleven years old, I'd taken at least fourteen medications, seen ten doctors, been diagnosed with six disorders, and gone to five schools. I guess you could say my childhood was not particularly normal. Through the nineteen years I've been alive, more of my time has been spent in doctors' offices, treatment centers, and hospitals than with friends. After coming home from my first treatment center at the age of fifteen, I decided the time had come to try to make sense of everything. And so I began the long endeavor of digging into my past, pulling up old memories from my childhood, and putting the pieces of my life back together. Another hospitalization and schoolwork interrupted my writing. I started writing again at the age of eighteen, at which point I ordered some of my past medical records.

I suppose you could say my endeavor was the equivalent of opening up Pandora's box. It's true—by writing everything down, I did have to replay every painful incident. But I didn't just want to try to understand what happened to me; I needed to understand to get well. In truth, writing has become one of my most central forms of nourishment.

I'm about to enter my junior year in college with the hope that I will be able to overcome whatever obstacles get tossed in my path.

However, what I cannot do is sit here and tell you honestly that I'm all better now; that would be a lie. Every day is still a struggle for me, but then again, who goes through life without struggles? What I *can* do is tell you that there is hope. The dyslexic girl with Tourette syndrome whose eating disorder almost claimed her life was able to complete her freshman and sophomore years of college as an honors student with all As.

(Not a) Cookie-Cutter Child

1

You know that excited feeling you have when you're little, as you wait on the front doorstep for the mail carrier to bring you a package? Every afternoon right when you get home from school, you run out and sit on that step for hours until the mail carrier tells you, "Sorry, nothing today." At first, you are hopeful and tell yourself that tomorrow will be the day. Then days turn into weeks and weeks turn into months; you begin to give up hope. It's been almost twelve years now, and I'm still sitting on my front doorstep waiting for my package to arrive. It's been so long that, for a while, I even forgot what was in that package. But today I know exactly what I have been sitting around waiting for: I have been waiting to live. LIFE is what that package contains, and once I have it securely in my hands, I know I won't ever let it go again.

I wasn't a cookie-cutter child; I didn't fit into the same mold as my eight-year-old friends. At least that's what having dyslexia and Tourette syndrome felt like to me. In second grade, my stomach twisted in knots every time the teacher asked the class to take out our readers. I came to detest those books about Jill and Jack with their dog, Spot. Who names their dog Spot anyway? The words printed on the pages of my reader were like puzzles my mind tried to solve but never could. As the teacher went around the room, calling on different people to read a passage aloud, I'd pretend to be invisible while praying that she'd skip over me. Eventually, the teacher would call out my name. The routine was always the same: I'd sit there for a few minutes making *thhh* or *mmm* sounds as I tried to sound out words like *those* or *much*. The teacher would stand in front of me with both hands planted firmly on her hips, tapping a foot up and down impatiently. Then, after I'd made a few hopeless attempts, she'd skip over me and move on to the next kid.

By midway through the year, not only had my reading skills failed to improve, but also I refused even to try sounding out a word when I was called on. The *harrumph* noise that escaped from my vexed teacher's mouth didn't bother me as much as the feeling of embarrassment and the sound of snickering classmates. When my parents realized that my reading problem wasn't something I would eventually work around, they decided to have me tested for a learning disorder. After running through a battery of tests, the specialist diagnosed me with dyslexia and suggested my parents look into placing me at a school for children with learning disabilities. My parents' decision to move me to a special school was encouraged by the principal, who told them the school was ill equipped to deal with children like me. A few years later, they also removed my younger sister, Samantha, from the same school. I say *removed* because the way she was treated resembles how people handle old, unwanted pieces of furniture they throw out the front door for the garbage man to pick up. I guess the school based its philosophy not so much on teaching, but on manufacturing cookie-cutter children. My sister and I didn't exactly fit into the school's ideal mold, though, because I couldn't read and Sam had cerebral palsy.

Of the three girls in the family, I would consider my older sister, Brooke, the "normal" child. Brooke was popular, smart, pretty, and accepted. Everything about her seemed so right, whereas Sam and I were sort of a mess. Sam stopped breathing when she was born, which caused mild brain damage. Primarily her motor skills had been affected, which turned walking into an arduous task. When Sam turned four, she had surgery to help her walk; the aftermath of that surgery was a painful experience for the entire family. I hated hearing her cry out in pain whenever she tried to take a step forward. Her piercing cries sent Brooke and me running into the safety of our small bedroom to escape the horrible noise. Ironically, it was because of Sam's disability that I was able to find my greatest love—horses. Brooke and I began taking riding lessons after my mother discovered a type of equine therapy that would ameliorate some of Sam's pain and relax her taut muscles. I fell in love with those gentle giants the very first time I walked into the barn. I liked the way my pony's sleek coat felt against my fingertips, and how the aroma of sweet hay filled the barn aisles. After a while, my pony's stall became my safe house, providing me with an escape from teasing kids and staring adults.

⁓

As the end of the school year approached, my ever-increasing anxiety about my inability to read only made my tics grow worse. It felt as though a battle was being waged between me and some other person who was relentlessly fighting to gain control of my body and mind. This fight for control became my new focus.

During class, I spent most of my time concentrating on making my body sit as still as possible. Every tic became a signal that I was losing the battle, causing a fresh wave of anxiety to rush over my body. I began to look for different ways I could at least control the things around me. I started organizing the books and pencils I kept in my desk at school. Books had to be arranged in a specific order, with the largest on the bottom and smallest on top. Each pencil needed to be perfectly sharpened, aligned, and ordered by length in the plastic pencil holder. *Books, pencils, pens; books, pencils, pens*—I'd repeat the mantra to myself as I went through the checklist of items that needed to be in order before I could begin working on an assignment.

Controlling books and pencils didn't satisfy me for long, though. What I really wanted was control over myself and, to me, the most obvious way to do this was by regulating what I ate. At first, I thought that by controlling what foods went into my mouth I'd be able to feel in control of my body again. The whole process was delightfully simple; I could choose to eat the grilled cheese sandwich my mother made for my lunch, or I could choose not to eat it. Generally, I preferred the latter since not eating provided me with a greater sense of control. I'd have to work actively at keeping the hunger pangs at bay, and yet the decision was entirely mine . . . or so I thought.

My parents noticed my apparent lack of appetite. At first, they thought I was going through one of those phases children sometimes go through. After all, I had always been a finicky eater, so my declarations of *I'm a vegetarian now*, and *I don't eat dessert anymore* weren't too far from the norm. With time, though, my parents came to realize that this wasn't just a phase—a phase didn't cause hip bones to jut out and ribs to protrude. Yet, my mother's suggestions of "Try a little more of this" or "Eat some of that" were always met by my protests of "I'm not hungry" or "I just ate," causing her to grow frustrated and drop the topic.

As my weight continued to drop, my mother's increasing concern caused her to approach my pediatrician to ask her if it was possible for a child my age to have an eating disorder. The pediatrician's reply was simple: "No, Mrs. Binstock, she's too young for that."

⌘

Eventually eating was no longer a choice for me. My mind became accustomed to denying food to my body. Even when I tried to eat, I was paralyzed by an inner voice that seemed to belong to a different person, yet somehow still resided within me. At first, this Sick Person merely whispered about gaining control over my mind and body. Over the course of several months, her whispers turned into hisses of failure and an inability to do anything right. And soon enough, those hisses escalated into screams of *Disgusting!* and *How can you feed your body when it's already layered with fat?* These were the messages I began hearing in my mind each time I tried to take a bite of food. After a meal, her voice became so loud that no other sound could be heard.

I tried to busy myself with whatever I could to distract myself from the Sick Person's cries. If my mother couldn't drive me to the barn, I turned to cleaning my saddle or organizing the tote full of horse brushes. I began cleaning my saddle so often that an oily residue started building up on the leather, which caused my riding pants to turn a putrid orange color. Once there was nothing left to clean or arrange, I had to find something else to do. I turned to pacing up and down the hallway next to the bedroom I shared with

Brooke, trying to think of a way to block out the thoughts. But no matter what I did or where I went, the insidious chant of *fat, fat, fat, control, control, control* followed me. Finally, out of desperation, I'd run into the bathroom, curl up in a ball on the floor, put both hands over my ears, and scream. I thought that maybe if I screamed loud enough, I'd be able to drown out the Sick Person's voice. But it was too late; she had already taken over.

It had only taken her six months to do so.

MELISSA, MEET MELISSA

2

At first, I thought of the Sick Person in my head as a kind of bully who got her pleasure out of tormenting me. We lived together in this one body, but I could tell we were two separate people. The real danger came when I began hearing her voice so often that the lines became blurry, making it hard for me to tell if we were one person or two.

Living with the Sick Person's tormenting voice was like having a part of myself that I really don't like, but in this case, that part of me was actually dangerous. As I look back now, I see similarities between myself with my eating disorder (i.e., the Sick Person) and a person with a drug addiction. I struggle with myself about whether to eat. The drug addict struggles with herself about whether to use drugs. Sometimes the healthy part of her wins out, but often the sick part of her does.

This merging of two girls was aided by the fact that I couldn't seem to see my body's proportions accurately. When I stood in front of the mirror, my stomach literally looked like it was expanding in front of me; my pants even felt tighter. The Sick Person's threats had come true. My body was growing larger before my eyes, and I was losing control.

My day became a strict routine of when to eat, what to eat, how much to eat, and what not to eat. I was only eight; I had no idea what calories or carbohydrates were. What I could understand was fat and sugar. I began to play around with numbers in my head, only allowing myself to eat things that had no more than twelve grams of sugar in them. The same rule was also applied to fat, but because fat seemed worse to me than sugar, I allowed myself only twelve grams of fat *per day* instead of *per item*. Twelve seemed like a good safe number. It was not too big or too small—it was just right.

The sack lunches I packed for the barn grew smaller. Peanut butter and jelly sandwiches turned into jelly sandwiches. Cookies turned into apples, which I fed to the horses or gave away. Mornings turned into a battle between the bedroom mirror and me. I put on shirt after shirt, trying to find one that didn't make me look huge. Eventually, I started wearing the same shirt every day because every other shirt made me look too big. The kids at the barn teased me while others tried to persuade me to change shirts, but no matter what they said, I just couldn't do it. I was convinced that my stomach was huge, and somehow this magical shirt helped hide the fat. At the time, I was eight years old, four feet eleven inches tall, and I weighed sixty-five pounds. God help me.

Sometimes I'd wake up in the morning and be content with what I saw in the mirror. On those good days, I could separate myself from the bullying Sick Person and I was daring enough to try to trick her. Since "the rules" said I could only consume something that had no more than twelve grams of sugar, water became the only acceptable drink. I sometimes allowed myself a small amount of milk if it was fat-free. I loved orange juice very dearly. I liked the citrusy smell and the feeling of pulp running down my throat. Nevertheless, orange juice has twenty-six grams of sugar, making it a big NO on my list. But if it was a good day and I didn't look too big, I would get up early in the morning and make myself fresh-squeezed juice. In my mind, I told the Sick Person that my fresh orange juice couldn't possibly have the same amount of sugar as the kind from the store because I hoped to trick her into thinking I was consuming less than I actually was. I was certain the producers of the juice poured in extra bags of sugar and other unhealthy things when making it. I might have had a suspicion that this was not the case, but the Sick Person never found out.

With the end of my second-grade school year came the usual grueling heat and humidity that never failed to accompany summer in Texas. I wanted the lazy summer days Brooke and I spent at the barn to last forever, and I dreaded the thought of beginning at another new school once fall came. Of course, I loved summer vacation for the same reasons other kids did. Getting a break from the mundane school days was always a treat, and I could spend my time doing things I enjoyed. However, my main reason for looking forward to the break was somewhat different from that of other kids. To me, summer was about finding relief from my tics, and about horses—especially Bailey.

Although she was just a lesson pony at the barn, I loved every-thing about Bailey. She was a tiny pony with soft brown eyes and a black coat that felt like silk beneath my hands. She was feisty and spirited, and I loved how she launched into a canter at the slightest touch of my heels and how she always cleared the fences with room to spare. Most of all, I loved how Bailey was always there for me.

Caring for her and riding her is a childhood memory so dear to me; this was a time when I actually felt alive and secure in my own skin.

Every morning right after getting to the barn, I'd wander out into the large horse field to catch Bailey. She was always in the very back part of the field, but I never had to walk far because as soon as she heard me calling her name, she'd come trotting toward me. After grabbing hold of Bailey, I'd tie my lead line around both sides of her halter and jump onto her sleek back. As she launched into a canter, I pretended to be a jockey, leaning low over her small neck while pumping my hands up and down to the motion of her steady gait. With my heels encouraging her onward, Bailey would extend each leg as much as her little body would allow. I enjoyed feeling the hot air lick at my face as we made our way through the field.

❧

One hot afternoon in the middle of the summer, our friend Laura invited Brooke and I to spend the night at her house. Brooke was ecstatic about the idea. I tried to act as excited as my sister was, but inside I was horrified. I had never been to Laura's house and didn't know what kind of food would be there for me to eat. I could hear the hissing of the Sick Person's voice as she warned me about going to an unfamiliar house. *How can you go to Laura's house when you know she won't have anything for you to eat? No, don't go. Stay at home where it's safe.* I knew I would probably be sorry later, yet my desire to be like Brooke overpowered anything the Sick Person said. The threatening thoughts continued to race through my mind, but no one noticed because by then I had mastered the art of hiding what I felt. I had recently developed a strategy I turned to whenever I was around other people. To avoid feeling overwhelmed by a flood of negative emotions, I'd distract myself by pretending I was on a stage performing a play. I even had a title for my play, calling it *Everything's Just Fine.* Each act would consist of me playing a normal, happy girl who was *just fine.* The make-believe play helped me mask my true emotions and subdue the pain of the Sick Person's relentless torments.

By the time we got to Laura's house, it was already late afternoon. I could feel the familiar gnawing sensation that accompanies hunger as my stomach began to ask for food. After dropping our bags off in Laura's bedroom, Brooke and I followed Laura as she trotted down the stairs.

"Do you girls want something to eat?" Laura's mom called out from the living room. I cringed at the mention of food. Since I was trying to ignore the sounds of my hungry belly, food was the last thing I wanted to think about. As we sat down at the dinner table, I could hear the Sick Person whisper into my ear. *Ask for water. Just chug a few glasses and you'll feel better. Go on! Trick the stomach into thinking it's full.* By the time I had downed two tall glasses of water, the pizzas Laura's mom had ordered for us arrived. As Brooke and Laura chewed on the greasy, cheese-covered bread, I sat watching in awe. I felt as though I was witnessing some extraordinary event. *How do they do it? What great skills do they possess that I lack?* I didn't know. All I could do was lick my lips and sip water, afraid to eat or touch anything else. I kept thinking that somehow the grease from the pizza had gotten onto the plate of vegetables that were sitting on the kitchen table. I lifted my hand to my mouth, intending to bite a nail but then thought that maybe I had somehow gotten grease on my hand.

Laura's mom kept asking me if I wanted something else to eat. Finally, she placed a peanut butter sandwich in front of me. My stomach growled as my mouth filled with saliva. I tore at the crust of the bread, lifting it to my mouth for a moment before dropping it back onto the plate. The Sick Person's screams were just too loud. No matter how hard I tried, I couldn't drown out her insidious chants of *fat, fat, fat, control, control, control!*

The next morning, Laura, Brooke, and I got up early so we would make it to the barn in time for our morning lesson. As we made our way down the stairs, the smell of homemade waffles and maple syrup filled the air. I didn't even attempt to ask the Sick Person for permission to eat a waffle. There was no point because I knew what the answer would be. Instead, I sat at the table and watched as Brooke poured thick, golden syrup onto a waffle that was coated in powdered sugar. Closing my eyes, I sat back in my chair and inhaled deeply, trying to fill my empty belly with the sweet aroma. That was the day I began to teach myself to enjoy food through smell instead of taste, knowing it would be the closest way for me to "consume" food without having to actually fill my stomach with it.

Once I was back at the barn, my body felt weak but my mind was at ease. The Sick Person's voice didn't chastise me because nothing had passed through my stomach to throw her into a rage. I hadn't eaten anything in nearly two days. My body felt light, almost as if it wasn't there at all. After riding Bailey, I walked to the equipment room to put my saddle away. The swarming black spots that appeared before my eyes made my knees wobble beneath the weight of the saddle I carried in my arms. I tried to lift the saddle up to place it on a rack; although it usually felt light, the saddle now felt like a 100-pound lead weight in my arms, causing both my knees to buckle. I fell in a heap on the equipment-room floor with the saddle lying across my chest. I'd had hunger pangs and the occasional dizzy spell before, but this was the first time I actually collapsed from not eating. Lying on the floor, I began to panic, fearing that I was going to die then and there.

Although I hate the feeling of a racing pulse and tightening muscles that accompany fear, I have also learned that fear can sometimes be my greatest ally. It was because of fear that I finally gave in and called my mother so I could go home to eat something. Once at home, I binged on cantaloupe and watermelon, knowing the Sick Person would return with a vengeance, but too damn tired and scared to care.

THE UNTAMEABLE BEAST

3

Like Pablo Picasso's blue and red periods, I suppose you could say that the summer before third grade marked the beginning of my white period. That was a period of time when I only ate white foods. Pasta, Cheerios, and cauliflower—those were my staples. My strict diet would sometimes make my mother so frustrated that she'd tell me I was turning the house into a jail where only three foods were served. If only she knew that, at the time, I really was becoming a prisoner of my own body and mind. Although my mother was concerned about my eating habits, she was comforted by the fact that I was at least eating something, and by the pediatrician's reassurance that I was just going through a phase. After all, Brooke had struggled with overeating for a while, and she had gotten over that problem. Mom decided my issues with food would blow over, too. No one in my family knew what was circulating in my head because I couldn't tell them. The only thing they could see was my odd behavior and lack of body fat.

Just before school started again, my family decided to take a road trip to San Antonio. We woke up early in the morning, piled into the car, and were on our way before 11:00 AM. As I sat in the backseat with my sisters, I jiggled my feet nervously. Lunchtime was approaching, which meant we were going to have to stop to eat pretty soon.

"Are you guys getting hungry?" My mother's question only intensified my anxiety.

Brook answered for both of us. "Yeah, when can we stop? The only place I've seen so far is that barbeque restaurant we passed." I wanted to put my hand over Brooke's mouth to make her stop talking. A barbeque restaurant—what could I possibly eat there? Because we were still two hours outside of San Antonio and there wasn't anywhere else to eat, my dad turned the car around and headed back toward the place Brooke had mentioned. Ten minutes later, we pulled into the parking lot of a dilapidated building with a sign in the front window that read STEVE'S FINGER LICKING BAR-B-Q. As I followed my parents into the restaurant, the aroma of cooked meat hit my nose. The smell sent a cold wave of anxiety surging through my body, making each hair on my arms stand on end. At the same time, though, I could feel my stomach grumbling in response to the smell of food. Physically, I was starving, but psychologically, I wanted nothing to do with food.

A hostess wearing a stereotypical Texas cowboy hat and boots greeted us and showed us to a table near the back of the restaurant. As my mother read the menu aloud, I sat on the edge of my chair, praying that there would be something for me to eat.

Please let there be something safe! Please, please! It was as though I was praying to the food gods, begging them with all my might to help me. When I heard my mother say they had baked potatoes, I let out a sigh of relief and sank back into my chair. Baked potatoes were safe enough if they didn't have anything on them. A few minutes later, the same woman who had greeted us came back to take our orders. When she got to me, I ordered a potato with a whole bunch of nothing on it.

Before I was done clarifying that I wanted absolutely nothing on the potato, the waitress interrupted, "Sorry kid, we don't serve potatoes on Thursday." My mouth slammed shut as soon as I processed what she'd said. I could feel the hairs on the back of my neck stand on edge. Panicked, I picked up the menu, trying to find something else Before I could even sound out the first item listed, my mother grabbed the menu out of my hand and told the waitress, "She'll have chicken soup." Without even thinking, the words "I won't eat that" flew out of my mouth. I said it again and again, but no one seemed to hear my voice. My sisters just kept staring at me as if I was some sort of nut case. After the waitress left the table, the smile slowly faded from my mother's face as she turned to me.

"Melissa, you're too skinny. I can see your ribs. If you don't start eating, we're going to put you in the hospital, and if you go to the hospital, there will be no horse for you!" When she told me I was *too skinny*, the words *thank-you* passed through my mind as if I had just received the best compliment anyone could ask for. But that was before hearing *no horse*. I didn't so much care about the threat of hospitalization as I did about losing my pony.

"I'll eat, I'll eat, I swear! Don't take Bailey away!" Tears began to run down my face and I licked my lips, the taste of salt evident on my tongue. When the waitress came back with our food, I played with my paper napkin, pretending to be invisible. Yet no matter how much I wanted to, I couldn't disappear. My mother kept throwing me anxious looks.

Maybe she'll stop staring at you if you just pretend to eat, the Sick

Person cooed in my ear. A half smile spread over my face as I reached for my silverware. I began playing with my spoon, filling it with broth and then turning it over so the greasy liquid splashed back into the bowl. The game, though, didn't stop my mother from glaring at me, and it certainly didn't put an end to the hunger that was gnawing at my insides.

Without looking up, I knew my mother's eyes were still fixed on me. I picked up the spoon again and dipped it into the steaming broth. Before opening my mouth, I made sure there wasn't any chicken mixed in with the broth I'd ladled out. Soon enough, though, my mother saw through my plan to avoid the meat and snapped, "You need to eat some of that chicken."

I could have fought with her, but I decided against it. I was too afraid of losing my pony, and tired of arguing with words that just seemed useless. By now, I had resigned myself to the Sick Person, who convinced me that no one would understand what I wanted to achieve. Sitting at that table made me feel like a foreigner surrounded by natives, unsure of their dialect; they didn't understand my language and I couldn't speak theirs. All we could do was use body language to show our frustration.

After giving my mother a few angry glares, I dipped my spoon into the murky broth again, filling it with both the brown liquid and pieces of chicken. I let the broth slide down my throat but kept the pieces of chicken lodged in my cheeks, like a squirrel holding nuts. Then I raised a napkin to my face to feign wiping my mouth and spit out the chicken into the napkin. My parents probably knew what I was doing, but they didn't say anything about the chicken bits that fell on the floor when we stood up to leave.

Attempting to control what I ate all the time made me feel even more out of control. Thoughts of gaining weight flooded my mind after every meal. I felt powerless over the Sick Person's incessant cries of *fat, fat, fat,* and the way I felt physically didn't help to reassure me that I wasn't expanding. After eating, the skin around my stomach would feel like it was being stretched out to make room for the fat molecules that would soon accumulate there. Panic sent me running from room to room so I could observe my body in different mirrors. I'd turn to the side, count each of the ribs, turn back, and then poke at the stomach that never looked quite small enough. The ritual usually lasted about twenty minutes. If I performed the ritual just right, I would be able to leave the house feeling somewhat satisfied with my size. Occasionally though, my obsessive thoughts and feelings of dread couldn't be assuaged by the mirror inspection, and I wouldn't be able to leave the house at all.

The beginning of third grade coincided with an increase in the frequency and intensity of my tics. The new twitching movements in my face made my desire for control grow stronger, but I was at a loss as to how to achieve that control. As the month of October drew to a close, my third-grade teacher, Mrs. Leonard, invited the class to a Halloween party. Mrs. Leonard was the first teacher I really liked. She was a young, vibrant woman who always seemed to be smiling. I loved sitting in her classroom, which was full of brightly decorated ornaments and wall posters that made everything feel cheerful and alive.

The night before the party I picked out my outfit, which only meant selecting a pair of jeans since I wore the same faded red and brown striped shirt every day. Wearing that same shirt was comforting to me, as I thought the colors and shape of the shirt safely hid the fat I believed was accumulating underneath. When I got home from the barn the next afternoon, I quickly took off the pair of riding pants and oversized shirt I had worn and folded them neatly on my bed. I picked up the blue jeans I'd chosen and examined the width of the waistline, trying to determine whether I was thin enough for them. As I pulled the pants on, I rubbed both hands against my hipbones that jutted out to either side. I smiled to myself as the Sick Person's voice praised me for not having to unzip the zipper of my pants to put them on. I picked my shirt up from the bed and began examining it, checking to see how big it was and how much smaller it—and I—should be. Before putting on the shirt, I glanced at the four-way mirror in front of me, noticing the visible backbone and ribs protruding from a half-naked body.

Adhering to my normal dressing routine, I ran both hands down my sides, feeling the indents between each rib bone. After putting my shirt on, I turned to stand in front of the mirror. I kept my eyes closed for a moment, hoping to open them and see someone acceptable staring back at me. I had no idea that *acceptable* really meant *not there*; at this point, I did not recognize that the Sick Person's death wish and determination to haunt me wasn't going to shut up until there was nothing left of my body or me.

When I opened my eyes again, I analyzed the girl peering back at me in the mirror. Her face made twitching movements and both her eyes blinked haphazardly. As I focused my glance downward, I saw a body that looked misshapen with a stomach that seemed too round and soft. *Disgusting! How can you let people see something so disgusting! Cover up! Hide yourself!* The Sick Person's voice caused a wave of panic to flood my body, sending me running into the bathroom down the hall to look in another mirror. Again, I closed my eyes for a moment, praying I wouldn't hear the Sick Person screaming once I opened my eyes again. But this time, not even changing the mirror helped allay the Sick Person's taunts or the feeling that my body was expanding. Both anger and fear overwhelmed me as I bit down hard on my lip. I wanted desperately to lash out, to scream at the top of my lungs for someone to do something. But that was impossible. I couldn't tell anyone what went on in my own head—the Sick Person had convinced me that no one would understand my concerns. Instead, I tried to keep the anger and fear at bay by distracting myself any way I could. Cleaning my room, organizing my closet—anything would do. I just wanted to keep myself busy so that I wouldn't have to feel. Yet the feelings just kept building up, as though the anger and fear had liquefied and were about to pour out of me like water from an overfilled glass. Thoughts flew through my mind as I stood there still gazing at the mirror. *Relief, relief! Where can I get relief?* The Sick Person replied to my angst almost immediately: *You can't be angry with anyone but yourself. It's your fault you are so disgusting.* I knew the only way to get rid of the negative feelings was if I took the anger out on myself.

Standing before the mirror, I began attacking my stomach with both fists, punching and scratching until my eyes filled with tears. I hated everything about the girl whose reflection peered back at me—her too large stomach, her red hair, her freckled nose. Yet more than anything, I hated how she couldn't make the Sick Person stop screaming. A few minutes later, I heard my mother calling out that it was time to go. Once more, the Sick Person's voice hissed in my ear, *How can you go out with a body so grotesque that you can't even look at it yourself?* Throwing my riding clothes back on, I walked into the kitchen to tell my mother I wanted to stay home. This wasn't the first time for me to miss an event because of my negative feelings about myself and my inability to get dressed.

In the past, my mother had tried to talk to me about what was wrong whenever I couldn't get dressed. She'd come into my room and sit down on the edge of my twin bed. Her concerned questions only made me more agitated and upset. I couldn't tell her what was wrong—I couldn't tell her about the Sick Person and how much she tormented me. My mother wouldn't understand. How could anyone understand something so insane?

"Melissa, don't you want to go to the party?" I could tell Mom was trying to keep her voice from sounding worried. I saw the corners of each eyebrow moving closer together, causing wrinkle lines to deepen on her forehead. Her eyes had a glossy sheen to them that told me she wasn't scowling out of anger but out of concern.

"No, I don't really feel like going. I'm kind of tired."

"Oh, that's okay. Do you want me to take you back to the barn instead?" While nodding in agreement, it occurred to me that my mother knew I'd lied about being tired. However, I still didn't give her the real explanation for why I couldn't go to the party. I knew my mother was worried about me, and she had even started taking me to see a therapist once a week. Yet, most of my sessions with the therapist consisted of me talking about how much I didn't want to be there, or about horses. Thank God for horses.

FRIENDS, OR THE LACK THEREOF

4

December brought Christmas vacation and cold afternoons at the barn along with it. I spent most of the break riding, going to horseshows, and trying to avoid Sherry. Sherry was a few years older than I was, and at one point, we had been friends. But when Sherry turned thirteen, something changed and she decided not to be my friend anymore. The escalating tension in her home may have fueled her cruelty toward me. Both of Sherry's parents were successful and career-driven, with her father increasingly absent physically and her mother often cold and emotionally removed. Sherry found me to be an easy target for her anger and frustration. Everyone else at the stable was older than me, and it wasn't hard to make fun of the odd movements my body made.

Sherry's favorite pastime was to see how many times she could make me cry in one day. The whole ordeal was a game to her, and once she started playing, all the other kids joined in, including my own sister. I'm convinced Sherry must have spent a good while psychoanalyzing me since she knew all of my weak spots. She made fun of my body, how I dressed, and she toyed with my emotions. Many of the other girls I rode with followed suit, although no one said anything as cruel as Sherry.

My head pounded with rage as Sherry and her gang circled around me like a pack of animals, laughing, spitting, and kicking dirt in my face. "Twitchy girl, twitchy girl, fat, ugly, twitchy girl," Sherry's taunts sounded like a nursery rhyme, albeit a menacing one. I always tried to think of something smart to say back to her, but the tears forming in my eyes sent me running to my pony's stall to hide. I didn't want Sherry to know that she'd upset me because that would only make her attacks all the more satisfying.

Instead, I hid in Bailey's stall with fat tears streaming down my face and the words *Help Me* running through my mind. I desperately wanted someone to help me. However, I didn't know who to ask or how to release the pent up words from my head. I knew what I was feeling, but I didn't know how to express my feelings in words.

When Sherry first started picking on me, I looked to Brooke to step in and say something, but after a while, I realized I was on my own. I know now that Brooke didn't say anything because she was afraid Sherry would turn on her as well. But at the time, I hated my sister for just standing there speechless while Sherry attacked me.

At one point, I became so desperate to find relief from Sherry's taunts and torments that I told my mother. She immediately came to my defense, confronting Sherry the very next day. Yet, the rebuke backfired. The confrontation only fueled Sherry's anger, causing her to tease me even more. After that, I stopped telling my mother about Sherry, Brooke, or any of the other girls, because I felt like no one could do anything to help me—I was alone.

As much as I didn't want to be at school, at least there I didn't have to fear people taunting me for having tics or not knowing how to read, because everyone in my class had some form of a neurological disorder or learning disability. No one made fun of anyone, because I guess all of us knew what it was like to be an outcast. Yet even though I could identify with my classmates, I still wasn't interested in getting to know them. The more preoccupied I became with food and with avoiding it, the less interested I was in making new friends. The Sick Person residing within me just wanted to be alone. All she desired was to turn my body into a lifeless shell that felt nothing, wanted nothing, and was nothing.

Sometimes, though, in the midst of the internal battle I would be able to break away from the Sick Person and subdue her voice for a while. When this happened, the old vivacious part of me that yearned for friendship, camaraderie, and companionship would reemerge. This was the real me; the me who had been taken captive by the Sick Person, the me who I could sometimes hear pleading, *I want to live! If I could just have a chance to live!*

During lunchtime for a few weeks before the end of the school year, the healthy person within me managed to show herself for a while. She encouraged me to sit with the other kids and even talk a bit. First, though, I was anxious to finish the fat-free strawberry yogurt I always packed. My concentration centered solely on taking the smallest spoonfuls possible so I could make the yogurt last longer. I savored each bite, moving the strawberry-flavored substance around in my mouth and trying to absorb every nuance of its taste before swallowing. After scraping every morsel from my container of yogurt, I began looking around the bustling cafeteria to see what the other kids were eating. Across from me, a boy with sandy blond hair sat dabbing his grease-filled pizza with a napkin, while the girl next to him noshed on a colorful Fruit Roll-Up.

Automatically, I pictured the nutrition label on a box of Fruit Roll-Ups—fat: none; sugar: thirty grams: calories: too many. (I knew all this because of the sugar-restriction game I played. Grocery shopping became like a scavenger hunt and if I got lucky, I would find a new food that fit my twelve-gram sugar limit.) After analyzing and calculating the nutrition facts for some of the other kids' lunches, I felt a wave of loneliness wash over me. The school year was almost over and I still didn't have any friends. *If I could just start talking to someone . . .* the thought made me turn to the girl who was eating the Fruit Roll-Up. I knew her name was Jessie although I had never called her by name before. Actually, I didn't call any of my classmates by their names because I never really spoke to them. That day at lunch, I tried to think of something to say to Jessie so that she would talk to me. I drummed my fingers on the lunchroom table as I thought. Finally, my mind centered on the boy I knew she had a crush on—so I asked her about him. Bad move. She responded by popping her sugar-sticky hand over my mouth to stop me from talking.

When I licked my lips, I could taste something sweet. Suddenly, the Sick Person in my head resurfaced and snarled: *Sugar, bad, out of control, fat, fat, you're going to get fat.* I panicked. I immediately jumped out of my seat, ran down the hall, and ducked into the girls' bathroom. After making sure that no one was inside, I turned on the water faucet and held my mouth under the spout, hoping to wash out any trace of sugar that I might have consumed. I stood there for ten minutes, rinsing my mouth until I was positive that the sugary flavor had gone away. I spent the remainder of the lunch period running laps around the small bathroom to burn off any calories I might have taken in. While walking back to class, I decided that trying to become friends with Jessie wasn't worth it after all.

Human
Guinea Pig

5

As the school year came to a close, I mourned the end of third grade as though someone very dear to me had passed away. The days spent in Mrs. Leonard's lively classroom were over, and now there was nothing to look forward to or to distract me from the tics that had been growing progressively worse for several months. By May, the seizurelike movements—the jerking arms, the flailing legs, the twisting torso—had gotten so out of control that they caused me to fall out of bed almost every night. After a while, I decided to move into the living room since the couches in there were lower to the ground than my bed was.

My parents were at a loss as to what to do. They took me from doctor to doctor, hoping to find medicine that would help manage the tics caused by Tourette syndrome. Yet none of the different drug cocktails prescribed to me seemed to work; they only made the tics worse or made me feel so drugged up and sleepy that waking up in the morning became impossible. Each time I had a bad reaction to a medication, my mother would frantically call my doctor.

"Hello, Dr. Johnson? This is Cathy Binstock. Melissa has been on the Zoloft for two weeks now, and it's not helping. She's so agitated that I had to pick her up at school early. She was tearing up her shirt on the ride home. What should I do?"

The doctor's responses were usually the same. "Oh, Mrs. Binstock, the drugs just need a little more time. Give it another two weeks and call back if she doesn't improve."

"What? No! I'm not keeping Melissa on this medicine for that long. For God's sake, she's tearing her clothing, and yesterday she was eating her dress."

My mother had been my strongest ally for a long time. She fought the doctors when they'd continue to insist that the drugs just needed "more time" and never allowed me to start taking a medication without first doing hours of extensive research. My mother's proactive and confrontational approach made me feel safe. I knew that nothing bad could happen as long as she was around to protect me. But after a while, I'd been through so many drugs that there were very few left to try. By then, my tics weren't the only cause for concern. I began throwing violent tantrums at random intervals throughout the day.

The anger I felt was so intense, so undeniable, and it hit me like a seething wave crashing against a levy until it burst wide open. I never knew where the feelings came from or how they took hold of me. All I knew was that I needed to get rid of the anger somehow, someway. After a while, the feelings became so intense that they sent me running through the house like some sort of wild animal, screaming, crying, and breaking everything in sight. I'd smash picture frames, hurl chairs across the room, and one time I even kicked a hole in the wall of the closet I shared with Brooke. No one was sure if the medication caused my tantrums or if I was just an incredibly disturbed ten-year-old. After learning about my violent tantrums, one of my doctors concluded that I was bipolar and suffered from a rage disorder. I don't think the doctor ever consider that my rage attacks might be a side effect of the drugs I was taking.

My next psychiatrist was no better than the first. He, too, doled out medication as though it was candy, even prescribing pills that hadn't been approved by the FDA for use in the United States. Somehow, he'd managed to get pills "under the table." Every morning, I choked down a handful of horse-sized pills while praying this would be the day the doctor's promises of making my tics better would come true. *Maybe this will be the day. Maybe, maybe!* Yet, when days turned into weeks and weeks into months, my hope turned into anger and my anger turned into a resigned sadness.

My third doctor didn't seem to be as pill-happy as the first two, and I liked him for a brief period of time. He told my mother we were going to try a different method—a method that involved injecting large quantities of Botox in my face to paralyze my facial tics. Well, the Botox did its job. I didn't have facial tics for about a month; I couldn't move my face much, either. I was incapable of creating facial expressions and I felt inhuman. I was an alien, a creature, a monster. Whatever I was, I most certainly didn't belong around other people who did nothing but stare, point fingers, and whisper about the odd movements my body made.

After visiting more than a few doctors, I began to loathe all men in white coats. Sitting in their offices made me feel like I was some sort of creature instead of a human being. They'd refer to me by my disorders instead of calling me by name. Once a week, I would go to these purported experts only to be placed on a high stool so the odd movements my body made could be videotaped for them to study. But the only outcome of these sessions was more medication.

The doctors continued to write script after script without the slightest hesitation or any warnings that a drug might not work. No one told my mother that the combinations of pills I ingested were not approved for use on children. She found this out only through her own research.

After a while, my behavior became so volatile my mother became desperate. She no longer argued with the psychiatrists when they advised her to keep me on a medication. Today I believe her desperation led her to trust the doctors to tell her what to do. But at the time, my mind was too overwhelmed and confused to understand she was trying to help me. I only saw her willingly acquiesce to the doctors and give me pills that made me feel sick. I felt betrayed by my ally who moved over to the doctors' side and no longer questioned their methods. And now, there was no one left to defend or protect me from being tested like a lab rat.

⸻

With my tics growing progressively worse, sitting still in class became an arduous task. The torso twisting, leg jerking, and arm flailing had become almost ceaseless, and I could no longer stay seated for more than ten minutes at a time. My disruptive behaviors didn't exactly make my fourth-grade teacher thrilled to have me as a student. But to tell you the truth, I wasn't exactly thrilled to have Mrs. Thomson as my teacher either.

Mrs. Thomson was a broad-shouldered, older woman with brown, shoulder-length hair that was turning gray at the roots. The sound of her voice was warm—sweet, even—but her words were icy and often cruel. A few weeks into the new school year, I could tell Mrs. Thomson was becoming increasingly bothered by my tics. I had recently developed a vocal tic that sounded somewhat like a person clearing her throat just prior to speaking. But unlike a normal person that clears her throat and then goes on to say whatever it is she was going to say, this sound lasted for minutes at a time, which caused the other kids in my class to turn around in their seats and stare. One morning in mid-September, I walked into class to find that my name tag wasn't on the desk where I usually sat. As I looked around the room nervously, I heard Mrs. Thomson's serene-sounding voice behind me.

"Good morning Melissa. How are you today? The weather is cooling off now, isn't it?"

I could tell something was wrong just by the fact that she was trying to have a conversation with me. Generally, the only time Mrs. Thomson talked to me was to tell me to "settle down" or to go to the nurses' station if my tics were causing me to become too loud.

"How come my name tag is gone?" My voice sounded shaky as I turned to face my teacher.

"Oh, it's not gone, Melissa. Look on that table." She made a motion with her hand in the direction of a table that was placed in the back of the room. As I glanced over at the table, I saw a name tag with *Melissa B.* printed on it in large purple letters.

"Should I move my name tag back to my desk?"

"Oh, well, I thought you might like to sit back here for a change." I was a little confused about the seating arrangement but decided it didn't really matter where I sat. I walked over to the table and started to sit down in a chair facing the front of the room when I heard Mrs. Thomson's voice again.

"Why don't we try and sit in the other chair, Melissa?" She pointed to a chair that was facing the wall. "I think it's best we sit here so we don't distract the class." I wasn't sure why she kept saying *we* since she really meant *me,* but I nodded my head and muttered an "okay" under my breath. At first, my new seating arrangement was actually somewhat nice; I didn't have to look at anyone and no one had to look at me. The only thing that really bothered me was that I had to strain to hear what Mrs. Thomson was saying. I guess I probably would have spent the entire year facing the wall had my mother not found out about the arrangement one day when she came into the classroom to pick me up early for a therapy appointment.

Once my mother discovered that I was sitting in a corner facing the wall, she scheduled a conference with Mrs. Thomson. After all, this was supposed to be a school that specialized in helping children with learning disorders, so my mother expected Mrs. Thomson to be understanding. Yet, Mrs. Thomson was anything but.

"Mrs. Binstock, Melissa needs her special seat because the other children get very distracted by her movements."

"But, she can't help it! Melissa has Tourette syndrome. Can't you let her sit at a desk like all the other kids?"

"I'm afraid I just can't do that, Mrs. Binstock. The other children need to learn, and I am here to do whatever I can to help them with that vital task of learning."

The meeting convinced my mother that I could no longer be a student at a school that hired teachers like Mrs. Thomson. She pulled me out of that school. And, because the large dose of antipsychotic drugs I was taking made waking up in the morning an impossible task for me, my mother decided she'd try home-schooling me instead.

Each day she set aside hours to work with me, but I was either too tired or too agitated to sit or listen for very long. My daily routine soon consisted of getting up around lunchtime, swallowing a handful of pills, eating some Cheerios, and then playing *Math Munchers* on the computer. During the course of the day, my tics would grow progressively worse, as I no longer had the energy to suppress them. Each tic felt almost like a sneeze I was trying to hold back. There finally came a point at which I just couldn't hold back any longer and the tics would explode from my body like water pouring out of a broken levy. When this happened, my mother always drove me straight to the barn. I think this was a reprieve for her as much as it was for me. Horses were my refuge; their mere presence put my mind and body at ease.

When I wasn't at the barn, I always had to be on guard—I worried about tics, other peoples' stares, and the Sick Person's cries. The constant worrying made me feel as though someone had tied metal wire tightly around my entire body, constricting every movement, every breath. Yet, when I was with the horses, something amazing happened—that constricting wire was cut, leaving me free to move and take in cool, deep breaths of blissful air. When I rode my pony, all I had to do was feel the rhythmical movements of her steady gait as we cantered toward a fence. As Bailey moved closer to the hurdle, I'd crouch down low over her neck, waiting for that awesome feeling of suspension in midair. It was during this brief, joyful moment that I actually felt light or even weightless . . . yet the momentary reprieve from my anxiety was only that. As soon as I stepped into my mother's car, the worries about tics, stares, and weight would hit me full force as the metal wire wrapped tightly around my body once more.

Two months before I began fifth grade, my mother took me to a new doctor who put me on a medication that came in the form of a patch. I don't know what it was; at that age, I didn't ask my parents the names of the drugs they were giving me, and years later when I asked, it turned out that my mother didn't know what it was, either. But that medication worked wonders. For the first time in a long while, I was actually awake. Getting up in the morning was no longer a battle, which gave everyone hope that I'd be able to return to school. In addition, my mother found a school that specialized in helping kids with neurological disorders. I was happy about starting at a new school, but more than anything, it was my new state of alertness that made me want to jump for joy. This reawakening made me feel as though someone had reached down and lifted me out of the medication-induced haze I'd been caught in for so long; God, it felt good to wake up in the morning.

VIOLATED 6

During the worst of the medication-brain fog I experienced, I hadn't been able to think about much of anything other than wanting to sleep; not even the Sick Person's voice could be heard. With the return of my ability to think, two significant things happened. The first I expected—the Sick Person returned. However, the second thing that happened was something I found to be extraordinary; I finally began to learn how to read. Because of my learning disability, looking at words on a page had been like looking at a foreign code of meaningless symbols. I just couldn't understand the relationship between letters and sounds or how the sounds could blend together to make words.

With my newfound ability, I'd sit on the floor in my bedroom with a book from the Pony Club series open on my lap, trying to sound out each word. Reading became like a math equation to me. I took a word like *math* and broke it into smaller portions of *ma* and *th*. Then I brought the two sounds together to make *ma* plus *th,* which equals *math.* I knew that Brooke, who would sometimes read to me, could get through the sixty-five page book in about an hour, whereas I took the same amount of time to read the first three pages. But to tell you the truth, I didn't really care; the door to a new world made of words was finally open for me to enter. I could step through the doorway anytime I wanted to and escape from everything. No one could enter my new world—not my parents, not Brooke, not Sherry; not even the Sick Person could force her way in.

I was excited about starting fifth grade at the Butterfly School, because I was finally getting the hang of reading, and because my parents had told me there would be other kids with Tourette syndrome there. I hadn't met others who had it, and I was interested to find out what they were like. I wondered if they experienced that same urging sensation—that same itch and tickle that could only be relieved by a specific movement, a specific tic. I wondered how many doctors they had seen and how many medications they had tried. Most of all, though, I wondered if they felt like outsiders, too.

However, I soon found out that the word *butterfly* could have both a positive and a negative connotation. Of course, to the naked eye, butterflies appear to be beautiful, delicate creatures, but their brightly colored wings can sometimes be misleading. You see, there are several types of butterflies that are actually poisonous, and I believe that this school was one of them. I knew that something was wrong the first week of class when I didn't receive any textbooks. But that was the least of it.

I didn't think there could be a teacher much worse than my fourth-grade teacher, Mrs. Thomson—but I was wrong. I do have to admit, Mr. Zimmer's disciplinary techniques were at least more original than Mrs. Thomson's. One morning about three weeks into the school year, I found Mr. Zimmer under a table sitting on top of one of the boys in my class. Later in the year, my mother watched as Mr. Zimmer chased another boy out to the front parking lot of the school. The chase went on for a few minutes before Mr. Zimmer caught up with the boy, knocked him to the ground, held the boy's hands behind his back, and sat on him. After seeing this, my mother had me transferred to another class.

My new teacher, Mr. Philips, didn't sit on kids, although his class wasn't much better than Mr. Zimmer's. I hadn't learned anything in Mr. Zimmer's class, and I became restless when all we did in Mr. Phillips's class for six weeks was learn how to bake bread. We still didn't use textbooks, and Mr. Philips didn't seem to be interested in making a lesson plan. I ended up spending the majority of the day either reading or watching the kids in my class build a K'NEX rollercoaster.

Because I was the only girl, I always felt a little odd in Mr. Philips's class. Every morning we'd all come into the classroom and sit around a circular table, waiting for Mr. Philips to mosey his way into the room. At first, I didn't notice that one of the boys in my class was interested in me. However, I became suspicious when day after day Adam would insist on sitting next to me. I wasn't sure how old he was, but I knew he had to be a few years older than me. I didn't really like Adam much and would arrive to school early so I could scoot my chair away from his. But as soon as Adam walked into the room, he'd move his chair right back to where it had been before I moved it. The gesture annoyed me, but I never suspected Adam would do anything other than move a chair or two to get closer to me.

December finally rolled around, and I was looking forward to the winter break that was approaching. On the last Friday before break, I arrived to school early, as usual. As I walked into the classroom, Mr. Philips still wasn't there, which wasn't unusual. After moving Adam's chair away from mine, I sat down at the circular table and pulled out a copy of *Black Beauty*. At the sound of footsteps in the hallway, I looked up to see Adam making his way into the classroom. That day, his unnaturally platinum blond hair was covered in gel and spiked at the ends. His new hairdo made me stare for a moment, and I rolled my eyes as Adam scooted his chair next to me.

I continued reading until I felt a warm, clammy hand rubbing my leg. I froze in my seat, scared and not sure what to do. Adam moved his hand higher until he had finally reached up my skirt and into my underwear. I froze in shock, and then a wave of angry fire surged through my body. I struggled to free myself of his grip, but he held me down, forcing the nails of his free hand into the skin on my arm. Finally, I picked one foot off the ground and slammed it down as hard as I could on Adam's foot. The boy's face grimaced as I jumped up and ran to the bathroom.

I never told anyone what happened that day. I was too scared that Adam would find out and do something worse. The Sick Person encouraged me to keep quiet, hissing that the whole thing had been my fault. *You shouldn't have let Adam sit next to you; you could have moved. If you had moved, none of this would've happened.*

That afternoon, my dad was supposed to pick me up from school. As I waited on the front porch of the building, I tried to block the thoughts of what had happened out of my mind. Ten minutes passed, and then ten more before I realized my dad must have forgotten about me. He wasn't in the habit of forgetting to pick me up. I guess I was just having a very unlucky day.

After calling my dad at work, I waited for another thirty minutes before a black Volvo pulled into the lot. My stomach dropped at the sight of the car; my dad had asked Jim, one of the guys who worked for him, to get me. Tears began to fill my eyes as I stuffed my backpack into the trunk. I carelessly wiped them away with my shirtsleeve and opened the car door. As we pulled out of the parking lot, I fought to keep the tears back, but my efforts were futile. Midway through the ride home, I broke out in sobs. Jim turned to me and asked what was wrong, but all I could say was "I'm just really tired." I wanted to tell someone, I really did. But I couldn't seem to muster up enough courage to talk or express how I felt.

The words and feelings were locked up within me, clawing at my insides until they festered with infection. I hadn't suspected Adam would hurt me, yet he had. How could I be certain that someone else wasn't going to hurt me, too? Images of Adam holding me down and forcing his hand inside of me bombarded my mind whenever I was around other people, making me wish for the comfort that solitude offered. Before the incident with Adam, I feared being around people because I didn't want them to notice my tics. After the incident, though, I developed a fear of people in general.

Even though the medication in the nicotine-looking patch allowed me actually to experience life instead of sleeping through it, I wasn't able to stay on the medicine for long. My tics had subsided for a while, but toward the end of fifth grade, the old familiar movements came back in full force with the addition of some new tics as well. During the middle of class, my face would begin to twitch while my arms and legs flailed in different directions. At least, these odd movements were relatively quiet. The most embarrassing tics were the strange new barking and grunting sounds that came out of my mouth without warning. After a while, I learned that the best way to control the vocal tics was by keeping my mouth shut tight.

Once again, I was placed on a new medication that was supposed to fix everything that was wrong with me. I waited in fear of the medication haze I thought was going to engulf my mind again. For a few days, nothing seemed to be different; it was only after about a week that I blacked out.

SPIRALING OUT OF CONTROL

7

To tell you the truth, I don't remember anything about that day. Brooke and my mother are the ones who have filled me in on the details. It was about a month before school let out when Brooke found me sitting on the floor in the living room staring blankly at the wall. She approached me and called my name, but I didn't respond. I was in some sort of weird state of psychosis, not recognizing anyone or anything. When Brooke realized I wasn't playing around, she yelled for my mother, who, in a panic, picked me up off the floor and drove me to the hospital where the doctors concluded that I was having an adverse reaction to the new medication. My pediatrician, Dr. Ingles, met us at the hospital, but the psychiatrist who prescribed the pills in the first place never showed up. When Dr. Ingles found out that I was on a strong dose of the mood stabilizer Haldol, his response was simple: "Get her off that stuff."

After the Haldol incident, I became even more resistant to taking medicine. But the new psychiatrist I was seeing, Dr. Adams, told my mother I needed medication—discontinuing the drugs was not an option. At almost every session, Dr. Adams would remind me of my options; I would have to take the pills or go to the mental hospital. I became so desperate to avoid taking my medicine that I tried to run away—but my mother just jumped in the car and drove after me. Once I was back at the house, there was nothing left for me to do but gulp down the colorful assortment of pills and wait for the haze to engulf my mind again. Within twenty minutes, everything began to feel slow and leaden. My mind became too clouded for me to even think, and my body grew so heavy and tired that I could barely sit up.

I didn't think of my pills by name but rather by what each one did to me. The three blue ones were the least bothersome; they didn't do much except make me a little groggy. I used to like to take the capsules apart so I could dump out the white powder all over the counter. After gathering the powder together in a neat little pile; I'd blow it into the air, pretending it was snow. The next pill was a white one, little and round. I always felt a strange sense of numbness after swallowing this one. You know that weird, numb feeling that you get when the dentist injects your mouth with Novocain to fill a cavity? Well, that's what I felt like, as though my whole body had been shot up with Novocain, making me numb to every feeling, sensation, or concern. It was almost as if I wasn't human anymore. The only part of me that felt alive was my stomach, which growled and clawed at me incessantly.

But of all the pills I had to swallow, the worst one was a large yellow pill that was coated with some nasty flavor that made me gag. I hated that pill most of all, because it made me feel ravished. In the middle of the night, I would awaken with the most intense hunger pains I had ever experienced. Nothing I ate could allay my hunger—not water, bubbly diet soda, Jell-O, or water-rich foods like apples. I was constantly starving. I started binging at night, first going through the trash can to find something; the Sick Person within me demanded that I only eat from the trash because I *was* trash. So I ingested the discarded remains of chocolate cake that was mixed in with coffee grounds and chicken skin.

Of course, there was food in the pantry, too, so if there wasn't enough to eat in the trash, I'd eat an entire jar of peanut butter, leftover pasta, or a box of Honey Nut Cheerios. I was like a mechanical robot programmed to feast. After a night's binge, I would wake up the next day in a panic. As I showered, I'd imagine that the water droplets falling from my body were fat molecules that I was washing away. But the nightly binging inevitably led to weight gain, and weight gain always led to pain.

My mind was somewhat sharper each morning because the effects of the medications from the day before had worn off. I could once again hear the Sick Person chanting: *Disgusting, disgusting, that's what you are. Disgusting, disgusting, that's what you are.* This was the rhythm I moved to until the pills I ingested in the morning took their effect, and I fell back into a clouded haze where everything was heavy, leaden, and slow. The effects of the medicine made me feel like someone was holding me underwater. I'd try to make my way to the surface only to be forced down again; I'd desperately gasp for breath. If I had to choose between living with the cruel, Sick Person or the drowning feeling, I would have gladly picked the former. At least I had some control over that voice; if I listened to her demands, I would be free to go about my day. However, the medication effects were out of my hands entirely, making it the worse of the two evils. As my hatred for medication grew, I began to desire the Sick Person as a companion more and more. If only I'd known that she really just wanted to kill me.

I desperately wanted to go back to those clearheaded days I'd experienced while wearing the patch medication. Yet I couldn't tell my parents how I felt. It's not that I didn't know what words to use. I knew exactly what to say because I'd played the scene over and over again in my mind: We'd all sit down in the game room on those old beat up couches that were covered by colorful quilts so that guests wouldn't know about the stains that lie beneath. I'd tell my parents about the drowning and that heavy, hazy fog that weighed down my mind; everything would be laid out for them to see. Each time I played the scene in my head, it always ended with my parents agreeing that I wouldn't have to take any more of the antipsychotics or mood stabilizers they thought were helping me.

Yet the conversation never happened; I couldn't force the words in my head to become audible so that my parents could know how I felt. The Sick Person convinced me that my efforts would be in vain, because no one would want to listen. The Sick Person convinced me that my parents no longer cared how I felt, because they were so adamant about following Dr. Adams's instructions. Almost every day, I would overhear my mother talking to my dad about my medication regimen. "Well, Dr. Adams wants this" and "Dr. Adams feels that" filled me with a hot, liquid rage that coursed through my entire body. No one asked what *I* wanted—no one asked me what *I* felt.

I'd do anything to escape when my mother approached me with the medication bottle in hand. Depending on where we were at the time, I'd either lock myself in a closet or run away. There were even a couple of times when I actually jumped out of a moving car in an attempt to escape. Understandably, my mother became frantic. Not knowing what else to do, she would call my psychiatrist. I do have to say that Dr. Adams was an extremely consistent man; his instructions were always the same. He told my mother that if I didn't calm down and take the pills, she should call an ambulance to take me to the hospital.

Instead of talking to my parents about my feelings, one morning I just refused to swallow any more pills. I locked myself in a bathroom, and my mother actually did call the police department to force the door open. As the sound of sirens drew nearer to the house, I sat on the bathroom floor holding both knees to my chest while sobbing and willing myself to be invisible. My mother pleaded with me to just come out and take my medicine, but I was tired of feeling like a drugged-up zombie all the time. I wanted to have complete control of my body, and the medication snatched that control away from me. When I heard the sound of footsteps approaching the bathroom, I felt like an escaped prisoner of war. The enemy had found my safe house, and now they were about to infiltrate. Even though I knew I would inevitably have to come out, I resisted giving myself over to the enemy.

I heard a man asking me questions through the door, but I refused to answer. Instead, I lay there on the floor, crouched in a tight ball, my hands over both ears. Ten minutes passed before everyone realized that I wasn't going to unlock the door and surrender. Through the door, I could hear the sound of clanging metal as though someone was digging through a tool kit. The sound sent a fresh wave of anxiety through me as I gripped my knees against my bony chest. I braced myself for the attack I knew was imminent. Moments later, a policeman unscrewed the doorknob. The doorknob fell to the ground with a loud *clank*. The battle was over, and I had lost. One of the EMTs rushed in, picked me up, and carried me out of my safe house. As the EMT listened to my pulse and checked my blood pressure, my whole body trembled violently.

The police officer asked me if I wanted to go to the hospital. Everything felt so unreal. I stared at his shoes without answering. They were black, old, and worn. It looked like he had replaced the laces recently because they weren't tattered like the shoes. He asked me several questions, but I never looked him in the eye; I replied by bobbing or shaking my head.

Finally, the police officer gave me the option of either going to the hospital or taking my pills. I could feel the hairs on the back of my neck standing on end. My body ached with fatigue, and my stomach was sore after sobbing so much. I was too tired to fight anymore and scared out of my mind. I stretched my arm out, took the pills from the EMT's hand, and swallowed the colorful assortment without water.

As the medicine took its effect about twenty minutes later, my head began to feel like a lead bowling ball had smashed down on top of me. All I wanted to do was go to sleep and never wake up again. I did get my wish in a way: for the next two days all I did was sleep, wake up, and then go back to sleep again—the EMT had slipped in an additional Valium when he'd given me my pills.

When I wasn't in a medication-induced haze, the Sick Person would scream in my ear about fatty flesh and losing control. I began to detest anything that revolved around food, including our family's weekly Shabbat dinners. Friday was my mother's favorite day because my dad would come home early from work and we'd all have dinner together. She always cooked a huge meal with all the traditional Jewish foods like challah, stuffed cabbage, matzo ball soup, and Israeli salad.

Friday was supposed to be a day of rest, but I could never rest because I was either too busy trying to block out the Sick Person's cries or struggling to subdue the hunger pains that unceasingly clawed at my insides. I began to fear hunger as though the sensation was a symptom of some deadly disease. Hunger became the ultimate sign that I was losing control of the one part of me that I still had command over, the part of me that still seemed to be mine. *Ignore the pains. Subdue the hunger. Control, control!* the Sick Person chanted in my ear.

Friday became the scene of a battle rather than a holiday for me as I fought my desire for food. I never knew when my dad would be coming home from work. Sometimes he'd be on time, yet more often than not he'd be late, arriving at the door at seven or eight. One Friday night was particularly bad for me. It was already 6:30 PM and my dad still wasn't home. Hunger began attacking my insides at 4:30 PM, but I refused to eat anything; instead I listened to the Sick Person's cries of lost control, soft bellies, and fat thighs. *You just need to sit down somewhere and breathe, forget about being hungry,* she hissed. Yet as much as I wanted to forget, I couldn't. As the hunger pangs increased, so did my pulse. *Thud, thud, thud* pounded in my ears as my breathing became shallower and beads of sweat accumulated on my brow.

"Air, air! I need air!" The words escaped out of my mouth as I looked around desperately for something to make the horrible feeling of not being able to breathe go away. I didn't really know what I was looking for, but I stumbled by chance upon one of Brooke's pink disposable razors sitting on a shelf next to the bathroom sink. I fixed my eyes on the sharp, shiny blade as I reached for the razor, gripping it tight in my right hand.

After closing the door to the bathroom, I sat down cross-legged on the cool tile floor and pulled one of my pant legs up above my kneecap, exposing my inner thigh. I ran the blade slowly over my skin, sending a stream of blood trickling down my leg and onto the tiled floor. I made a long U-shaped pattern on my inner thigh, then dropped the razor. Leaning back against the wall, I closed my eyes and inhaled deeply. Finally, I had found a release. Twenty minutes passed by before I opened my eyes again. I looked down at my blood-stained sock and the splattered floor, but I felt neither pain nor fear from what I had done.

Once the bleeding stopped, I wadded up some toilet paper, wrapped it around my thigh, and rolled down my pant leg. Another hour passed before I heard my dad pull up the driveway. By this time, my self-inflicted wound had begun to sting, but I didn't care. I welcomed the pain because it distracted me from the hunger pangs that gnawed relentlessly at my stomach. Yet, more than anything, I welcomed the pain, because it distracted me from the Sick Person's searing cries.

The rest of the summer passed by almost as usual. On the days that I wasn't too tired to get up, I'd go riding and continue on with my normal routine; only this summer, Brooke wasn't a part of it. Since Brooke began middle school the previous fall, she spent less and less time at the barn. On rare occasions she'd go out with me, but most of the time Brooke was busy with friends from school.

Her absence wasn't the only change that summer; in the middle of July, I stopped taking medicine. My decision wasn't exactly medically advised. Actually, my mother didn't even know what I was doing. I'm not sure if she just trusted me or if she was just so fed up that she purposely stopped watching me take my pills; I suspect the latter. Since my mother didn't see what I was doing (or not doing), she could pretend everything was all right. Every morning I walked into the kitchen, went over to the cabinet, and pulled out the pill case that was imprinted with the different days of the week. I collected the colorful assortment of pills in my hand and walked out of the room. I never told my mother that I was flushing them down the toilet.

Actually, by then, my mother and I never really talked about anything at all. She had become the pill forcer, the caller of the police, and the enemy. When we conversed at all, it was about medicine, and our conversation would turn into a screaming match that always ended with a ceremonial slamming of doors.

Before my mutiny, the fight was the same every time: I refused to swallow the pills, my mother threatened to call the police or put me in the hospital, and then I'd scream at her and say I wanted to be left alone. After that, she'd storm out of the room and I'd wait for the sound of her bedroom door slamming shut. I always yelled at her to leave me alone, but in reality I just wanted her to hold me close and make the hurt go away, if only for a little while. Yet I could never tell my mother what I needed from her. For some reason, the words just wouldn't come.

MEETING MELANIE

8

I felt like I'd been submerged under water for years, and now that I had stopped taking the pills, I had finally reached the surface and could take deep breaths again. The world seemed new and bright; I actually felt alive, much like that brief, blissful period of time when I was wearing the patch medicine. But my spirits somewhat dampened as the summer came to a close. I dreaded starting sixth grade, because I knew I would have to begin all over again at a new school.

My mother had wanted to pull me out of the Butterfly School since the parking lot incident when Mr. Zimmerman sat on a student. At the time, there wasn't another place to send me because the semester was already half over. Besides that, attending a "normal" school just wasn't an option for me. I still struggled to read, I couldn't multiply or divide, and on some days I couldn't even sit in the classroom long enough to get through a lesson because of the tics that consumed my body. Instead of trying to move me in the middle of the year, my parents decided to look into schools I could attend once fall came around. Moving around from school to school had become almost a custom for me. Between my first elementary school and sixth grade, I had attended six different schools.

The only thing that remained stable in my life was the love I had for horses. Horses taught me how to have fun, how to love, and how to just be. I had decided long ago that all I wanted to do with my life was be around them. There was one thing, though, that constantly ate away at me: I was afraid that I was getting too big to ride Bailey. I knew my fear wasn't unreasonable because for a time Brooke had also been worried that her legs were getting too long for her pony. Although Brooke's fear dissipated after a while, I couldn't get the thought out of my mind. I felt as though someone had recorded a message that was playing in my head like a mantra: *You're too big, you're too big, you're too big!* I abhorred hearing the recording, but the *off* switch was inaccessible to me.

In my attempts to make myself look smaller, I'd hike up my stirrup leathers so my legs didn't reach so far down Bailey's side. At every riding lesson I took, the recording went off in my head, becoming so loud that I would have to ask my instructor for reassurance that I was the right size for Bailey. One of the girls I continually asked was Jessie, whose reply was always the same: "No, Melissa, you aren't too big. Please stop shortening your stirrups." She'd get annoyed with me for asking the same question over and over again because she didn't understand my fear.

I never explained how I felt to her, or to anyone else for that matter. None of the other kids seemed to have the same interminable worry, and I was afraid that everyone would think I was even more weird if they found out. At the same time, I hated frustrating Jessie because I wanted so badly for her to like me. She was the best rider at the barn and got to ride the nicest horses. Jessie seemed so cool with her baseball cap, oversized T-shirts, and black riding pants. Everyone looked up to Jessie; not even Sherry was above her in status.

One Saturday morning while Bailey and I were warming up for our morning lesson, I knew that my fear of getting too tall for her had finally come true. As we made our way toward a red and white fence, I hovered low over her neck, waiting to experience the awesome sensation of being launched into the air. When I felt Bailey's front legs leave the ground, I shifted my hands forward on her neck and sank all of my weight down into my heels. Bailey was midway over the jump when my left heel caught the top pole, sending it to the ground along with one of the white standards the poles had been resting on. No matter how much I hiked up my stirrup leathers, my legs were still too long for Bailey's tiny frame.

The realization that my worst fear had come true made me feel as though someone had struck me hard in the stomach. As I got off Bailey, the pain reverberated throughout my body, making me want to cry out as my eyes filled with fresh tears. The pain came from multiple sources, one of which was the realization that the Sick Person had been right; I was getting too big, too large to ride my tiny pony. Yet, the main source of the pain came from the realization that things were going to change. My pony—my stability, my rock—would have to be sold if I couldn't fit on her anymore.

Luckily, my parents were able to sell Bailey to the head trainer at the barn, which reassured me that I would always be able to visit her. As an early birthday present, my parents bought me a new horse named Ace. Ace had beautiful soft brown eyes and a deep chestnut coat that matched the color of my hair almost exactly. The first show Ace and I competed in was my most successful one to date. We won all our over-fences classes and placed third in the under-saddle class.

Horse shows had become my ultimate source of fun. Walking around the picturesque show grounds where everyone slept, ate, and breathed horses made me feel like I had entered a world where I actually belonged. I was one of them, not some outcast whose body made strange movements. On Friday afternoons, everyone from the barn would drive out to the show grounds to set up our stall area and get the horses comfortable with the competition arena. Everyone was always in a great mood as we piled fresh-smelling shavings into the horses' stalls.

One of the best things about horse shows was that Sherry never tormented me. It was as though we had gone back in time to the days when we were friends. The two of us would sit side-by-side, laughing and joking with one another as though we'd never fought at all. I was so relieved when Sherry was being nice that I pretended she'd never teased me or kicked dirt in my face. But Sunday would come and the show would end, and we'd all go home. The next time I'd see Sherry I always hoped that maybe she'd be the girl I used to know. Yet as soon as we got home, our roles would resume—she was the cool one, and I was the freak.

That summer, as I watched the show-jumping portion of the Olympic Games in Atlanta, I began dreaming about competing in the Olympics one day and owning my own barn full of sleek-coated horses. I wanted to learn everything there was to know about horses and riding. Two weeks before sixth grade started, I convinced my parents that I needed to move to a new trainer if I ever wanted to ride in the Olympics. The move was a big deal because my new trainer charged twice as much as my previous trainer. However, I think my parents were so relieved that I was medically stable that they didn't protest.

Willow Wind Stables was a small barn with a tiny indoor arena and dilapidated stalls. My new trainer, Melanie, had just purchased the place and was planning to remodel it. I picked Melanie's barn after searching all the local stables. For weeks, I perused the Willow Wind website studying pictures of Melanie jumping a muscular bay horse that was clearing a five-foot fence with room to spare. I read all about how she had grown up in Germany, competed at the Grand Prix level (the level that included the Olympics), and trained amateurs to become top-notch riders. Moving to Willow Wind was like a dream come true—or so I thought.

Melanie replaced Jessie as my role model. Eventually, though, Melanie became much more to me than just a mentor; in my mind she became my mother. The years of fighting with my real mother had left me believing that I couldn't be loved by her. Our relationship was just too damaged, too broken to ever be fixed. At the same time, though, I was only twelve years old; and I hungered for love, so I began to look for someone who could replace the mother I thought I had lost. Melanie became that replacement.

My heart would jump for joy as soon as I heard Melanie pulling up the gravel drive each day in her old white Dodge truck. Every afternoon I went to the barn and spent countless hours watching Melanie ride and handle her glossy-coated horses. I analyzed all of Melanie's moves and tried to mimic her riding style. I even went as far as selling all my old equipment so I could buy the brands Melanie liked. I desperately wanted her approval and was willing to do anything to get it. I always got ready for my lesson at least forty-five minutes early. Ace had to be impeccably clean, my equipment needed to be polished, everything had to be perfect. I relished the praise Melanie gave me for being so meticulous and for mimicking her riding style. I couldn't believe someone was telling me I was doing something right for once.

The first horse show Melanie took Ace and me to was even better than the shows I had been to with my previous trainer. No jump seemed too big or too challenging for us. When the announcer read out the results, I could feel tears form in my eyes. Ace and I had won every class in our division. Things had been so hard for so long, and now I was actually succeeding at something. I had no idea everything was about to come crashing down.

Melanie broke the news to me gently: if I ever wanted to make it to the top, Ace would have to go. Her tone of voice was full of care and concern, as if she knew how much her words hurt me. When I first moved to Melanie's, I thought of Ace as my teammate. Everything about the two of us just felt so right. When we went to shows, people told us we even looked alike. His eyes were large, brown, and soft; mine were hazel. His coat was chestnut colored, my hair was red. I loved Ace immensely, yet my love for Melanie was greater. In the end, I betrayed my teammate in the hope that Melanie would love me back.

I had already stopped talking to my mother before moving to Willow Wind. Once I met Melanie, though, silence turned into detachment, which then turned into hatred. My mother first became my enemy because she made me swallow pills or eat. Now she was the enemy because Melanie said so. *You have to convince your parents that you need a new horse and fast. Ace just isn't good enough to get you to the Grand Prix level. If you don't get a new horse, you will never succeed.* This was the new recording that played in my head, orchestrated by Melanie. I could only think about failure, the end of my dream, and the end of my future. Without horses, there was nothing left for me to hold on to; my life would be meaningless.

These horrible thoughts sent a wave of panic rushing through my body as I tried to muster up enough courage to ask my dad for a new horse. If my parents wouldn't let me get one, I believed Melanie wouldn't want to train me anymore. I would just be a waste of her time. My fears were confirmed when Melanie began saying that she was "losing interest" in me. I cringed at her words, feeling as though I had been abandoned by my own mother.

Even when Brooke and I were little, we would run to our dad first if we wanted something. We knew he was a softie and would give in to our demands for new Polly Pocket watches or the latest Beanie Baby. When I worked up the courage to ask for a new horse, I reverted back to the days when I would crawl up on Daddy's lap, smile real big, and ask if we could go to the toy store. Now though, I wasn't just asking for a teddy bear—I was asking for an expensive horse that had to be shipped from Europe. As soon as my mother found out about my request, the first word out of her mouth was no. At the sound of my mother's voice, I snapped my head around and stared at her coldly. As far as I was concerned, she was an unwelcome intruder who hadn't been invited into our conversation. Regardless, there would be no new horse.

At the time, my parents' initial refusal to buy me a new horse drew me even closer to Melanie. We'd sit in her office devising new schemes to change my parents' minds. Melanie offered to meet with my dad and make the case for a horse from a trainer's perspective. I thought she had a great idea and continually thanked her for her generosity. Her promises to help me reach my goal of becoming a Grand Prix rider made me smile as I thought about all Melanie was willing to do for me. I thanked her repeatedly for everything, clasping both hands together with my head bent down low as though I was giving thanks to the gods.

"Don't worry Melissa. We will get everything worked out. Just make sure your mother doesn't come to our meeting. You know, Melissa, I am more of a mom to you than she is. I spend the most time with you. I'm the one who drives you to horse shows and takes care of you when we go out of town. Your mother almost never comes to see you ride. She's just not interested in you." I nodded my head in agreement the whole time Melanie spoke. Melanie was right. My real mother didn't love me. All she ever did was push pills in my face and call the police to take me away. As I reviewed the past few years in my mind, I believed my mother hated me and I hated her.

Our original plan was to have my dad come to my Saturday lesson and watch me ride Ace so Melanie could show him how limited Ace was, but my dad had to spend most of the morning at the office and wasn't able to make it to my lesson. I wasn't surprised by the change of plans, since I was well aware of my dad's preoccupation with work. Yet I couldn't help feeling a pang of sadness when I found out he wouldn't be coming to watch me ride. The feeling quickly dissipated, though, when I saw Melanie walking up the barn aisle. Melanie always watched me ride; Melanie always wanted to help me.

Around 11:00 AM, I saw my dad's car turning into the parking lot of Willow Wind. The sight of his gray Explorer caused my stomach to twist in knots as every muscle in my body grew rigid. I prayed that my mother hadn't come along, and breathed a sigh of relief when only my dad stepped out of the car. For the past few days, Melanie and I had practiced what she was going to say to my dad, so the whole visit was almost like some sort of theatrical performance.

My dad exchanged a few greetings with Melanie, and then we followed her to her office. As we sat down, Melanie cleared her throat and began talking to my dad in her thick German accent. "Mr. Binstock, I know that paying for horses, training, and horse shows is very expensive. But you must understand—this is what

Melissa excels at and has chosen for a profession. Ace is a wonderful horse for beginners, but Melissa has outgrown him. To move up, she really needs a horse that is more suitable for higher jumping divisions."

Melanie's tone of voice was sweet yet forceful at the same time. Everything she said just seemed to roll off her tongue as if she'd had this conversation with a thousand other parents. When my dad finally agreed to buy me a new horse, I wanted to jump up, hug Melanie, and tell her to take a bow. Her performance had been brilliant.

As the weeks at Willow Wind went by, my attitude toward horses slowly began to change. Once Melanie had told me that Ace wasn't good enough to take me to the higher divisions, I started noticing his faults more and more. Melanie was right about Ace. He was lazy and stiff. He couldn't do all the fancy dressage moves her German horses could do so easily. Ace didn't have beautiful gaits, and he couldn't jump very high. My view of him had completely changed. I began to view horses as tools that I needed to get to the top level. I could love them only as long as they could give me what I wanted.

STARVING
FOR LOVE

9

Sixth grade started off smoothly at my new school, Cornerstone Academy. Most of my classes were one-on-one with just me and the teacher, and generally the day ended by 1:30 PM. Other than that, though, Cornerstone wasn't too different from a regular school. I had books for each subject, assignments to complete, and I even had my own locker. In the beginning of the year, I looked forward to school and was excited to learn, but soon my excitement shifted to agitation and then to fear. Math, the subject I had loved the most in Mrs. Leonard's third-grade class, became one I learned to despise. My teacher continually snapped at me for counting on my fingers and threatened to make me wear a pair of gloves if I didn't stop. I wasn't all that sure what good gloves would do, but the constant threats were enough to annoy me. My frustration only grew when my teacher tried to teach me how to do long-hand division, because I had no idea how to divide in the first place. In reality, it wasn't really my teacher's fault for moving through the material so quickly. She had no idea that I had just spent the past three years in either a state of medicated oblivion or in a school with no textbooks. I never told her about my past, so she didn't know how to help me. My mother explained my situation to the teacher during the fall parent-teacher conferences. After that, my teacher's brusque demands of stop it or quit that whenever she saw me counting on my fingers were replaced by a silent scowl and an impatient tap of the foot. Her body language told me she was still miffed at me, but at least now she was relatively silent about it.

At the end of every school day, I changed into my riding clothes and waited on the front steps of the school for my mother to pick me up and take me to the stable. The horses continued to serve as an escape for me. At first, horses had been a comfort solely because I could go to them and feel completely at ease with myself. Now, though, being around horses was a comfort because they gave me a reason to live by providing me with a purpose. I guess you could say that horses are what saved my life.

As I got more serious about my riding career, the healthy person within me became stronger and stronger until she overpowered the Sick Person, allowing me to begin to look at food differently. The peanut butter sandwich I packed for lunch was fuel and without it I knew I wouldn't have the energy to perform well. As I got stronger, the Sick Person began to hush. At first, it was strange to have so much energy. The chant of *fat, fat, fat* that I was used to hearing after eating was replaced by a sweet sounding voice that whispered *You did well today.* Sometimes, though, the Sick Person would regain her power over me, which she did one afternoon toward the end of November.

It was noon, and I had just gotten out of English. All through class, I had listened to my stomach growling as my teacher read the last chapter of *The Outsiders* aloud. When the bell finally rang I picked up my book bag and made my way back to the small junior high study hall. On the way, I saw two of the middle-school girls I had PE with. Tia and Kylie were the cool girls everyone seemed to like. I had always been the odd kid, but there was a part of me that wanted to be considered "cool." After we all arrived in study hall, I summoned the courage to ask Tia if she wanted to have lunch with me. But before Tia could respond, Kylie jumped in to say, "Sorry, we don't eat lunch."

Those words unlocked a door I had been trying to shut tight to keep out an unwelcome visitor. The Sick Person barged her way through that door and made her presence very clear to me. All I could hear for the rest of the day was her hissing, *We don't eat lunch, we don't eat lunch, we don't eat lunch.* Yet the *we* was no longer referring to Tia and Kylie; the *we* was the Sick Person and me.

The return of the Sick Person sent a wave of panic crashing hard through my body. How could I eat with the Sick Person constantly screaming in my ear? If I didn't eat, how could I have the energy to ride? No, I couldn't let that happen, not when everything was finally going well! Somehow, I would have to find a way to shut the Sick Person out. And the only way I could think of doing that was to focus even more on the horses, performing, and being perfect for Melanie.

My new horse arrived from Germany in late December. After my dad had agreed to buy me a horse, everything seemed to just fall into place. Melanie had been planning to take a trip to Germany anyhow, and now she could just pick out a horse for me while she was there. All my dad had to do was wire over the money.

When I first laid eyes on Apollo, I couldn't help but gasp. He was a beautiful horse with a sleek bay coat, long graceful legs, and an elegant head. When Melanie brought Apollo to me, I felt as though she was putting my shattered world back together. Everything was finally going right. I had the best trainer and a great horse. On top of that, I was actually making friends at Willow Wind. It felt so good to feel like I belonged to something, to feel like I was normal. I wish I could just end my story here in this happy world I found myself in for a while. But that was far from the reality of my life; I would just be lying to you.

For a while the Sick Person was quiet again. Now and then I heard chants of *fat, fat, fat,* but over time the sound of the Sick Person's voice became nothing more than a barely inaudible whisper. I began traveling to out-of-town horse shows more often, and since my parents couldn't come, Melanie made a place for me in her car. On the way to the shows, I sat in awe as Melanie told me all about her fabulous life in Europe and how she competed at the highest levels. I heard all about the great and many horses she had and the famous people she trained with. Soon enough, my life became a nonstop cycle of horse shows, training, and obsessively worrying about whether I was Melanie's favorite or not. My worry turned into terror when Emily moved to Willow Wind.

The first time I saw Emily, I knew we couldn't be friends. It was mid-January, and as I stepped out of my mother's car, the chilly air nipped at my face and gloveless hands. Everything seemed calm and quiet until I turned into the barn to see a girl with long brown hair swept back in a ponytail; she was brushing a horse in Melanie's grooming stall. The sight of the girl caused something inside me to yell, *Intruder!*

I felt like the two of us were competing predators in the wild and that Emily was about to invade the niche I had already claimed as my own. But as much as I wanted to chase Emily away, the rational part of my mind told me that I couldn't. Instead, I decided to talk to her so that I could get a better feel for how big a threat she was going to be. As I walked up to Emily to introduce myself, I saw a petite woman with graying hair and bright red lipstick standing beside her. She didn't look much like Emily, who had a boxy frame and broad shoulders. The woman was the first to say hello, introducing herself as Ms. Sindy. As I began asking a question, Ms. Sindy interrupted me to ask how long I'd been training with Melanie. I threw an anxious glance at the woman, realizing that her agenda was the same as mine; she was sizing me up. All the while Ms. Sindy and I questioned one another, Emily continued brushing out her mare's long brown tail, appearing to be totally disinterested in the conversation.

Toward the end of February, the atmosphere at Willow Wind was thick with excitement as everyone began preparing for one of the biggest shows of the year. The Pine Hollow show brought people from all over the country together to compete for the $25,000 that was offered to the winner of the Grand Prix. I was excited because Apollo and I would be competing in a new division for the first time. Although my riding career was beginning to take off, my growing hunger for love distracted me from enjoying what I had. More than anything, I wanted Melanie to love me. I yearned for the special type of love that only a mother and daughter share. I wanted to grab hold of that love, hold it safely in my arms, and never let it go. I thought if I could just secure Melanie's love, I would be complete.

Yet no matter what I did, I couldn't seem to hold on to Melanie's love. At times, she would offer it by giving me a pat on the back or calling me *daughter,* but then she'd snatch her affection away, uttering cold comments of *not good enough* and *worthless* whenever I didn't perform just right. I felt like a hungry dog constantly being tempted with food that would be pulled away at the last second. But I kept reaching out because I was ravenous and starving for love. The thought that Melanie could hurt me never crossed my mind. In my eyes, she could do no wrong. At the time, I didn't realize she was purposely pairing me up with Emily for lessons because she knew how jealous I was of the girl. During our lessons, Melanie would tell us to watch each other, scoffing when one of us messed up, and making comments like "See how she did that totally wrong?" Lessons were turning into torture sessions. I couldn't wait for the thirty minutes to be over so I could either walk away in victory or kick myself for being such a screw up.

The weekend of the Pine Hollow horse show finally came. On Friday morning, Melanie and I arrived at the show grounds while it was still dark out. The smell of clean shavings hit my nose as I walked down the Willow Wind aisle. Most of the horses were still dozing quietly but a few were sticking their heads out of the stall window, waiting for their morning grain. After feeding Apollo a carrot, I walked down to the arena in-gate to look at the jumps. The brightly colored poles and standards were already set up for the first division of the morning. As I walked around the arena, I examined the height of all the jumps and concluded that Apollo and I could master the fences.

After giving Apollo a pat, I walked over to sit down next to Melanie, who was relaxing in one of our barn's monogrammed chairs, smoking her morning cigarette and drinking a Coke. Emily and a tall, blond girl named Amanda were also sitting nearby, busily putting on their boots and riding hats. After Melanie flicked her cigarette butt into a trash bin, the four of us got up to walk the course of jumps we would later take. While we walked, Melanie told us what the fastest route was going to be, where to turn, and how many steps our horses should take between each fence.

"Emily, your mare can do five strides here. Don't hold her back too much. Amanda, don't go too far into the corners. You might get time faults. Melissa, don't pull on Apollo's face." I began to wonder if there was a meaning behind why Melanie addressed me last. Did she like me less than the other girls? *Melanie can't like Amanda more than me. I know she can't because she always talks about how Amanda is a brat. What about Emily? Melanie never talks badly about her. She must like Emily better than me. She does, I know she does!* I could feel my anxiety increasing at the thought of losing Melanie to Emily. I had to prove to her that I deserved to be talked to first. If I could just win this class, then she'd see. Preoccupied with the thought of losing Melanie, I stopped paying attention to the course of fences I was supposed to take. By the time we had passed the last jump, I had no idea what the correct path was. My mind began to buzz. Even when I reviewed the course on a slip of paper, I was still having a hard time remembering where I was supposed to turn or what jump I needed to go to next. The jump course seemed impossibly long.

It always amazed me how Emily and Amanda could review the jump course once or twice and know exactly where they needed to go. For me, learning a course took at least thirty minutes of reviewing and making up some sort of mnemonic to help me remember. Even then, I would sometimes forget where to turn, and forgetting would send me into a panic as I frantically scanned the arena for the next jump. What I didn't know at the time was that I had a working memory issue, and instead I believed I just wasn't as bright as the other girls.

As I led Apollo down the barn aisle, I went over the course again and again in my mind, trying to convince myself that everything was going to be okay. By the time I got to the warm-up area,

Amanda was already trotting her big bay mare around the arena while Emily was in the middle of the ring adjusting her helmet. After a few warm-up jumps, the three of us headed to the show ring, my stomach doing flip-flops all the while. Emily was the first of us to go, and she completed the course with a fast time. As she made her way out of the ring, I saw Ms. Sindy clapping and jumping up and down in the stands. Secretly, I had wanted Emily to fail. I hoped that she'd get a rail down or that her horse would refuse a jump. I didn't really care about how Amanda did. She wasn't a big enough threat for me to worry about; Melanie didn't love her. Finally, it was my turn.

As we made our way into the show arena, I squeezed my legs around Apollo's sides, signaling him to pick up a trot. A buzzing noise sounded, meaning that we had one minute to get to the first jump. I moved Apollo into a canter, and we began heading toward a blue-and-white colored fence. As we got closer to the jump, Apollo's ears pricked forward before he launched into the air. Before I knew it, we were on the other side of the fence and heading toward our second jump. Everything went well—until about midway through the course, when I forgot where we were supposed to go.

Panic took over as I heard Melanie's brusque voice. "Turn, turn! Yellow stone wall!" After frantically looking around the arena, I finally figured out where we were supposed to go. But the jump came up too fast, causing Apollo to take off at an awkward distance so that he knocked the top pole down with his hind legs. I was slightly shaken by the sound of poles hitting the ground, but I managed to remember that we were supposed to take the water jump next. As we approached the fence, I felt Apollo shorten his stride as he tried to swerve away from the formidable-looking jump. I squeezed my calves hard against his side, yet he didn't respond. All of a sudden there was a skidding of hooves and a loud crash as Apollo slid through the fence. Losing my grip, I flew over Apollo's head and landed on top of the fallen rails. I lay there for a moment with my eyes closed, trying to catch my breath and wanting nothing more than to just disappear. I didn't care to look up to see where Apollo had run off to. All I focused on was trying to make myself become invisible. A few minutes passed before I finally forced myself to stand up, walking out of the arena horseless and covered with dirt.

As I made my way back to the barn, I could hear the Sick Person hissing in my ear. *Failure, failure, failure—you are a failure! How could you think you would succeed? Worthless girl; pitiful, worthless girl!* I didn't even try to counter the Sick Person's sneers. She was right; I was a failure. Melanie met me at the stalls where the groom had already unsaddled Apollo. Seeing Melanie's angry scowl and piercing blue eyes scanning me up and down made me feel as though someone had stripped me naked, exposing me for the world to see.

"Melissa, how could you forget where you were going?" Melanie growled at me. "You reviewed that course for half an hour, damn it! Didn't you see Emily's round? Didn't you see that? God, I don't know what to do with you. How can I work with someone who can't even remember where she's going?" Melanie's searing words felt like burning oil being splashed against my bare skin, making me want to cry out in pain.

"I'm sorry, I'm sorry! I'll do better next time. I promise I'll do better next time!" I hiccupped as I tried to hold back the tears that were stinging my eyes.

"Go shower your horse, Melissa. I don't want to talk to you anymore."

As I walked away from Melanie, my body felt heavy and slow, as though someone had tied fifty pound weights to my arms and legs. When I got to the wash racks, Emily offered me a pat on the back and a promise that things would get better. I tried to muster up a smile in return to Emily's kindness, while simultaneously feeling guilty about how much I secretly despised her.

Saturday wasn't much better for me. No matter how hard I tried, I couldn't remember the jump course. Round after round I'd forget where to go midway through the course, causing my anxiety to increase a little more each time I had to enter the show arena. The fences seemed to grow in size before my eyes. Each jump became an insurmountable wall that I was asking this horse to carry me over. My fears seemed to be justified: after a while, Apollo refused to jump.

The old courses I used to ride with Ace and Bailey were simple and straightforward hunter courses, with the judging based on how graceful you and your horse looked. Now that I was competing in the show-jumping division, everything was fast, hard, and complicated. Show jumping was all about getting over the jumps as quickly as you could without knocking anything down. I missed the slow, rhythmic movements of hunters, yet I could never admit that aloud. Melanie thought hunters was pointless, boring, and slow. More than anything, I wanted her approval, so I never spoke up. As far as I was concerned, going back to hunters would mean failure.

THIS TIME WILL BE DIFFERENT   10

I was relieved when summer finally came. Everyone at Willow Wind was getting ready for a show in San Antonio, the first since my embarrassing debut with Apollo. I wasn't looking forward to forcing Apollo back into the show ring. He seemed to now detest jumping as much as I feared it. At every lesson, terror cut away at my insides as Melanie raised the jumps higher and higher. Yet I wouldn't let anyone see my internal wounds. I remained calm on the outside, sometimes even asking Melanie to raise the fences higher, thinking that would help me earn her love and approval. Even though I wasn't looking forward to competing, I was ecstatic when Melanie offered to drive me to San Antonio.

Amanda and Emily's parents were taking them to the show, but neither of my parents could go. Things were different now. When Brooke and I were little, horse shows had been like family weekends. Our parents would wake up at 4:00 AM to drive us out to the competition grounds. My mom always got us up extra early so we would have time to stop at Starbucks and pick up hot chocolate and blueberry muffins. On the way to the show, Brooke and I would eat our oversized muffins while belting out our favorite country songs. But now things were different. Brooke hadn't ridden in almost two years, and my parents were too busy with other things to watch me ride. They still drove me to some of the in-town shows at odd hours in the morning. But Brooke had been replaced with an empty seat, and blueberry muffins were exchanged for bottles of water and Diet Coke. There was no one for me to sing country music with. Now, horse shows were business affairs, not fun.

After a five-hour car ride from Houston, Melanie and I finally pulled into the show grounds. I was relieved because for most of the drive, Melanie wasn't interested in talking to me much. Each time she said my name, I sat up a little straighter in my seat, but usually "Melissa" was followed by "Hand me a Coke from the back." I kept waiting for some guidance, or at least a lecture, about the upcoming show . . . at least, that's what I thought a good trainer would do . . . but Melanie basically ignored me.

My first class was another disaster. I managed to stay on Apollo's back this time, but we were disqualified after crashing into a jump. As we walked out of the arena, I finally broke down. Hot tears streamed down my face, dripping onto my navy show jacket with a splash. As we walked out of the arena, the sound of Apollo's hooves hitting the ground matched the beat of the recording that was going off in my head that shouted *failure, failure, failure.* I wanted Melanie to tell me everything would be okay, yet when I looked around the in-gate area, she wasn't there. I walked Apollo around the show grounds for another twenty minutes until I was sure that my eyes were no longer red. As we walked, I held my reins in one hand while pinching the skin on my thigh with the other. I wanted to feel pain. A cold sounding voice within my mind told me that the only thing I deserved was pain. This voice belonged to a second Sick Person; a Sick Person who told me how I would never be loved, yelling at the top of her lungs, *You unlovable, disgusting girl! How could you let Melanie down again?* This other person was loud and demanding, making me run myself ragged until she was certain that I had pleased Melanie. Her voice was the one that yelled, *Not good enough! Not good enough!* causing me to tear at my skin until it bled. I began to experience an omnipresent battle taking place inside my head between two sick people, each one trying to scream louder than the other. Both of them, though, shared a common goal: they wanted complete control. One wanted control of food, the other of love. In the midst of the feud, though, I never realized that both wanted to kill me.

The more I tried to ignore them, the louder the words in my head became.

When I got back to the barn, I jumped off Apollo's back and handed him to the groom. As I walked away, I felt a stinging sensation in my thigh. Looking down, I noticed blood had soaked through my breeches. Unconsciously, I had clawed at my leg until it bled. I changed out of my show clothes, putting on a pair of jeans and an oversized white sweatshirt that had the Willow Wind emblem printed on the front. Standing at the bathroom sink, I scrubbed at the bloodied pants leg with a bar of glycerin saddle soap, but the stain wouldn't come out. I finally gave up and tossed the pants in the trash. When I got back to the stalls, Melanie was writing the next day's schedule on her dry-erase board. I was too afraid to talk to her about what had happened. I was a complete disappointment, and I knew it. Later in the day when Melanie tried to talk to me, I couldn't look her in the eyes, much less answer her questions. My failure to respond only made Melanie angrier.

"God damn it, Melissa, you are ruining that horse. If you keep crashing, he's just not going to jump anymore. I think the time has come for you to sell him because from the looks of it, he's pretty fed up with you." Melanie's words were like knives in my side, causing me to almost double over in pain. I felt hot tears fill my eyes again until everything was blurry. I didn't love Apollo, but I didn't want to go through the pain of selling him, either. It's not that I would miss him or anything; I just knew there was no way my mother was going to let me get another horse.

Melanie didn't know why I was crying. I think my tears just fed her fury, and when Melanie noticed that I was wearing a Willow Wind sweatshirt, she snapped and yelled, "Take off that sweatshirt and go sit in the dirt where you belong!"

I never told my parents about most of the comments Melanie made. If I let something slip out, I knew they wouldn't let me travel with Melanie anymore. Without Melanie, there would be no one to take me since most of the time my dad was too busy with work and my mother needed to stay home with Brooke and Sam. At one point, I deeply wanted my mother to come with me to the shows like Emily's mom did. I hated Ms. Sindy, but it was only because I didn't have what she gave Emily—love. I wanted to be loved, to feel something besides hate, sadness, or anxiety. Love became a tangible object I thought I could reach out and grasp in my hands. I wanted love so badly that everyone who had it or whom I thought was impeding me from getting it became my enemy. Ms. Sindy and Emily had exactly what I couldn't get, and I couldn't help but hate them both for it.

Even though Melanie had all but convinced me that my mother didn't love me, a small part of me held out hope that perhaps Melanie was wrong. At the end of the summer, I begged my dad to take me to a horse show that was coming up in Louisiana, knowing that he wouldn't go without my mother. When my dad finally agreed, I felt a strange warming sensation ripple through my body as a smile spread over my lips. For the first time in a long while, I was happy. My happiness, though, was overcome by annoyance once I found out that my sisters were tagging along. I didn't really want anyone there but my mother. I thought that if I could just have her there and no one else, everything would be like it was before we stopped talking.

The scene played in my mind like a movie. My mother would drive up to the show in her old gray Expedition. We wouldn't talk at first, but after listening to an Alison Krauss CD or two, my mother would comment on something stupid, like how the man at the gas station looked like Barbara Walters. We'd both laugh for a while, and then I'd tell her how sorry I was for everything. She'd say that everything in the past was over with and not to worry. Then the moment I had been waiting for would come. We'd pull over on the side of the road, my mother would wrap me in her arms, and she'd whisper, "Melissa, I love you." I imagined how it would feel to hear her say those words. Love would finally be mine. But my dream world was only that. I never told anyone what I wanted, so the car ride I had so carefully planned out in my mind never happened. Instead of taking the Expedition, we took a plane; instead of only my mom and I going, the whole family came.

The first morning of the horse show arrived, bringing a warm September breeze along with it. The warm air felt good against my face as Melanie and I walked the course for my class. *This time it's going to be different. My mom's here this time. Everything is going to be okay.* The mantra played in my head as we walked from fence to fence. Melanie's tone of voice was soft and sweet sounding as she explained what path would be best for me to take. Part of me knew she was only being this nice because my parents were two feet away, but at that moment I didn't care. As soon as we finished walking the jump course, I ran back to the barn to collect Apollo from the groom. I had to be certain that Apollo looked beautiful. His coat glistened in the warm sunshine and the new white saddle pad looked lovely beneath my mahogany colored saddle. Apollo was a gorgeous horse, and as I looked over him, I was proud to say he was mine. But to tell you the truth, I still didn't love him.

The warm-up area was crowded with horses, while trainers called out instructions to their students. As I squeezed Apollo into a trot, I couldn't help but think how cool Melanie was. She was leaning against a jump standard, smoking a cigarette and talking to an odd-looking man who was wearing tan-colored jodhpurs and a worn-out cowboy hat. My warm-up session with Apollo went off without a hitch. Apollo's gait was smooth and rhythmic as we approached each fence. I could see my mother out of the corner of my eye. I smiled to myself, feeling as though I had finally entered the fantasy world I had created in my mind. As Apollo trotted into the show ring, I wrapped my legs firmly around his sides, cueing him to pick up a canter. A buzzing noise sounded overhead; and after circling around once, I guided Apollo to the first fence. As we approached a green and white colored jump, the sound of barking dogs and shouting trainers suddenly became inaudible, as though someone had pressed the mute button on a TV that had been blasting moments before. The only sound left was the rhythmic *pat, pat, pat* of Apollo's hooves against the ground and a voice in my head saying, *If you do this right, she might love you.* As Apollo's front hooves left the ground, I pushed my hands up his muscular neck while sinking all my weight into my heels.

The second fence was a green box with fake flowers placed on top. I felt Apollo hesitate when he caught sight of the flowers, but I encouraged him forward with my legs. He cleared the jump with ease. Everything up to fence ten seemed like a dream to me. For the first time, Apollo and I were actually a team. Yet my little fantasy world evaporated as we approached the next jump—the water jump. The voice inside me yelled, *You're going to mess this one up, too!* A moment later, there was the all-too familiar sequence of events: the sound of sliding hooves and splitting poles, the last attempt to clutch Apollo's neck, the hard landing, and the inability to get in a breath of air. All of this had become routine to me; the only difference this time was that my mother was there to see it all.

I lay on the ground for a minute, trying to take in a breath, all the while wishing I was invisible. The arena sand felt soft under my body. I pretended that I was back at home in my bed. The sand I clutched in my hands was really the pink and white down comforter that sat on my twin-size bed.

Yet as soon as I heard my mother's voice at the in-gate, I realized that what I held in my hands was just dirt. I wanted so badly to just disappear. I couldn't wrap myself up in a cocoon of warm blankets because I was prone on the arena floor next to a pile of fallen standards and broken poles. I lifted my body off the ground, not the least surprised to see that Apollo was nowhere in sight. As I made my way out of the arena, my mother rushed up to me to ask if I was all right. I nodded my head silently. She was there for me, but I couldn't think about anything other than disappointing Melanie.

If I could just find Melanie and tell her I was sorry for being such a screw up, she'd help me make everything right again. My mother was reaching for me, and I pushed her away. Her hug felt cold and foreign to me. She wrapped me in her arms, but I didn't feel that warm sense of happiness rush over my body. All I could think of was Melanie—where had she gone?

I walked back to the barn with my mother a few feet behind me, listening to a voice in my head that sneered, *Your mother doesn't really love you.* Melanie was sitting in her usual spot on one of the red and gold chairs that had WILLOW WIND printed on the back. All I could think about was running up to her to tell her how sorry I was, but my thoughts were interrupted by the sound of my mother arguing with Melanie.

"Melanie, how could you leave her there like that?" My mother's words sounded both angry and cold to me. I wanted to yell at her to leave us alone. It was my fault for messing up; Melanie didn't have anything to do with it. I wanted to scream for her to stop talking, fearing that my mother's outburst would make Melanie even angrier at me. Even though I heard the words sound off in my head, I couldn't force them out.

I could see Melanie getting angrier and angrier with each word as my mother continued, "It's your responsibility as a trainer to make sure Melissa is safe. You put her in a class that was too difficult. Those jumps were too high, and that horse isn't safe." I could feel hot tears pricking at my eyes, but I forced them back. If I started crying, Melanie would think I was upset with her. I couldn't cry, not now.

"Well, Mrs. Binstock, if you don't like my training methods, you are free to take Melissa and leave." The word *leave* echoed in my ear. Where would I go? Who would take me? Who would want me? I felt like I was being forced out of my home with no one to go to for help. The thought of not making it to the Grand Prix level crossed my mind, but more than anything, I feared losing Melanie. I tried to focus on something other than the sound of angry voices.

I concentrated on working the toe of my boot into the sand, seeing how deep a hole I could make. So many words swarmed around my head. I wanted to scream them all, but the only words to escape from my mouth were "Please stop." No one seemed to hear me.

Later in the afternoon, my dad returned with Brooke and Sam in the jeep we had rented. My dad was smiling and joking with Brooke about how she had almost driven the jeep into a ditch. As I watched them, I wondered, *What do they have that makes them so happy? Where did they get it, and why don't I have it?* The laughing stopped, though, when my mother told them what had happened. That was the last horse show my parents attended.

CREDIT LIMIT   11

Almost an entire week passed before Melanie spoke to me again. Thursday afternoon was an especially long day at school. For the entire week I thought about what to say to Melanie and decided that Thursday would be the perfect day to tell her how sorry I was. I could talk to her during my lesson and everything would be okay again. The words I would use were all picked out and neatly organized in my head like a script; that was the way I prepared for everything. That afternoon, I sat rehearsing my script in the PE room just before class began. A few minutes after the bell sounded, the gym teacher—a small spunky woman with bright red hair—made her way into the gym. Mrs. Keller was an interesting woman with a step so full of enthusiasm that whenever she entered a room it seemed like she was bouncing instead of walking.

Everyone looked forward to gym because Mrs. Keller never made anyone work very hard, and once in a while she would even take us to the pizza place down the street. I never got very excited about our little field trips since I wasn't going to eat greasy, fattening pizza anyway. On this day when Mrs. Keller led us to the pizza parlor, I especially wasn't in the mood to watch other people eat pizza when all I could think about was what I was going to say to Melanie.

I stayed a few paces ahead of everyone else and pretended to be alone. As soon as I walked into the pizza parlor, the smell of cheese and marinara sauce filled the air. Automatically, I took a deep breath in, trying to satisfy my growling stomach with the rich smells. I still heard the Sick Person's voice whispering cruel things about my body every time I ate or looked in the mirror. Lately, though, the louder voice yelling unceasingly was the second Sick Person, the one who demanded love. Although her words were often cold and cruel, I looked at her as an ally and even yearned for her companionship. When this second Sick Person was present, the screams about food and weight became nothing more than whispers. The best thing about allowing this second person to have control over me was that she actually let me eat—God, it felt good to eat.

Pizza is a food I love and fear at the same time. That day, when the waiter brought over everyone's meals, I picked up a slice of cheese pizza and tore off a piece of crust. I was allowed to eat the crust, but nothing more because these were the rules of the diet game the Sick Person had configured. I was extremely grateful the Sick Person allowed me to eat pizza at all.

Only a few years earlier, bread in any form had been completely forbidden. When I began focusing on my riding career, I started to look at food as energy and, in a sense, as medicine I needed to take to succeed in the show ring. Doing well at horseback riding had become more important to me than pleasing the Sick Person, which allowed me to ignore her screams for the most part. Now I had some leeway and could nibble on some crusts.

It seemed like something bad always happened whenever pizza

was in the picture, though. While I silently rehearsed my script, I took a bite of the crust, chewed for a few seconds, and then swallowed it. But as I felt the crust make its way down my throat, I was struck by a wave of panic. I didn't know where the feeling came from or how it took hold of me. All I knew was that right before the feeling hit me, the words *disgusting pig* had sounded off in my head like a chant, each time louder than the last. My head began to pound from the noise until I couldn't stand it. Every sound seemed magnified to the extreme; the voices, the clinking of glasses, even the sound of people chewing became unbearably loud. All I could think about was getting relief from the noise and the screaming voice. Anything would do; I just wanted to make it stop.

I jumped up from the table and dodged into the bathroom, splashing cold water on my face. Yet the water didn't help ameliorate the panicky feeling as the words *filthy, disgusting girl* continued playing in my head like a tape recording. I desperately wanted to get rid of the horrible, panicky sensation that made me feel as though my stomach was coiled into tight knots and the crust was stuck in my throat, but I didn't know how to make it go away. Finally it hit me: I could throw it up. Yes! Yes! Throw it up; that was the answer! Walking into the farthest stall, I knelt down while tying my hair back with a rubber band I had on my wrist. The rest is so predictable that it's unnecessary to even detail. All I wanted was some sense of relief from the horrible feeling and blaring sound of the Sick Person's voice. Throwing up did that for me. When I stood up, I felt light and at ease again; I didn't realize I had mistaken the feeling of emptiness with relief.

The conversation with Melanie I had planned out in my head never actually happened. I couldn't tell Melanie how I felt or that I was sorry. The words just wouldn't come. As the weeks passed by,

Melanie's comments became more piercing and hurtful to me, "Melissa, I'm losing interest in you. You are careless, just careless! Your horse is ruined, and I can't train you anymore unless you convince your father to buy you a new horse." As visions of Ace appeared in my mind, I also heard the sound of my mother's voice shouting, "How dare you ask for anything else!" The same old panicky feeling passed through my body as I thought about making my mother angry and the possibility of Melanie giving up on me again.

History was repeating itself. Melanie planned another meeting with my dad to persuade him to buy me a new horse. The only difference was that Melanie's script had changed. This time, instead of saying that I had outgrown my horse, Melanie talked about how I had ruined my horse, referring to horses as "credit cards" that have set limits. I had used up all of my extra credit by crashing Apollo into jumps or pulling too hard on his bit whenever I forgot where I was supposed to go on the course. Melanie's script was carefully planned out from start to finish. She sounded so sincere when she spoke to my father.

"If we are not careful, Mr. Binstock, Apollo's price value will fall too low and we will not be able to sell him. You see, horses are not very forgiving, and Melissa has made a lot of mistakes that have shaken Apollo's confidence. We do not want Melissa to lower Apollo's price value any further. We can spend the money that we get from him on a new horse, and you can make up the price difference by agreeing to a payment plan." Once again, my dad gave into Melanie, agreeing to buy me yet another new horse. By the time eighth grade began, Apollo was sold and replaced with a honey-colored mare Melanie named Cadence.

Cadence was beautiful, even more so than Apollo. Her eyes were big, soft, and brown. She had a coat that shone with the signs of health and good feed. There was something about Cadence that just seemed special to me. The first time I sat on her broad back and felt her powerful step, I knew something was finally going right. It was as though we had just melted together into one body, no longer two separate entities.

After two short weeks, the show day at Pine Hollow arrived. It felt strange to be back at Pine Hollow with Cadence. A year had passed by since my first disastrous show with Apollo. By the time I got to the show grounds on the first Friday of the show, the aisles were bustling with activity. Amanda and Emily hadn't yet arrived, but the grooms already had our horses saddled up for our morning class. As I patted Cadence's soft honey-colored neck, she tossed her head and let out a high-pitched whinny. The sound of footsteps made me turn around, and I saw Melanie coming down the aisle with two Jack Russell terriers trailing close behind.

"'Morning, Melissa. It sounds like Cadence is ready to get going. Why don't you go down to the arena and learn your jump course. I really hope you can remember it this time. I don't want any more of your disastrous rounds."

"Sure, yeah, okay. I'll go do that now. I promise I won't forget this time, Melanie." As I walked toward the arena, the words *I promise, I promise* kept running through my mind.

My initial class with Cadence on Friday morning seemed unreal to me. I could hardly believe I had actually completed the jump course without forgetting where I was going or ending up on the ground. I had been practicing for weeks to improve on memorizing jump courses, and my ability to remember them had improved, although it still took me significantly longer than Emily and Amanda. With Apollo, competing had become a business affair, no longer a happy occasion filled with anticipation. But with Cadence,

I felt like I had gone back in time to those days when I looked forward to riding and truly enjoyed it.

After we had taken the horses back to Willow Wind on Sunday afternoon, Melanie offered to drop me off at my house. Just as I stepped out of Melanie's old dodge truck I heard her say, "Melissa, well done." I was flooded with a warm wave of happiness. The words *well done* echoed in my head again and again, intermingled with *She loves me, Melanie loves me*. This sense of happiness was so overwhelming and strong that it left me feeling sedated. My body was light, my mind at ease. There were no voices yelling now, almost as though nothing bad had ever happened.

Walking into my parents' room, I held out my ribbons to my mother as though they were peace offerings. The word *look* came out of my mouth as I gestured to the offering with my eyes. I wanted my mother to reach out and take up the ribbons in her hands, to accept the peace offering. But she never reached out. She just glanced at the pile, then returned her gaze to the quilt she was patching. I heard her speak words of congratulations, but they were meaningless and drowned by the thoughts that ran through my mind. *She doesn't want them. Why didn't she take them? She doesn't want me!* I walked out of my mother's room while she was still in midsentence, and I muttered something about being tired and needing to sleep.

UNWELCOME 12

The hot summer weather began to dissipate as fall approached. Melanie asked me to work for her, grooming and tacking her horses. I was thrilled she singled me out for this honor. I would arrive at the barn extra early on the weekends. With the annual two-week Dallas horse show fast approaching, every horse needed to be bathed, their manes trimmed short, and their whiskers clipped. On the Saturday before we left for the show, I arrived at the barn around 6:00 AM to groom all of Melanie's horses before she arrived. I read the list she had posted for me on the dry-erase board in the grooming stall. A total of twelve horses were listed under the "Needs to be groomed" section, along with a note that said, "Please clean my tack" under it. My pulse began to race at the thought of trying to get everything done before Melanie arrived. Grooming her horses was not just a matter of lightly going over their coats with a brush for five minutes. Melanie had numerous sets of brushes, mitts, mane and tail combs, hoof picks, and polishes to use on every horse. To do the job right, each horse would take about a half an hour. My arms usually ached by the end of the process.

I heard Melanie's truck pulling up the driveway around nine o'clock. She was neatly dressed in tan pants, and her black polo shirt had the Willow Wind emblem printed in the left-hand corner. Her hair was pulled back in a tight braid held in place by several bobby pins. As she walked up the driveway, I tried to smooth my own hair, which was damp with sweat and hanging loosely on the nape of my neck.

"Melissa, can you get Lena out for me please. We need to clip him for the show." I jumped at her request and pulled out a small bay gelding from the first stall. Lena was Melanie's new favorite. He was small but had a long stride and a powerful jump. I had taken extra time that morning to make sure that his coat shone and that his tail was free of shavings. Our usual routine was for me to hold a horse while Melanie clipped the hairs around the muzzle and ears with an electric clipper. But as I brought Lena into the grooming stall, Melanie handed the clippers to me and announced, "You can do it this time." I beamed as the words *She trusts me!* echoed in my head. I felt like someone had just put their life in my hands. This was Melanie's best horse, and she was letting me take care of him. It was a test, and I had to pass.

I could only hold the clippers in one hand since I had to hold Lena's head steady with my other. After a while, the huge set of clippers began to feel heavy in my hand, but I wanted Lena to look perfect. I was almost done when Lena spooked at the sight of one of Melanie's Jack Russell terriers running down the aisle. As he shied away from the dog, I accidentally ran the clippers backward against his muzzle, making a strange Z-shaped pattern across his nose. I panicked at the sight of the lines that I had created, knowing

Melanie would notice right away. And did she ever notice.

"Melissa, what did you do?" she screamed in near-panic. "Everyone at the show is going to see this. You're just a careless girl, aren't you? I shouldn't have let you do this. The *one time* I trusted you with my clippers, you messed up." The rest of the morning was filled with a continuing barrage of "Everyone is going to see this mess you made" and "How could you?"

"I'm sorry, I'm really sorry; I didn't mean to," was all I could say, and I kept repeating it over and over again, almost forgetting what I had done in the first place; I just knew that I was sorry. I knew that Melanie's love for me hung on a delicate balance, a balance that tipped closer or farther away from me depending on how perfect I could be. The line in Lena's muzzle was so much more than just a little line; it was the force that tipped the balance and took Melanie's love away from me. I felt sick as Melanie's angry words sounded in my ear. As soon as she excused me, I escaped to the bathroom to throw up.

≈

The first few days of the show were always my favorite. Melanie and I would get to the grounds on Monday, and I had almost two full days to spend with her until the other girls arrived. Most of the girls would be accompanied by their mothers—everyone except Olivia and me. She and I always had to find someone else to take us and to stay with once we got to the show. I think that's one of the reasons I felt so close to Olivia; unlike the other girls, we were alone. Usually things worked out well. Everyone stayed at the same cheap hotel, so for the first few days I either shared a room with Melanie or stayed by myself. Then when everyone else came, I'd move into a room with Ms. Sindy, Emily, and Olivia.

The tension I felt around Ms. Sindy and Emily made staying with them difficult. Every time I saw Ms. Sindy embrace Emily or ruffle her hair, jealousy would gnaw away at my sides. I smiled and joked with Emily, but inside I was hoping she would fail. I knew Ms. Sindy was doing the same thing with me. She and I were sweet to each other's faces, but we both knew the truth. Ms. Sindy and I were like war enemies, only our fight wasn't physical; it was mental. I'd purposely tell Ms. Sindy that I was going up to the show early with Melanie, knowing that the information would tick her off. Ms. Sindy would counter my attack within the next few days. Sometimes she'd repeat one of Melanie's comments, like how great Emily was or that she was going to move up a level at the next show. This passive-aggressive mental battle went on and on until I couldn't stand it anymore. My breaking point came only a few days before leaving for the Dallas show: Ms. Sindy told me she and Emily had attended Melanie's wedding, and I hadn't even been invited.

I drowned Ms. Sindy out as she cooed about the ceremony and how beautiful Melanie looked. I wanted her to stop talking so I could think. What had I done wrong? Why didn't Melanie tell me about the wedding? I ran through the past few weeks in my mind, trying to pinpoint where I had messed up. The only thing I could think of was the grooming fiasco and the lines imprinted on Lena's muzzle. My body suddenly felt heavy with guilt.

I never asked Melanie why she hadn't invited me because I was convinced of my own deficiencies. I was second best to Emily, and it was just time for me to realize that I would never be good enough, fast enough, or careful enough. I wanted to yell at Ms. Sindy for telling me, to scream at the top of my lungs, *You don't know! You don't get it! I need this. Why do you keep trying to take my love away? You already have it, don't take mine, too.* I wanted to get down on my knees and plead with her to just leave me alone; I was so hungry for love.

Ms. Sindy didn't know I was desperate and starving for love. Instead of sharing my insecurities, I retaliated. It was during the first few days of the Dallas show that I carried out my counterattack. This time Melanie provided me with the blueprints of my plan.

The day before everyone else arrived at the show, Melanie approached me with a proposal. She began with a compliment, which I hungrily accepted. "Good ride today, Melissa. You and Cadence are really doing well. Hey, I wanted to ask you if you'd be willing to do me a favor." I sat up a little straighter in my chair. At that point I was willing to consider almost any request to redeem myself in Melanie's eyes. "I've heard from a few people that there has been some gossiping around the barn. I'd really like to know who's talking about me, and I think you are the only one who could tell me. Keep a look out for me, would you? If you hear Emily or someone else talking poorly about me, you need to let me know."

A smile spread over my lips when Melanie said she thought Emily was talking badly about her. I didn't hesitate to bob my head in agreement. This was yet another way I could prove to Melanie that I was worth something, that I was loyal. It never occurred to me that Melanie had mentioned Emily's name in an effort to rattle me.

For the next few days of the Dallas show, I stayed close to Emily, analyzing everything she said, picking apart each sentence, and reporting back to Melanie any negative comment she'd make about Willow Wind or Melanie. I'd try to provoke Emily by bringing up issues she'd talked about in the past like why we had to keep selling and buying more horses from Melanie. I was so desperate to please Melanie that I didn't think about what would happen if I exposed Emily. The only thing on my mind was Melanie's love and how I could get it.

On Thursday afternoon when everyone was done competing, Emily received news that one of her friends back in Texas had died of cancer. Not even this sad news stopped my efforts to sabotage Emily. I focused solely on pleasing Melanie. On Friday, Olivia and I were sitting in front of the Willow Wind stalls, trying to get the splattered sand off our horses' equipment with a bar of saddle soap. I looked up when Melanie came to sit down in the chair next to us. She was sipping a Coke and dangling a cigarette butt in her other hand.

"Olivia, you are a reasonable girl. I want to ask for your opinion about something," Melanie said. I looked up from the boot I was scrubbing, wondering what Melanie was going to ask. "Melissa tells me that Emily has been making some crude comments about my training methods. Do you agree? Tell me, what have you heard?"

The look Olivia gave me made my whole body ache with pain. Her face was so sad, so full of disbelief as she said, "Melissa, what did you do? Why would you do that? I thought we were friends. I won't forgive you for this. How can I trust you?" Olivia sprang up from her chair as though I was some sort of contagious disease she had to get away from. More than anything, I wanted to reach my arms out and cry for her not to leave me. Hot tears filled my eyes before overflowing onto my cheeks. I wanted to say something—anything—to make it better, but no words would come. I closed my eyes, imagining that I was invisible to everyone. Sobs began to escape from my throat as the Sick Person hissed in my ear. *You're alone now. No one wants you, you disgusting freak! How could you ruin the one real friendship you had, and for what? Where's Melanie now, huh? Not even she wants you; no one will ever want you.*

In the evening, when I got back to the hotel, all of my things had been put outside the room I had been sharing with Emily, Olivia, and Ms. Sindy. I gathered my belongings hurriedly, hoping to escape without seeing anyone. My efforts were futile, though; as soon as I had my things together I saw Ms. Sindy coming back to the room, holding her dachshund in one arm. I kept my head down low as I passed, pretending to be invisible. As I walked away, I heard Ms. Sindy's cold voice behind me, "You'd better find someone else to take you back to Houston because you are not welcome here."

I was only fifteen, so there was no way I could rent a car and drive myself home. I rented my own room and just sat in bed, running my hands up and down my empty stomach while feeling the soft babylike hair that was beginning to grow in small patches. I spent most of the night flipping through TV channels, trying to find something comforting to watch. At home, I'd gotten into the habit of leaving the TV on because the noise was soothing. I could fall asleep feeling as if there was someone with me when in truth I was alone. That night, though, every show just made me antsy. I felt like my body was on fire. Cool beads of sweat began to accumulate on my back and forehead. Each sound in the room seemed to be magnified: the ticking clock, the pipes in the wall, my stomach growling. I couldn't stand it. I felt so alone, so empty.

At some point during the night, I must have fallen asleep because I woke up to the sound of my alarm clock going off the next morning. My pajamas were damp with sweat, and when I got up, I noticed that all of the bedcovers were piled in a heap on the floor. Grabbing the clothes I had laid out the day before, I headed to the bathroom to change. When I took my pajama top off, I saw the word *empty* written across my stomach in permanent marker.

The funny thing is that I didn't even remember writing it.

I managed to arrange a car ride back to Houston with an Italian couple who rode at Willow Wind. At first, my thoughts after the Emily incident were accompanied by the usual voice of the Sick

Person who resided within me shouting, *Careless girl, stupid, stupid girl!* But then a different voice, the voice belonging to that healthy person I hadn't heard for so long, began to cry, *Melanie called me daughter, she called me daughter! Then she turned on me.* A deep sadness ran through my entire body, chilling every bone. Melanie didn't love me, and for the first time, I was angry at her.

The feeling filled and overwhelmed me like a hot, burning liquid. I wanted to lash out, to cry, to stomp my feet in rage. How could Melanie use me; how could she manipulate me to betray the two girls who wanted and tried to be my friends? And, yet, I had let her. *I had let her.* It was my fault. *You can't blame anyone but yourself. You stupid, stupid girl.* The Sick Person hissed in my ear like a snake. I turned the anger I harbored toward Melanie back onto myself, making me pinch my skin and pull at my hair.

Arriving home didn't stop the voices, either. Relentless guilt built up inside me, engulfing me and replacing my feelings of anger. I felt as though I was choking, choking on guilt. *Relief, relief! Where can I get relief!* My desperate thoughts were immediately answered by the Sick Person's seductive reply—*punish yourself. You need to be punished. You'll feel better; I promise.* The promises of relief sent me searching for a way to fulfill the Sick Person's demands. The memory of my sister's pink disposable razor with its shiny, sharp blades flashed in my mind, and I remembered the relief I had experienced after cutting into my skin. *You could cut yourself. Yes, yes, cut yourself! You can hide it; no one will even know.*

I locked myself in my tiny bathroom and sat on the cool tile floor with a razor in hand. I welcomed the sting that followed the cut, the feeling of release that followed the initial shock. I imagined the blood that flowed down my arm was guilt draining from my body, and it felt good. Yet, the feeling of relief only lasted a day or two, and the self-loathing that returned sent me back to my bathroom to cut again and again. I ached for that feeling of relief, that sensation of *everything's going to be okay* more often as the days went by. I wanted to empty myself of the feelings of guilt and loneliness that suffocated me; and when cutting myself wasn't enough, I turned to throwing up. *Yes, yes! Throw the feelings up. That's how you can get rid of them! Good girl!* The Sick Person purred in my ear like a cool alley cat. My bathroom became a sort of temple; a temple where I would go to purge myself of any negative feeling by cutting or vomiting.

FROZEN 13

Just prior to the start of the school year, I reached one of those milestones every teenager dreams of reaching—I got my driver's license. For most teens, getting a driver's license means staying out later with friends, taking road trips, and experiencing new-found freedom. But for me, getting a driver's license just meant one thing—access to the grocery store. The first thing I did after getting my license was to drive to the grocery store by my house. I spent hours walking up and down the aisles, stopping at the bakery to deeply inhale the aroma of fresh-baked bread and gingerbread men. I began to frequent the store almost every afternoon, and stockpiled my room with soy crackers, apples, and Diet Coke. It felt comforting to have food near me, knowing that in case I got hungry I could reach under my bed and pull out a soy cracker. True, there was food in the kitchen, but it wasn't the same as having the food close by, safely tucked away so that no one could take it. My hoarding behaviors made my parents vacillate between frustration and worry.

"Melissa, you can't keep all these open packages of food in your room. We are going to get bugs. Can't you put your things in the kitchen?" My mother's furrowed brow and pursed lips told me she was tired of my idiosyncratic behaviors. I'd answer her with a languid "I guess so." I got the feeling, though, that my mother knew just as well as I did that nothing was going to change. Although my mother didn't succeed in getting me to stop hoarding food, she did manage to get me to talk to a nutritionist about my eating habits. Once a week, I'd sit down in the nutritionist's small office that smelled heavily of incense and lavender. She'd ask me what I'd eaten in the last twenty-four hours, and I'd ramble off an imaginary menu I'd carefully constructed before the visit. Nothing came out of those visits except empty lies and false promises that I would "work on myself."

Another summer came to a close and the school year began again. I generally looked forward to starting a new school year because school meant reading and reading meant distractions. This year, though, I wasn't all that excited about starting tenth grade. There just wasn't anything to look forward to in the school day. I didn't get to have my favorite English teacher, Mrs. Tiltman; I hated geometry; and my chemistry teacher spent the entire class period playing with water bottles that she thought represented the shape of an electron orbital. My monotonous daily routine consisted of sleeping, going to school, riding, and sleeping again. I was bored with everything and reluctant to do anything. Even riding had become a chore.

On the weekdays, I left the house extra early so I would have time to eat a semifrozen apple once I got to school. Freezing food became a new passion of mine. I'd go to the store, buy a huge bag of red apples, get home, and stick the bag in the freezer. It takes an incredibly long time to eat a frozen piece of fruit, but that's what I liked about it. Every morning I woke up, threw on some clothes, and ran to the kitchen for my apple. While I drove to school, the apple would sit in a glass dish that balanced on one of the cupholders. At each stoplight, I'd eye the fruit, feeling my mouth begin to fill with saliva at the sight of sweet food. The drive was just long enough for the apple to thaw out so I could eat it once I arrived at school. If I was lucky, the apple wouldn't have any rotten spots hidden beneath the frozen outer skin. If part of the apple was rotten, it didn't matter. I would rather eat a rotten apple than nothing at all. Even if the taste made me gag, I'd hold my nose and continue my apple feast. Taste was irrelevant to me. Food was food no matter how rotten it was. The "rules" formulated by the Sick Person allowed me to eat an apple and only an apple in the morning. I yearned to put something in my mouth, to chew and swallow.

Being at school made me feel like I was trapped in a box with nowhere to go and nothing to do except watch the clock. The box that was my classroom was always freezing, no matter how many layers of clothing I piled on. By 10:00 AM, my hands—the only exposed part of my body—would begin to turn purple. Then numbness would set in, making me feel like I'd been sticking my hands in a pile of snow for too long. I'd rub both hands together or stick them in the pockets of my jacket, but no matter what I did, I still felt like I had frostbite. After my first class, I'd escape into the bathroom to run my hands under hot water. I yearned for the warmth of a window sill or something hot to drink. I wanted to go outside and just lie on the warm pavement with my eyes closed and arms stretched out. It felt so good to get outside at the end of the school day. On the way to the barn, I'd just zone out. The drive took thirty minutes, and the majority of the time I could put the car on cruise control and just stare at the empty road.

I went to sleep at night semihoping not to wake up in the morning. I didn't necessarily want to die, but the idea of death wasn't unwelcome, either. If I was dead, the voices would stop and I would feel no pain. To me, pain was life and life was pain. Of course, there was the physical pain stemming from the open sores on my arms and legs from cutting that wouldn't heal and the cuts on my hands from scraping my knuckles against my teeth while purging. Yet the pain that hurt the most was the emotional pain of loneliness, weakness, and, worst of all, the pain of feeling unlovable. I despised the daily torture, aches, and throbbing. But then again, if I had been numb to these feelings, I know I would be dead by now. The pain is what made me want something better, even though I wasn't sure what *better* consisted of. I was waiting for something to happen. Whether that something was fantastic or horrible, it didn't matter as long as it was something.

Part of me knew that the only remedy for my pain resided in good, healthy food and rest. Yet the Sick Person continued to overpower my reasonable thoughts for nourishment. I was so far removed from my family and everyone else at that point, I didn't think anyone cared and I cared even less for myself.

The next horse show I attended was in Mississippi. After a long car ride to get there, I helped the groom set everything up, as I always did, while Melanie disappeared to the show office, as she always did. Bags were unloaded, horses were brushed, and tack was cleaned as usual. Melanie still dangled love in front of me periodically, almost allowing me to grab on before snatching it away again. I expected everything to play out like a continuous loop, repeating the same things that always happened at the shows—the early mornings and late nights, the long days of schooling and classes, and the ever-looming anxiety over whether I did well enough to please Melanie; I expected it all to be the same.

The second day of the show started off cold and rainy. It was one of those January days where I just wanted to stay in bed and hide under the warmth of the covers. I walked the jump course by myself that morning. At each step, the wind blew against my body, unbalancing me and chilling every bone. I couldn't wait to get the competition over with so I could find somewhere warm to go. As soon as we entered the show ring, Cadence pulled at the bit and leapt into a jolty canter, but every movement I made felt mechanical. By the third jump, my body was already exhausted. I hadn't eaten anything that morning; Cadence's strength seemed to double in the freezing weather, but mine dwindled. The cold weather made it almost impossible for me to feel my feet, and as we came off the fourth jump, my heels came up, knocking me off balance. As Cadence bounded forward, I fought to regain the stirrup my foot had slipped out of. I squeezed my calves hard against her sides as we approached the next fence, causing Cadence to launch forward and take off at an awkward distance. As we landed on the other side, my upper body fell forward onto Cadence's thick neck. For a second, I thought maybe I could force myself upright again if I just tried hard enough, but I had expended all my extra energy during the fight to get my stirrup iron back, and now there was nothing left.

I expected the impact of the fall to be painful, but it wasn't. The arena sand was soft against my face. I had no desire to get up. I just wanted to lie there and sleep for a while until some of my strength came back. The only thing that made me want to get up was the thought of Cadence; I didn't know if she was okay or if anyone had caught her after my fall. A wave of panic rushed over me as I tried to organize my cold limbs and force myself to stand. I attempted to push myself up, yet my body wouldn't cooperate. My efforts failed as the blowing wind kept tipping me off balance. Lying there on the arena floor, it hit me for the first time that I'd lost control of absolutely everything.

I finally gained my footing and walked out of the show ring as tears filled my eyes. I knew Melanie would be angry at me for this public display of emotion, and I was already expecting her usual rant of how I was an embarrassment. I didn't look for Melanie at the in-gate; I was used to her disappearing act whenever I fell. When I got back to the barn, Cadence was in the tacking area with the groom. I ran my hand over her muzzle and neck, brushing off some of the sand that had splattered onto her honey-colored coat.

At the end of the aisle, I heard voices and laughing. Emily and Ms. Sindy were talking to Melanie. I walked forward but stopped when Melanie turned to look at me. The usual thoughts I had after falling streamed through my mind: *Now you're going to get it. She's going to yell at you for being such a screw up.* But I was wrong this time. Melanie glanced at me for only a moment before turning away again. Her eyes didn't seem to register that there was a human standing there; it was like I wasn't there at all.

When I got back to the hotel, I collapsed onto my bed without even changing out of my muddy show clothes. Part of me was thankful for not having to hear Melanie's angry voice, but then again, I would have preferred she yell than not acknowledge me at all. At least when she was shouting, Melanie showed that she was still interested in me. I was worthy enough to evoke her anger, which meant that I had to mean something to her. In a sense, I misconstrued Melanie's anger as a form of love for me. By not yelling, it was like she was saying, "You're worthless." I was no longer good enough even to be angry at. I felt empty, but it wasn't the sweet, light sort of emptiness I got from denying myself food. This emptiness was the torturous feeling of desperation and neediness that sent me searching around my room for something to fill it. I threw pillows and sheets around the room and dumped everything out of my duffel bag. The remaining bags of soy crackers fell out of one of the pockets along with a few empty Ziploc containers and cans of Diet Coke. My mouth watered at the sight of food. The crackers didn't taste like anything, but I didn't care. I wanted something to fill up the empty hole. After I'd wolfed down three bags and chugged a can of Diet Coke, I got up off the floor, walking over the pile of scattered clothing, and went into the bathroom to throw up. The crackers came up along with splatters of blood. The sight of the blood brought fresh tears to my eyes.

"I don't want to do this anymore!"

The words spilled out of my mouth before I even realized what I was saying. I was so sick of being empty. I just wanted someone to pick me up and carry me away somewhere. There was nothing left for me here, and there was no one to stay around for. My cell phone was lying next to a dirty pair of riding pants. I picked it up off the ground and dialed my home number, praying that someone would pick up.

"Hello, Melissa? Honey, why are you crying?" The sound of my mother's voice on the other end made me sob even harder. I didn't know what to say. I wanted to talk to her, but I couldn't get any words out. Instead, I just sat there on the phone, sobbing.

HUMPTY DUMPTY 14

The original plan had been for me to go back to Texas for a few days and then leave again for another week of showing. But when I got home on Sunday, my parents told me I wouldn't be leaving for another competition any time soon. Part of me was relieved. The thought of rest and sleep was intoxicating. I wouldn't have to train or wake up at 4:00 AM . . . but then I began to think about Melanie. What would she say? What would she do if I told her I wasn't allowed to compete? Panic set in as I thought about how angry she would be. I heard Melanie's voice sound off in my head: *You are of no interest to me. Every horse I get for you ends up being ruined because of you. Take off that Willow Wind sweatshirt and sit in the dirt where you belong!* Anger consumed me until every muscle, organ, and limb was swollen with it. The feeling overwhelmed me, making me want to scream, stomp my feet, and pull at my hair. There was no escape. I couldn't leave Melanie because I had no place at home, and I had no place at home because I couldn't leave Melanie.

That night, my parents and I fought for what seemed like decades. I needed them to understand that I had to go back to the horse show. I yelled and screamed random things about Melanie hating me and messing up Cadence. I was shouting at the top of my lungs, trying to get them to see that I had to go back. But none of the words that came out of my mouth conveyed that message. Instead, I just kept crying and screaming about Melanie while my parents stared at me like I had gone mad. I only stopped my tirade when my throat began to sting.

The momentary pause allowed my dad to finally speak. "Melissa, you've got to stop crying. We can't let you go back next week. I'm sorry, but we just can't. You don't need Melanie. What you need is help. What you need is to get treatment." My dad's voice suddenly faded into the background as feelings of dread and panic intermixed with guilt hit me like a surging wave crashing against a seawall. The guilt hit me hardest of all. I felt guilty about everything—betraying my friends, lying to my nutritionist, constantly asking my dad for money. More than anything, though, I felt guilty about having ruined my relationship with my mother. The sickening feeling almost made me double over in pain, and I fumbled through the kitchen cabinet, looking for something to relieve the sensation. Pulling out a knife, I pressed the steel blade against the skin on my arm, stopping only when I saw a stream of blood trickle down onto the oversized T-shirt I was wearing.

My mother's voice crackled with fear, "Okay, fine! You can go. Just drop the knife!" When I heard the sound of her frantic voice, the knife fell out of my hands clattering as it hit the ground. At that moment, my mother flew across the kitchen and emptied the drawer where all the knives were stored into an empty grocery bag she grabbed from under the sink.

"Bob, Bob, will you get the Valium? I need you to get the Valium." My mother's voice sounded strange and childlike to my ears. Silently, my dad rummaged through the medicine cabinet and pulled out a bottle.

"Here, Melissa, take this. Please take this."

I had never seen my dad's hands shake like they did that night. His usually bright, jovial face suddenly looked very old to me as he handed me a glass of water and some pills. Twenty minutes later, I slipped into a heavy sleep for the rest of the night.

I didn't leave my room the next morning until I was certain my dad had gone to work and my mother had taken Sam to school. The drive to school seemed to take forever. I usually had the radio blaring, but today I wanted quiet. The previous night's fiasco kept replaying in my mind's eye. The yelling, the anger, the knife—all of it seemed too unreal, too insane. I just kept thinking, *It wasn't me. I didn't do that. Only an insane person would cut herself in front of everyone.* As I tried to convince myself that nothing had happened, I began to wonder if I was insane for trying to convince myself that nothing had happened. That morning, the apple was left sitting in the glass bowl.

Although my body was physically present during history class, my mind was elsewhere. I kept revisiting the portion of the previous night's conversation where my dad had talked about getting me treatment. What did he mean by "treatment"? Who could even help me? The only "treatment" place I knew of was some Christian dude ranch out in New Mexico. How could going there make me better? What were they doing to do, give me a new brain that couldn't hear the voices? They couldn't do that, and they most certainly couldn't get Melanie to love me. The only good thing about the idea of treatment was to get far away from everything and everyone. Something about being a long way from home was appealing to me. I'd be gone long enough for people to forget about me. I could come back a new person and start every relationship from scratch. It would kind of be like having a do-over. After class, I walked into the school office instead of heading for my English class, and I dialed the number for my dad's cell phone.

"Hello, Melissa." I'd heard his voice so many times, but I still didn't know anything about the person behind the deep-sounding *hello*. I wrapped the phone cord around my fingers as we sat there for a moment in silence. "Hello? Are you still there?" he asked.

"Yeah, sorry, I'm here." My voice sounded strange and unsteady. I was used to always asking, needing, or wanting something from my dad, usually involving horses, but today we weren't going to talk about horses. I forced the next words out of my mouth as quickly as possible, fearing that I'd back down and hang up the phone.

"If I have to go to a treatment center, can I at least pick where I want to go?" There, the words were out, my job was done. Now I just had to wait for my dad to say something. I could feel my pulse speed up when he didn't respond right away. I heard the sound of my own breathing until my dad finally spoke. His usual jovial voice was quiet and somber.

"Well, I guess so. Where do you want to go? There's a place in Florida your mother and I looked at a couple of months ago. Is that what you're thinking about?"

"What? Oh no, I wasn't thinking about Florida. There's this place in New Mexico I read about. It's warm there, and they have horses."

"Yes, I think your mom told me about that place. She wanted to go up and see it. I'll make some phone calls and try to get you in there. Where are you? Are you at home?"

"No, I'm at school. I think I'm going to leave, though." A moment later, I hung up the phone, walked out of the office, and made my way into the English wing. I wanted to say good-bye to my favorite English teacher, Mrs. Tiltman, before leaving. Her door was closed when I got to her room; I realized it was Tuesday, and she always left early on Tuesdays.

Mrs. Tiltman was one of the few people I actually wanted to remember me while I was gone. I needed my family to forget me because our relationships were too broken to fix. They had to forget me so that I could start over as a new person when I got back. I finally scribbled down some words, folded the paper in half, and pushed it under her door. As I walked away, I wondered what she'd think in the morning. What would go through her mind when she unfolded the piece of paper and read, "By the time you get this, I'll be in New Mexico, working on putting myself back together again."

❧

I left school after slipping the note under Mrs. Tiltman's door. When I got home, my mother was standing near the front door.

"A bed's opened up. I called," she announced breathlessly. "Everything is already taken care of. We can leave tomorrow." My jaw dropped as I took in her words. *Tomorrow—we can leave tomorrow. How am I supposed to respond to her? Do I say thank-you? Do I say I'm sorry?* I didn't know because, frankly, I had no idea how to talk to my mother. So I just stared at her until she walked away.

I spent a few hours packing that night, but my duffel bag wasn't full of the usual things I brought to competitions; all the show shirts and riding breeches stayed hanging in the closet. I glanced at the array of colorful show shirts while I tossed a few pairs of jeans and sweatshirts into the bag. The shirts reminded me that there was still one more phone call I wanted to make before leaving. Grabbing my cell phone off the desk, I dialed Emily's home number. Emily was the one person I trusted to take care of Cadence for me when I was away. I was jealous of Emily and couldn't stand being around her, but it wasn't because she was annoying or a bad person. We could have and would have been friends if I hadn't been so damn jealous of the love she had from Ms. Sindy. I was surprised when she picked up the phone. I was afraid that my number would flash on her caller ID and she'd ignore the call. When I heard her voice on the other line, my first instinct was to beg Emily to forgive me. To tell her how sorry I was over and over again, and that I would fix things. Yet I knew she wasn't interested in hearing empty versions of "I'm sorry." At the time, my feelings were genuine, but I knew if another opportunity arose to grasp onto Melanie's love, I'd betray Emily again if I had to.

"Emily, I was wondering if you would take care of Cadence for a while. I'm leaving tomorrow to go to a treatment center in New Mexico. I don't really know when I'll be back. I know this is short notice, and I know it takes some nerve to ask you to do me a favor when I've done nothing but hurt you. But I don't trust anyone else to ride Cadence." I had to stop talking because my voice was beginning to shake at the thought of leaving Cadence for so long. I didn't hear anything on the other line for a few moments, and I figured she was going to say no. But she didn't. Emily responded in her usual way, with a soft voice and few words. "I'll take care of Cadence. Go get help."

That was the last time I ever spoke to Emily.

THE
TREATMENT
CENTER

15

During the flight to New Mexico, my parents and I didn't say much. It still hadn't registered that I was going to an eating disorder treatment center. Instead, I just kept thinking about how odd it was to travel long distance with my parents instead of with Melanie; I tried to remember the last family vacation I'd been on. When we arrived at our destination, the airport was teeming with activity. The baggage claim area was full of people in business attire and casually dressed mothers holding onto the hands of screaming children. A woman near one of the doors held a sign with "Binstock" printed on it in big black letters. She was an older woman whose brown, wrinkled skin told me she spent a lot of time outdoors. As we approached her she said, "Hi, you must be the Binstocks. My name is Leslie, and I'll be taking you all to the ranch." The car ride was long and bumpy, which made me bounce around in the back-seat. My dad tried to strike up a conversation with Leslie, asking her about the weather and good restaurants in town. Nothing about the trip seemed real to me until Leslie pulled into a large gravel parking area. I climbed out of the van and looked around at the cactus-filled area. The main building looked brand new with a stucco exterior and red tiled roof. A woman with curly red hair and reading glasses came out to meet us.

"Hello, my name is Terri. I'm going to be Melissa's nurse." Her words hit me like a brick in the face. Terri began to talk about some of the rules and regulations, but I didn't hear any of it. I could only think about the fact that I was in the middle of nowhere on some ranch in New Mexico and that I wasn't going home. The realization caused the hair on my arms to stand on end. Had I made a mistake in coming here? How could I trust that these people would know how to help me? Could anyone help me? *You stupid girl. No one can help you. You're too far gone for that. They are just going to make you eat and get huge. Stupid, stupid girl.* The Sick Person's hisses cut me like the cold blade of a knife, making me want to wrap up into a ball to defend myself against further attacks.

"Mr. and Mrs. Binstock, if it's all right with you, I'll give you over to Vicky. She'll show you around while I ask Melissa some questions." Before I could even look at my parents, Terri was already leading me into the main room of the red-roofed building. Rows of tables and chairs were set up, and it reminded me of the elementary school cafeteria I used to eat lunch in.

"This is where the girls eat their main meals. Breakfast is at eight, lunch at twelve, and dinner at five. Snack time will be held in the house." The mention of meals and snacks caused me to panic. I should have been expecting to hear about food—I should have been ready. Yet, nothing could ever prepare me for the Sick Person's angry screams. *You're going to get huge and disgusting!* I wanted to cover my ears and yell at the top of my lungs. I tried to drown out the Sick Person's voice by listening to Terri, who was talking about the daily religious services the girls attended.

Terri led me into one of the side rooms next to the dining area. It looked like a typical doctor's exam room, which I thought was somewhat strange since it was next to the area where people ate. I wondered, *Do they examine you after eating to make sure you don't hide any mashed potatoes in your cheeks like a chipmunk?* Before Terri could say anything, my parents returned from their tour, and now they needed to say good-bye.

I stood up when I saw my mother at the door. Part of me wanted to beg her not to leave me with that crazy nurse. *Take me home please! I promise I'll do better. Anything, I'll do anything, just don't leave me here.* I heard the words blaring in my head as feelings of anger boiled inside of me like hot molten lava. I was angry; angry at my parents for even thinking about dumping me in this place. True, I had asked to go to the ranch. But, there was still a part of me that expected my parents to know how to make me better so that I wouldn't have to go to treatment after all. That was the part of me still holding on to the childish belief that my parents were superhuman and supposed to be able to fix anything.

Yet, the anger began to slowly dissipate as it dawned on me for the first time how vulnerable they looked. My dad, who was always so strong and tough with his serious visage and deep-throated courtroom voice, suddenly looked tired and old. And, my mother—my never-flinching mother. The way she grasped her forearms with either hand made it look as though she was desperately trying to hold onto something, to anything. I guess I had expected her to play the "I'm concerned about you" game, where you look sad on the outside, but on the inside you're really jumping for joy at the thought of finally getting rid of the person. However, something about her eyes told me that my mother wasn't playing any sort of game; she actually didn't want to leave me. A sob escaped from my throat as I began to furiously wipe tears away from my eyes. There was no way I could beg them to take me home; I was going to stay here, and they were going to leave me.

After a few solemn good-byes, Terri led my parents to the exit, shutting the door behind them. "Melissa, I'm going to need you to change into this gown now. We need to examine you." She handed me a frumpy blue and white hospital gown that looked like it'd been worn by a thousand other girls. A knock at the door made me think for a moment that my parents had come back for me. I got up from the chair I was sitting in, only to sit back down once I saw that it wasn't them.

"Hi, Melissa, I'm one of the other nurses here at the ranch. You can call me Jane." The woman extended her hand, but I didn't move. When she realized I wasn't interested in shaking her hand, she pulled it back and said, "Okay then, go ahead and get changed."

I stood up again with the frumpy gown in my hands, expecting the nurses to leave the room so I could change. But they just looked at me without saying anything.

"Er . . . um, where do I go to change?"

"Oh, well, we actually can't leave you by yourself," Jane answered. "Go ahead and change here." I thought maybe she was kidding, so I waited a few minutes to see if they were going to leave. I wasn't going to take off my clothes with people around. What were they thinking?

"Come on, Melissa, we'd like to get you back to the house before dinner." I stubbornly waited another five minutes; I finally realized the women weren't leaving and I wouldn't be leaving either, until I did what they wanted.

From that moment on, I thought of my body as some kind of art piece that was being examined for flaws. As Terri looked me up and down, she spoke aloud to Jane as though I wasn't in the room. "Ah, there's a scar here, Jane. Make sure you document that blister on her right foot. Did you get this scratch on her arm?" Terri's high-pitched voice was irritating, but it was her hand running over my skin that really made me want to scream. Every time she tried to move the frumpy hospital gown up, my death grip around it tightened as I scooted away from her, almost falling off the edge of the exam table. But they finally accomplished their mission: by the time thirty minutes had passed, almost every freckle, scratch, and scar had been accounted for.

When Terri finish the examination she said, "Okay, Melissa. We just need to ask you some questions," I gathered the back of the gown in my hand and sat up with my back leaning against the wall. Terri spoke first.

"Melissa, do you have a history of cutting? Can you point to each scar and describe the cause of the injury? Do you want to die?"

Her questions sent me into a rage. *Why the hell did they scrutinize me first and then question me about scars second? Couldn't they have just asked me to begin with? Did I have to show them every inch of my body? What kind of question is "Do you want to die"? Is that why they think I'm here—because I have some sort of death wish?*

After glaring at Terri for a moment, I decided how to answer her questions. "I have scars on my leg because I got stitches when I was little; there's a scratch on my arm from one of my dogs; that blister is from wearing riding boots for too long, and no, I do not want to die." For another thirty minutes they continued to ask what I considered to be ridiculous questions about what I liked to do, where I went to school, and what my favorite subjects were. All of it seemed trivial to me. Why did it matter what subjects I liked in school?

Had I come to this place only to be asked stupid questions like *what's your favorite color?*

Jane popped out of her seat. "All right, young lady, you can come with me now. The girls are anxious to meet you."

"What girls?" The words were out of my mouth before I even knew what I was saying.

"Well, in the house where you'll be staying there are about twenty other girls. You will be sharing a room with three of them." Jane led me through the dining area I'd passed on the way in. As we approached some windows, I could see it was getting to be late afternoon. Outside, there was a woman sitting in a golf cart, scribbling something down on a clipboard. She looked up at the sound of the door opening. I began to walk past her, but Jane grabbed me by the arm. "Melissa, this is Mona, she's going to be taking you to the house in the people mover." I guessed that "people mover" was synonymous for "golf cart."

"It's okay, I can walk. I don't need someone to drive me." Mona got up from where she was sitting and patted me on the back.

"It's all right, Melissa, it's just protocol until we get you in to see one of the doctors." I found something about Mona to be calming. Her voice was soft and gentle, not like the aggressive-sounding nurses I'd met so far. I preferred to walk, but the way Mona extended her hand and patted my back reminded me of the few times Melanie had done the same.

"Okay then, I'll go with you." The drive to the house took longer than it would have if we had walked. Ten minutes later, the golf cart pulled up next to a house that looked almost identical to the one I'd already been in, its cream-colored stucco surrounded by tall, leafy plants that looked awkward next to the barren cacti.

The inside of the house was furnished like a typical living room.

Looking around, I expected to see some of the other girls, but the room was empty. Mona explained, "Everyone is at chapel now. They'll be back before dinner. Your parents brought over your bags. I can take you upstairs to unpack them in a few minutes. Go ahead and take a seat for the time being." I flopped down on one of the couches and waited for Mona to return. My thoughts were interrupted by the entrance of a girl who looked to be about seventeen and had short blond hair that curled around her face. I was surprised to hear her voice; she sounded so happy.

"Hi, I'm Courtney. What's your name?"

I stared at the girl for a second before telling her my name as I tried to keep my voice steady. Courtney went on to tell me about the program, what her roommates were like, and about the art therapy session she had earlier in the day. Midway through her description of the painting she'd been working on, I interrupted her.

"How long have you been here?"

"Two months. I'm going home this weekend. I think I'll kind of miss this place. Everyone here is so nice."

As I went upstairs with Mona, I wondered if Courtney was just happy because she was getting to go home.

Upstairs there was a nurse's station in the front portion followed by a long hallway that eventually led to the different bedrooms. After walking down the hall and passing a few of the bedrooms, Mona stopped. "Here we are. This is where you'll be staying. Your bed is that one in the middle." She pointed to a bed that already had my duffel bag on top of it. I stepped inside the room and looked around. There were four beds situated around the room; each one had a matching solid lavender bedspread and white pillows. Two of the girls had stuffed animals on their nightstands alongside pictures of friends and family. The sight of the framed pictures made me wish I'd brought a few more things from home. All I had were clothes and some old tennis shoes. It didn't take long for Mona to go through my bag to make sure I didn't have any contraband, like food or razors.

As she reached into each of the pockets on a pair of jeans, I looked outside the window and saw horses grazing on a paddock. The sight made my stomach twist. What was Cadence doing? Did she miss me? Did she even know I wasn't there? I pressed my hands against the glass windowpane, wishing I could reach out and touch one of the horses' coats.

"Do you like horses?" Mona's voice made me jump up. "Sorry, I didn't mean to scare you. I was just wondering if you liked horses. You seemed interested in the ones outside."

"Um, yeah, I have a horse at home."

"Oh, that's nice. You'll fit right in here. Once you get your doctor's permission, you can go to equine therapy. All the girls really enjoy it."

"How long will that take? When can I go see the horses? Will I get to go tomorrow?" Mona smiled at my questions. I guess she wasn't expecting me to talk much. "No, darling, tomorrow is Saturday. None of the doctors will be here. You'll have to wait until at least Monday, and even after that you won't be able to go right away. Things take time. We have to make sure you're healthy enough to walk around first."

Why did I have to come on a Friday of all days? I was going to have to ride around in that damn golf cart until Monday. By the time Mona had finished sorting through my luggage, I heard the sound of the door downstairs slam shut, followed by the din of voices. "Ah, the girls must be back from chapel. I think we're just about done here." Mona was about to say something else when she was cut off by a collective shout of "Hello, new girl!" that echoed from downstairs.

"Well, I guess we should go down now. You can put your things away after dinner," Mona said.

The voices grew louder as we made our way down the steps. There were two girls already standing at the foot of the stairs as I came down; the short one with blond hair and green eyes shouted up at me. "Hi, I'm Ally! What's your name? Where are you from? How old are you?" The excitement and barrage of questions caught me off guard. Why would so many people be excited to see a complete stranger? It seemed so odd to me. They didn't even know me, and here they were jumping up and down in excitement to talk to me. Before I could answer any of their questions, a woman's voice drowned out all the other sounds in the room.

"Girls, circle up for dinner." A hush fell over the room as everyone gathered next to the couches. Tonia, a small Mexican woman with wide hips and red cheeks, came out from behind the nurse's station. The booming voice didn't seem to fit with this woman; she looked so sweet and charming. But when she belted out "Prayer time," I knew it had to have been her. Everyone gathered together, clasping each other's hands as a tall girl with shoulder-length brown hair began to recite something about "Our Father." The thought of holding a complete stranger's hand was not appealing to me, so I decided to take a few steps back from the circle. Once prayers were over, everyone gathered by the door.

"Can we go now?" Ally asked Tonia, who replied, "One moment Ally, I need to find Mona to take the new girl in the people mover." I watched Mona as she walked out of one of the side offices and approached me. She was older, but her upturned lips and loosely tied hair made the lines on her forehead less perceivable. It annoyed me that everyone else was able to walk over to dinner, but having Mona around made the feeling subside. I found her presence comforting. "So how are you doing so far?" she asked. "Have you gotten a chance to meet any of your roommates? Has anyone told you about your option at this first meal?"

I stared at Mona for a minute before answering, "No, no one has explained much of anything to me."

"Well, tonight's dinner is what we call a grace meal. You can eat if you want to, but you don't have to." The Sick Person in my mind shouted in triumph, *You're safe tonight! You can rest easy. There won't be food in your stomach to weigh you down.* The idea of not having to eat was so calming. For the first time since arriving, I could finally take in a deep breath as the anxiety that had been gnawing at my stomach abated.

LEARNING THE PROGRAM

16

The dining area was loud and teeming with people. There were tables and tables full of girls. Some of them looked healthy; their faces radiant with color, and they even appeared to be happy about eating. Others, though, made me gasp. I couldn't help but stare at the skeletal bodies wandering around the room. One of the girls who sat at a table near the door was especially shocking. She was tiny with pale skin so paper thin it was almost transparent. Her eyes were huge and catlike with darkened circles gathered underneath like pools of black ink. A yellowish tube extended from the girl's nose and was taped to the right side of her face. I studied the girl for a moment, watching as she sat poised with a knife in one hand and a fork in the other, as if about to begin a meal. As I watched her, it dawned on me that she wasn't going to eat. The girl just continued to sit in her chair as if frozen.

"Melissa, come on, you're sitting at our table!" I turned at the sound of my name being called by a girl with long, jet-black hair. "Hi, I'm Jessie. You're going to be rooming with me."

Ally, the girl I'd met earlier, stepped forward, grabbing Jessie's arm. "Aren't you going to introduce me? I'm her roommate, too!"

"Oh yeah, sorry." Jessie turned her attention back to me. "I thought you'd already met the person who is currently cutting off the circulation in my arm, but anyhow, we're going to be your roommates. Come on, we'll show you where to pick up your tray." Jessie and Ally led me over to a counter that resembled a concession stand. Kitchen workers dashed back and forth with plates full of boiled meat and mashed potatoes. One of the workers called out Jessie's name and handed her a tray. As she walked past me to get back to the table, I heard her muttering something about the large amount of fat in ranch dressing.

A woman wearing a black hairnet called my name. I watched her as she placed a bowl of what looked like watered-down broth onto my tray. As I moved to pick up the tray, the woman grunted, "Now don't you forget these crackers here." She reached out and placed two packets of saltines next to the soup. By the time I got back to the table, almost everyone was already sitting down.

"Melissa, here, you're going to sit next to me." Tonia pointed to an empty spot at the table where there was a yellow index card with *Melissa* spelled out in black marker. As I sat down, I looked around to see what the other girls were eating. Most of their plates were identical—meat, some mashed potatoes, and a salad. Some of the girls had juice, while others had additional crackers or cookies on their trays. I glanced down at my bowl of broth and wondered why I had this putrid-smelling stuff while everyone else had something that at least looked edible.

"They've got you on the refeeding plan. I was on the same thing when I got here. My name's Tiffany, by the way."

"I'm Melissa. What exactly do you mean by the 'refeeding plan'?"

Tiffany kept her eyes on her plate as she talked. "It's something they make you do if you haven't eaten in a while. They don't want you to go into shock or something. It's kind of gross, but hopefully you can get to solids soon."

"Tiffany, you know we aren't allowed to talk about food," a tall girl with curly brown hair snapped.

"Sorry, Shelly, I was just trying to explain the rules to the new girl."

Tonia broke up the conversation. "Girl, that's enough. I will explain the rules to Melissa; everyone else can continue eating." Tonia turned back to me and described how the meals were set up.

"Everyone has thirty minutes to eat. Fifteen minutes into the meal, I'll call half time so that you'll know how well you're doing with pacing. You must finish everything on your plate. If you have condiments, you must use them all and show me the containers when you're done. I also need to see everyone's bowls, plates, and cups. If you spill something, I need to know about it. You cannot use your napkin unless you ask my permission. That means all napkins must stay on the table at all times. If you fail to eat all of your food or if you are unable to finish on time, there will be consequences: you will have to drink a supplement when we return to the house and your refusal to eat will be documented. Also, we do not allow conversations about food, calories, weight, or exercise. Do not compare what you are eating to anyone else, and do not make any sort of reference to weight loss. You will be supplemented if someone catches you hiding food, exercising, purging, or anything of that nature. Do you understand?"

As Tonia went on about the rules, I stared at the broth circling around my bowl. *I wish she'd just shut up already. Doesn't she know how loud she's being?* My thoughts were interrupted by an "ahem" followed by "I said, do you understand the rules?" I looked up from gazing at the brown mixture and after a moment, I mumbled an unenthusiastic "Yes." In truth, I really could have cared less about hearing the rules. A part of me was still convinced that I wasn't going to be staying around very long.

After Tonia's introduction, the girls launched into a table game of "would you rather," with Chris asking each of us if we'd rather be stuck in a car with the most annoying person in the world or sit outside in the cold for three hours. It didn't surprise me that everyone chose the former; since their lack of body fat would make the cold unbearable.

"All right, we are out of time. I need to see everyone's hands, napkins, and dishes." Tonia systematically made her way around the table. She stopped when she came to a girl who was sitting at the far end.

"Maggie, you need to finish your salad dressing." I was surprised to see the girl lift the plate to her mouth and lick off the remaining dressing. As soon as she licked the dish clean, she showed the plate to Tonia again.

"I'm not going to get supplemented for that am I? See, look, I got it all off the plate. I didn't mean to leave it."

"No, Maggie, I won't make you drink Ensure this time, but I will if I see this happen again." The girl's frantic look subsided when she realized she was safe.

By the time we made our way out of the dining hall, Mona was already waiting for me in the golf cart outside.

"How was your first meal? Did you meet more of the girls?" Mona was about to ask another question before I interrupted her.

"Does anyone ever get out of here after a week?" I kept my eyes on the ground as I asked, already anticipating the *no* before it came out of Mona's mouth.

"I've been here ten years, Melissa, and have never seen anyone go home after only being here for seven days. The first two weeks are always slow for everyone, but things will get better once you get used to the program. You know, on Sunday you get to call home and talk to someone for ten minutes. I bet you'd really like to talk to your mom." The familiar pang of guilt set in at the mention of my mother. That ten-minute phone call would be the longest conversation we'd had in years without any yelling, crying, or reference to Melanie. What were we going to talk about? I wasn't sure. Without horses, what was there left to say?

By the time we got back to the house, everyone was already sitting down in the common area. I looked at the clock on the wall and saw that it was only six. How much longer were they going to make us sit around? I was dying to go upstairs and put my things away. That way, I could at least move around a bit. At eight o'clock, Tonia called out from behind the front counter, "Come on girls, it's time for a snack." I followed Ally into the back room where a long picnic table was situated against a wall. Colorful drawings hung from the walls along with a dry-erase board that had "weekly goals" printed at the top along with a list of the girls' names followed by handwritten goals. Most of the girls listed things like "be more positive" or "be supplement free." Some of the goals were indicated by initials or acronyms, like Jessie's goal of working on her "BI," which I knew stood for body image. I was amused at Ally's goal; she had written, "Ally will not pull out her hair this week."

After everyone was seated at the table, Tonia came into the room carrying a tray full of different snack foods. Mona was right behind her, holding a water pitcher in one hand and a can of chocolate Ensure in the other. As everyone began to line up, I stayed seated at the table, reading over the rest of the affirmations. I had made it to

Mariah's goal when I heard Tonia calling my name. "Melissa, please come and get your snack." I grimaced, both at the sound of Tonia's booming voice and at the thought of having to eat. As I walked over to the table, I prayed that Tonia was going to tell me that my snack was optional, just as dinner had been. The only things left on the tray were a few bananas and a package of red Gushers. I silently willed Tonia to give me a banana, but instead she handed me the bag of Gushers. As I sat down next to Ally, I looked around the table at the array of packages filled with nuts, yogurt-covered pretzels, graham crackers, and something called gorp, which appeared to be a trail mix of raisins, peanuts, and chocolate. "Okay everyone, you have fifteen minutes to eat. Go ahead and begin." As Tonia said *begin,* everyone tore into their bags.

A girl wearing her hair in two long braids turned toward me and said, "I guess we should all introduce ourselves. My name is Cory. I'm sixteen years old, and I'm from Connecticut." Jesse went next. "We've already met, but I'll tell you my name anyhow. I'm fifteen years old, my name is Jessie, and I'm from Florida." One after the other, each girl took a turn introducing herself to me. No two girls had come from the same state. The girl who lived closest to my home state of Texas was from Louisiana. Her Southern accent was unmistakable as she introduced herself as Caitlin. When the circle of introductions made its way around to me, I felt my stomach turn over as if I was about to give a lengthy speech to a massive audience.

"Err . . . umm . . . I'm sixteen. I live in Texas, and my name is Melissa." When I finished, the room went quiet again. The only noise I could hear was the soft rustle of a bag and the sound of chewing. The silence was broken by Tiffany, who was sitting across from me. She leaned toward me and whispered conspiratorially.

"I would eat those Gushers if I was you. The Ensure they make us drink is really gross. They keep it warm on purpose so that it tastes bad."

"I thought today was my grace day or whatever it's called." I could hear my voice begin to shake.

"Well yeah, but you already had your grace meal at dinner. Now you have to eat or they'll make you drink Ensure."

I could see the nutrition label for Gushers in my mind. Ninety calories, one gram of fat, sixteen grams of sugar—all of it was too much. The Sick Person began to shout about fat and flesh and my disgusting body unworthy of food. Slowly, I opened the package of sugar-filled candies but was too afraid to pick one up. What if the calories could somehow be absorbed into my skin?

Tonia's voice rang out. "All right, snack time is over. I need to see everyone's bags." Tonia walked around the table like an inspector, checking over our work of eating. When she got around to my seat, I heard a disapproving hiss escape from her lips.

"Melissa, you didn't eat your snack. Please wait here while everyone else goes into the other room." I bit down hard on my lower lip. What was she going to do to me? I frantically looked around the room for some mode of escape—a door or window, anything I could sneak out of. Cory must have recognized the frantic expression on my face, because when she walked by, she leaned over and whispered, "Don't do it. I tried to run away, but they caught me three miles from here."

After everyone left the room, Tonia nodded for me to follow her. She led me to the makeshift exam room behind the nurse's station. "Please sit down while I measure out your supplement." Tonia's voice sounded cold and slightly vexed. She removed a cup and a large plastic bottle filled with thick white liquid from one of the overhead cabinets. I watched as Tonia filled the cup three-fourths of the way. "All right, you have five minutes to drink this. If you don't get it all down, there will be consequences."

My gaze shifted back and forth between the robust woman and the cup full of thick white liquid, not really sure what the stuff was or what she meant by "consequences." What more could be done to me that hadn't been done already? They'd already humiliated me by scrutinizing every inch of my body. I'd been poked and prodded, thrown on a scale, snapped at for not cooperating. Hell, someone had even gone with me and watched as I went to the bathroom. I wasn't going to drink that stuff. She couldn't possibly take any privileges away from me because I didn't have any in the first place. I crossed my arms and stared at Tonia, trying to tell her with my body language that there was no way I was going to pick up that cup. Tonia grinned at my attempt to look tough.

"You realize, Melissa, that we could take away your phone call this Sunday." The phone call! I had forgotten about the phone call! It was the one thing left that was still mine, the one thing I could still look forward to. I felt my face begin to twitch at the thought of losing the one chance I'd have to beg my parents to let me come home. Tears began to overflow as I reached for the cup. I couldn't help but feel angry at myself for not eating those damn Gushers; at least I knew what was in them. The liquid was thick and warm in my mouth. The stuff was supposed to be vanilla-flavored, but it tasted more like sour milk that had been sitting out in the sun all day. After taking a sip, I began to gag.

"It's bad, isn't it? Well, we do that on purpose because if we gave you something good, you'd never finish your meals. You have to get used to eating solid food. We can't have you on a liquid diet forever, it's not normal."

I glared at Tonia before picking up the cup again. This time, I held my nose and poured the remaining liquid into my mouth. Once I had finished, Tonia rose to her feet and patted my leg.

"Good girl, now you may go back into the common area." I felt like a dog being praised for sitting on cue.

THE NEW GIRL 17

"Come on, girls, line up for meds." It was 9:00 PM, and a petite woman with long blond hair peered out the window of the nurse's station as she slid it open. She had a thick Southern accent that reminded me of one of the girls I used to ride with. I didn't know if I had medication to take or not, but everyone stood up and walked over to the window, and the prospect of standing up was irresistible to me. One by one, each girl was given a tiny cup filled with water and a container with an array of colored pills. I heard the nurse call out the names of the medicines: "Okay, Courtney, you have Benadryl, Seroquel, and clonazepam. Ally, you have Ambien and clomipramine."

When I got up to the counter, the woman smiled. "You must be the new girl. Hi, I'm Dora. I'll be one of your nurses. Let's see what we have for you today." She ran her hand down a list, read something, and then pulled out a little cup of pills. "Okay, you only have Benadryl tonight. I see that tomorrow morning you get some other meds." She handed me the Benadryl and a cup of water. I gulped the pills down and crumpled up the paper cup in my hand.

"Can I please see your mouth?"

"What?" I looked at Dora, thinking maybe I'd heard her wrong.

"I need to see your mouth, darlin'. Please open it." I stood back and opened my mouth. "All right, thank you ma'am. I just need to make sure you aren't hiding any pills in your cheeks or something. You girls have a tendency to do that." I wanted to snap at her for insinuating that I was a pill hider. My face felt hot as I walked away from the nurse's station, musing to myself, *Why would she even think that I would hide pills? I haven't done anything sneaky yet.*

The word *yet* made me stop walking for a moment. Was I already subconsciously planning to manipulate the system? I hadn't done anything sneaky *yet.* Her words echoed in my ears; *You girls have a tendency to hide pills.* She'd never met me, but my face must have told her that I'd hidden medicine before. In a sense, I felt as though I had been caught. And yet, for the first time, I was happy about it. I abhorred the blunt numbness, the lethargy, and the ravishing hunger caused by my medications. Plus, the years of hiding pills and lying to my parents had left me feeling weighed down with guilt that I couldn't seem to shake. The nurse's comment left me feeling lighter, as though the idea of being caught had drained some of the guilt that was weighing me down. As I sat down on the couch, I couldn't help but grin. That nurse was good; she was really, really good.

Thirty minutes later, Mona announced that it was time to go upstairs. I was relieved, since going upstairs meant I could finally brush my teeth. Even after drinking a cup of water, I hadn't been able to get rid of the Ensure's rotten-milk taste. As everyone headed to their rooms, Mona stopped me. "Melissa, have a seat at the nurse's station until someone can monitor you while you get ready for bed." I plopped down on an old cot and waited.

"Hey, you must be Melissa," smiled the tall, broad-shouldered woman who approached me. "My name's Martha. We can go to your room now if you're ready." Faking a smile, I stood up from the cot and followed Martha down the hall.

The rest of my roommates were already in their pajamas when I walked through the door. The area around my bed looked empty: no stuffed animals or colorful frames with pictures of family members. I didn't even have a throw blanket from home. All I had brought were clothes and toiletries. A wave of sadness flooded over me; I had never wanted to go home so badly in my life. The sound of Martha's high-pitched voice pulled me out of my thoughts.

"Are you going to take a shower? Do you want to change?"

I turned around to face her again and took a deep breath before replying. "No, I just want to brush my teeth."

Martha glanced at me suspiciously. "You mean you don't want to change out of those jeans? They don't look very comfortable."

"It's all right, I sleep in jeans at home all the time," I lied. I just didn't want to have to change in front of another person. Martha followed me around the room as I brushed my teeth and threw the rest of my clothes into a drawer. After I was done, I climbed into bed and pulled the covers over my head, waiting for Martha to get the message that I wanted her to leave. "Good-night then, Melissa." Martha finally left the room, and as the sound of her footsteps faded, I began to think about the possibility of sleeping away the time I had to spend at this place. The idea was childish and impossible, but it helped me to relax and fall asleep.

I didn't sleep much that night. Every sound in the room seemed magnified. Even the other girls' breathing kept me awake. At midnight, the door opened and Dora, the nurse, came in, rolling a strange-looking machine behind her. I sat up in bed, keeping my eyes halfway closed until they grew accustomed to the light that was coming from the hallway. As Dora came up to my bed, I saw the machine behind her was some sort of mobile blood pressure monitor.

"I'm just checking on you. Can you give me your arm, please?" As I complied, she handed me a thermometer.

"I feel fine," I said. The nurse made a clicking sound with her tongue before answering in her Southern accent, "I know, darlin', but we just want to double check." As I placed the thermometer in my mouth, the machine made a beeping noise. Numbers flashed on the screen, which the nurse wrote down on a clipboard before asking me to stand up. As I complied, I tried to look over what she'd written under my name. I could only make out what looked like a patient identification number next to a comment that said, "heart rate: on the low end." The nurse completed taking my standing vitals, and then left. By that time, I was too awake to sleep anymore. I spent the rest of the night watching the minutes change on Ally's digital clock.

I must have fallen asleep around dawn, because I woke to the sound of shuffling feet and loud voices shouting, "Time to get up!" A woman I hadn't seen before came into my room wheeling in the same mobile blood pressure machine the nurse had used. The woman looked younger than any of the other nurses or staff I'd met so far. Her blond hair was cropped short and pulled back by a headband that matched the color of the green Puma tennis shoes she was wearing. I found her overly cheerful personality a bit irksome.

"Good morning sunshine, one and all! It's time to get up, up, up!" Her singsong voice reminded me of some sort of Disney character. As the woman rolled the machine over to my bed, Ally began to complain about the noise and the light. I couldn't help but laugh under my breath. The woman introduced herself as Rochelle before taking my vitals.

"I'll be watching you this morning while you get ready. Did you sleep in those jeans?" I looked down at my pants, forgetting that I hadn't changed the day before.

"Um, yeah, I was really tired yesterday."

"Well, okay. You can change after you get weighed this morning, but first let me go ahead and get your vitals." My stomach dropped at the mention of being weighed. The sinking feeling remained as Rochelle led me down the hall and into the weighing room where Terri was standing beside a large digital scale.

"Ah, Melissa, good to see you, good to see you. How was your first night? Did you sleep?" Before I could answer, Terri disappeared into a large white cabinet and reappeared with a blue-and-white pinstriped hospital gown.

"Here, you need to change into this so I can weigh you. Why are you wearing jeans?" I took the gown from Terri without answering any of her questions. I just wanted to get out of there as fast as possible. Before Terri closed the door for me to change, Cory came into the room. She was already wearing a hospital gown identical to the one Terri had handed me.

"Oh, Melissa, do you mind waiting outside for a minute while I get Cory's weight?" Before Cory stepped onto the scale, I heard Terri say, "Shoulder and hip please." I watched as the girl unflinchingly lifted up her gown to display a bare hip. After Terri nodded, Cory rolled down the top portion of the gown to show Terri her shoulder. I assumed the shoulder and hip routine was to ensure we weren't hiding any clothing underneath our gowns so we'd weigh in heavier than we really were. Of course, the logic behind weighing more was simple—if we had gained weight, we wouldn't be forced to eat as much. I wondered if Cory had always been so comfortable displaying her body like that. Her movements were mechanical, almost as if she'd stopped thinking.

After Terri closed the door behind Cory, I began to fumble with the button on my jeans. I wanted so badly to copy Cory's nonchalant manner. *Don't think, just don't think.* The words kept running through my head. Yet the more I tried not to think, the more rapidly the thoughts came. *She's going to see the layers of fat and the expansion of flesh. How can you stand there like that? Cover up, hide yourself!* The Sick Person's voice was so loud that I could feel my head begin to throb. The day had just begun, and I couldn't wait for it to be over.

After I was weighed, Rochelle came by to walk me back to the room. I grabbed the first pair of jeans and shirt I could find in the drawers I'd stuffed my clothes into the night before. Rochelle followed me into the bathroom where Ally was poised in a crouching position on top of the counter. "Ally, what are you doing up there? Silly whim, you need to get down and stop messing with your hair." At first, it didn't seem like Ally was aware of our presence. She continued making faces at herself in the mirror while pulling out individual strands of hair. As I stood there watching the curious expression on Ally's face, I suddenly remembered the goal board I'd read the night before: *Ally will not pull out her hair this week.* At the time, I had thought Ally was just using a figure of speech, but I guess she really wasn't.

"Hold on, Rochelle, I'll get down in a minute. I just want to get this last one. . . ." After pulling out another hair, Ally climbed down from the counter, giggling ecstatically. I couldn't help but smile at Ally. It felt nice to be around other girls who weren't exactly "normal." For the first time in a long time, I felt like I actually fit in.

Back in Texas, things were different. In Texas, I had always been the odd girl with tics, or the stupid girl who couldn't read; the butt of other kid's jokes, or the source of teachers' scorn. As I watched Ally climb down from the counter, I began to think that being at the ranch might not be so bad after all.

By the time I got downstairs, most of the other girls were already gathered outside of the nurse's stations. As soon as I lined up behind Jessie, the glass panel slid open. "Mornin' y'all!" Dora's now-familiar Southern accent rang out from behind the nurse's station.

"Do you ever go home?" Jessie asked Dora in a joking tone of voice—although part of me thought she really meant it.

Dora smiled in response, then turned to me and said, "Hey, Melissa, how are you doing today? Let me see, what do we have for you today?" Dora pulled out a small paper pill cup and began rummaging through a cabinet. "All right, here you go, young lady." As I took the cup from Dora's hand, I noticed a few large pills I hadn't seen before. I eyed them suspiciously as Dora handed me a cupful of yellow liquid.

"What's this?"

"Oh, didn't they tell you about the Gatorade?"

At that moment, the Gatorade was only a secondary concern. "No, I mean, what are these?" I pointed to the small white medicine cup she'd given me.

"Well, the white one is a Caltrate and the red one is a multivitamin."

"I don't want these. Nobody asked me if I wanted to take calcium." Dora stared at me for a moment before making a huffing noise and responding, "Oh, come on, hun, they're good for you." I could feel my heart rate begin to speed up.

In my mind, I went through all the doctors who'd told me the same thing: "Here, Melissa, these pills are going to help you. They'll stop the tics. Here, take these, *they're good for you.*" They were all liars—every single one of them. I felt my face grow hot with anger. How dare she lie to me and tell me that pills are "good" or "helpful." She didn't know about the ambulance, the police sirens, or the doctor who pushed needles into my face while promising I'd feel better. I wanted to throw the pills back at her and run away. I was about to crumple up the cup, but then out of the corner of my eye I saw Tonia. All I could think about was losing my phone call, the one source of freedom I had left. I had to protect what was still mine.

Dora smiled at me after I had gulped down the pills along with the cup of Gatorade. "There see, it's not so bad. Good job!" Her praise made me grimace. I felt as though I was a toddler being praised for not wetting the bed.

The call for prayer time came a few minutes later. As they had the night before, everyone formed a circle near the back door and began to sing while making hand gestures that corresponded to the different parts of the song. Their prayer circle was unappealing to me. Even if I'd known the words, singing about Jesus Christ wasn't something a Jewish person was supposed to do. And I still had no interest in holding someone else's hand. Ally saw me standing outside of the circle and motioned for me to join. When I didn't move, she walked toward me.

"Come on, we all know this is kind of stupid, but at least when you're signing you can forget about being here for a few minutes."

"I don't know the words or the hand motions."

"So? It doesn't matter."

"I'm Jewish."

"Really? That's cool!" Ally's reaction was unexpected. I had never been "cool" before. As I began to smile, Ally tugged on my hand, pulling me into the prayer circle.

The Serious Business of Eating

18

My breakfast that morning consisted of watered-down oatmeal, a carton of milk, and some cottage cheese. The food wasn't even appetizing to look at. The other girls at my table had bowls of granola mixed with yogurt and fruit. I eyed Caitlin's tray, wishing I could swap my cottage cheese for the piece of toast on her plate. I picked up my spoon and began to stir the lumpy-looking cottage cheese.

"Melissa, please do not play with your food." I looked up and saw Tonia glaring at me. I laid the spoon back down and picked up the carton of milk instead. The nutrition label for 2 percent milk popped into my head: calories: 120; fat: 5 grams; sugar: 11 grams. Years of playing the grocery-store game had made me a pro at storing nutrition facts in my head. I could look at someone's tray and add up the calories, fat, and sugar content for each dish. The only foods I couldn't do this with were the ones I had no desire to ever eat, like cottage cheese.

"Melissa, please eat your meal. It's almost half time." Tonia's voice was beginning to aggravate me. I picked up my spoon again and dipped into what looked like oatmeal. But when I placed half a spoonful into my mouth, I began to panic.

"What is this?" The words flew out of my mouth automatically. The formidable expression on Tonia's face told me I was pushing her patience to the limit.

"It's grits. Haven't you ever had grits before?" I shook my head back and forth, indicating that I hadn't. The conversation at the table seemed to die down at my explosion. The only audible sound was the soft clanking of silverware.

"What are grits?" I demanded, my voice shaking.

"Melissa, we can't talk about food. If you have a problem with grits, you need to talk to your nutritionist about it."

It was Saturday morning. That meant I would have to face at least six more meals plus the snacks they were going to make me eat before I could even talk to anyone.

"You all have five minutes." My pulse sped up at the thought of not finishing in time. The taste of warm, rotting milk was already on my tongue. One of the girls sitting in front of me chewed so loudly that the noise made my head ache. Each time she bit down on an apple, I could hear the Sick Person in my head chanting, *fat, fat, fat* to the rhythm of her chewing. "Shut up, shut up!" I mouthed the words I wanted to shout at her, wishing I could yell out loud. There was no point in trying to finish now, time was up.

Rochelle drove me back to the house after breakfast. She tried to strike up a conversation with me in her singsong voice, but I wanted no part of it. Tonia called me into the same exam room I had been in the day before. Again, the thick liquid was measured out and poured into a plastic cup for me to drink. I didn't even resist this time. After gulping down the contents and gagging a few times, I shoved the cup back in Tonia's direction. She peered into the cup and nodded, signaling that I was done. As I walked back into the common room, I could hear the sound of music playing. Some of the girls were sitting in front of the TV watching *The Lion King*. Jessie waved at me from the couch she was sitting on.

"They let us watch movies on the weekends. We can only see G-rated films, but it's better than nothing." I sat down next to her, crossing my legs over each other to sit cross-legged.

"Don't sit like that."

"What? Why not?" Jessie's comment startled me.

"They get mad at you if you sit like that. It looks like you're stretching or something. You have to sit with your legs down." Looking around the room, I noticed that every girl was sitting the same way with both feet planted on the floor. I uncrossed my legs and thanked Jessie for warning me.

Everyone spent the rest of the morning watching *The Lion King*, making necklaces, or coloring. My whole body was stiff from sitting so long. At noon, Rochelle took me back over to the dining hall in the golf cart.

"Is there anything else to do here on the weekends?" I think it surprised her to hear me talk.

"Silly whim, there are plenty of things to do! You could color or make bracelets. Have you written any letters yet?"

"I thought about writing to some of my teachers, but I don't have any stamps."

"I can fix that for you. After lunch, come over to the front desk and I'll give you a pack." Rochelle's voice was annoying and bird-like, but I was beginning to enjoy her ebullient personality.

The smell of cheese pizza hit my nose as we entered the dining area at lunchtime. For the first time, relief flooded over me when I picked up my tray. In place of the greasy cheese-covered pizza the other girls were eating was a bowl of vegetable soup next to a plate of watermelon. Maybe being on the liquid diet for a while longer wouldn't be too bad if I could get out of eating things like pizza, boiled meat, and mashed potatoes. When I got back to the table, a few of the other girls were already sitting down. I saw my yellow index card lying on the table next to Tonia's seat. I was beginning to wonder if she put it there on purpose. As I sat down, I glanced at Jessie, who was sitting across from me with a repugnant look on her face. In addition to the slices of pizza, she had a plate of hash browns, thick-looking pudding, fruit compote, and a bag of potato chips. My jaw dropped when I saw her tray. How could anyone eat that much?

"Okay, girls, you have thirty minutes." I picked up the green napkin that was sitting beside my tray under a spoon.

"Melissa, did you ask me if you could use your napkin?"

"Sorry, I forgot." After putting the napkin back down, I ladled some of the soup into my spoon. I could hear the Sick Person's voice in my head get louder as I lifted the steaming contents to my mouth. *You don't know what's in that soup. They probably filled it with fattening things—lardy, disgusting, fattening things!*

Stop it! Shut up! I told myself, but I knew that my efforts to silence the Sick Person were futile. I felt as though a ceaseless screaming match was taking place in my head, pitting me against the Sick Person.

In the end, I submitted to the Sick Person's demands, dropping my spoonful of soup back into the bowl and picking up a piece of watermelon instead. The fruit was safe since there were only fifty calories and nine grams of sugar in an entire cupful. I had eaten about half of the watermelon when Tonia's voice sounded in my ears again. "Melissa, you need to mix your food groups." I paused, having no idea what she was talking about. "You need to mix up what you're eating. Have some soup and then go back to the watermelon again."

As I looked around the table, I noticed that none of the girls had finished one dish entirely. On Cory's tray, a half-eaten slice of pizza sat next to two-thirds of a fruit compote. She was working on getting in a few bites of ranch dressing–covered salad before returning to a glass of V8 Juice that sat in front of her. "Melissa, focus on your own plate, please. You need to mix your food groups and take bigger bites."

Tonia's constant nagging was beginning to make me more irritated than scared. Why did she need to dictate *how* I ate? As long as I got the food down, why should anyone care how I cut up my watermelon or how much soup was in my spoon? I wanted to yell at her to mind her own business, but there was no point; I knew she was in control of me. That sudden realization only fueled the Sick Person's anger, causing her to rant and rave until she drowned out every other noise in the room. *They are going to make you huge! Don't you get it? Don't you see it? Huge!* I clenched my jaw at the sound of the Sick Person's cries, trying to drown out her voice by focusing on the game Ally had started playing. Halfway through the meal, everyone's attention focused on Jessie, who had thrown her plate of hash browns on the floor.

"Jessie, I hope you didn't do that on purpose," Tonia snapped.

"There's too much food! I can't eat all of this." A hush fell over the table at Jessie's outburst. Everyone stopped eating and looked down at their plates. I glanced up for a minute to study Jessie's face. I knew that expression so well; it was the expression that reflected the fear, anger, and pain of wanting to eat but not being able to.

When I woke up on Sunday morning, my stomach felt awkward and distended, as though my skin was being pulled across an area that was too large for it to cover. I was full, and I hadn't even eaten yet. I spent the next couple of hours watching the clock, waiting for the morning to be over so I could make my first phone call. I tried to imagine the conversation my mother and I were going to have. What were we going to say to each other? I couldn't just act like a whiny child who stomps her feet while demanding to go home. No, I would need to be calm and assure her that I was better, the treatment had worked, and now I was ready to come home.

There was another bowl of cottage cheese on my tray at breakfast. This time, instead of just poking at it with my fork, I actually tried to eat a bite. I spooned a small amount into my mouth and gagged. Ally, who was sitting in front of me, scooted her chair back, fearing that she might get hit by projectile vomit. I was surprised at my response to the cottage cheese. The years of purging had left my gag reflexes weakened, making gagging or throwing up difficult and sometimes impossible. I thought about the last time I had actually purged, which was after the horse show in Mississippi. A picture of the hotel room came to mind. I could see the clothes scattered around the room alongside empty bags of soy crackers. Then there was the white-walled bathroom where I sat, gazing into a pool of vomit and blood. The vision made my body feel chilled even though the room was warm. I never wanted to see that hotel room again.

The thought of being able to tell my mother that I'd eaten an entire meal made me want to finish the cottage cheese. But the bowl was deep and filled to the brim with the curdled stuff. The monitor of the table advised me to sprinkle some salt and pepper onto the dish, but I ignored her suggestion. Sodium would only make me feel even more bloated, and a dash of pepper wasn't going to mask the revolting flavor of cottage cheese. After half time was called, I decided against trying to finish the meal. There was no point; if I was going to be supplemented, I might as well just not eat anything else. Luckily, Tonia was off on Sunday so I didn't have to watch her smirk at me while I downed a glass of warm Ensure. When one o'clock finally came, I went to the front desk to ask about my phone call. Terri handed a portable phone over the counter.

"You have ten minutes to talk. You must use those minutes to call home." Terri's instructions about only calling family members really didn't matter to me. Who else was there for me to talk to? It would have been nice to call up Emily and ask how Cadence was doing. But what else was there to say? Calling Melanie wasn't an option either. I didn't want to talk to her now for the same reason I didn't speak to her the night before I left for New Mexico. I knew I had failed her. After college, I wouldn't be going into business with Melanie or competing at the Grand Prix level. The days of training, horse shows, and travel plans were over now. I didn't want any of it because along with the glory, ribbons, and prize money came grief, pain, and empty hotel rooms. Hearing Melanie's voice would only reinforce what I already knew—I was a failure.

My hands shook as I dialed home. The phone only rang once before I heard the soft, delicate voice say, "Hello, Melissa?" It was a familiar voice, and I could easily identify who it belonged to, even in a room full of people. Yet the owner of the voice was still a stranger. I sat there for a minute, still unsure of what to say. I'd planned something out during breakfast, but now I couldn't think of what it was.

Mom continued, "How are you? We miss you. Daddy and I checked on the horse. Don't worry, she's just fine." The mention of Cadence sent a sharp pain down my body, as if someone was slicing me in half with a kitchen knife. I leaned my head against the back wall, trying to force back the tears that blurred my vision. When I didn't respond my mom asked, "Melissa, are you okay?"

I had to say something. Anything was better than sitting there in silence. "Yeah, I'm okay."

"What have you done so far today?" she asked. I ran through the day's events in my head and summed everything up to one activity. "I ate today." The words almost sounded foreign to me: *I ate today.*

"That's great, honey. What did you eat?"

"I don't want to talk about it."

"Oh okay, well what do you want to talk about?"

"I—I don't know." I spent the rest of the conversation listening to my mother tell me about the various things my family had planned for the upcoming week. Brooke was busy studying for finals, Sam liked her swimming lessons, and my dad had a business meeting in North Texas. The details were not really important to me; I just wanted to feel close to my mother. There were so many things I wanted to say to her, but the barrier between us inhibited the flow of words. Instead, we talked about trivial things, like two strangers having a conversation about the weather. After we said good-bye, I stayed on the line until I heard a clicking noise followed by a long dial tone, and then the operator's recorded voice saying, "If you would like to make a call, please hang up and try again."

For a while, I held my knees against my chest, cradling the phone in my arms as though it were a beloved rag doll. Sobs began to escape from my mouth and were accompanied by a stream of tears that ran relentlessly down my face, hitting the faded blue carpet. I had no desire or energy to suppress them anymore. Several of the girls came up and asked if I was okay. I nodded my head in assent and answered that I was just homesick. Homesick, I knew, wasn't the right word. I wasn't homesick because I had no home to miss. The house that I lived in back in Texas didn't feel like my real home; it was just the place I slept in between horse shows. To me, the feeling of being at "home" was equivocal to the feeling of being loved. Home could be anywhere love resided, but if a place was devoid of love, it could not be a home. When I said I was homesick, what I really meant was that I was sick of feeling unlovable.

On Monday morning, I woke up to the usual knock on the door and the sound of complaining about the bright lights. Monday was the day for everyone, not just the new people, to get weighed. As I walked out of my room, I saw a line of girls in hospital gowns stretched down the hallway, and I was shocked by how similar everyone looked. Bodies were no longer hidden beneath layers of clothing; faces weren't covered up with foundation or bright eye shadow. We were all naked, covered only by a thin blue sheet pulled tightly around skeletal bodies that shook in the cool morning air. Our faces had the same wan expressions and haunting catlike eyes. Every time a gown was rolled down to show a bare shoulder or hip, the same display of protruding bones could be seen. We were all just standing there, a mesh of bodies—tired, undernourished, and utterly naked.

I could already tell that the day was going to be a bad one. The Sick Person's voice was beginning to shriek at me for my failure to suppress my stomach's growling. *Concentrate! You're just not trying hard enough. How dare you let your stomach ask for food. Unworthy girl—filthy, disgusting, unworthy girl.* My stomach wasn't supposed to growl. Growling meant that my body wanted and expected to be fed; growling meant that I no longer had control over my body.

While standing in line for medicine, I tried to think of the last time I'd felt that rumbling sensation. I remembered how, during the early years of starvation, hunger pangs would drive me to search for food late at night. But after a while my body gave up, realizing that no matter how much it begged, I still wasn't going to give it anything to eat. After that, the rumbling ceased and was replaced by a hollow sensation that left me feeling light and at ease. Now that I was eating again, the hunger pangs were coming back as my body began to beg for food again.

As I followed Ally downstairs, the voice in my head grew more livid. *How dare you be hungry. Can't you see the fat and flesh that covers every bone? Look! Are you blind? Look at yourself! Disgusting girl.* I began to panic and started looking around the room for something to appease the Sick Person.

"Melissa, stop wandering around." Tonia's voice reminded me how much trouble I could be in if I kept walking around in plain sight. I sat down, but the desire to move only increased as the Sick Person's hisses became intolerably loud. Desperately looking around the room for something to do, I noticed that one part of the back room was partitioned off by a wall just wide enough for a person to stand behind without being seen. Now that everyone had congregated in the front room, I could sneak behind the wall and get away with running in place for a few minutes. I wouldn't run much; I just needed to move around long enough to assuage the Sick Person. A smile tugged at my lips as I slowly rose and walked into the back room. Now was my chance. With my eyes shut tight, I imagined being outside on an open stretch of road, far away from the building that had become my jail. I was like a little child playing a game of pretend. When I opened my eyes again, I saw Tiffany staring at me.

The Rules of the Game 19

I lifted a finger to my mouth, signaling for her to keep quiet. If she told anyone, I knew there would be a big glass of Ensure with my name on it. For the rest of the morning, I sat as still as possible on one of the couches in the front room. Anxiety welled up inside of me each time my name was called. I could only breathe again when I realized that the nurse just needed to give me a cup of Gatorade or that Rochelle only wanted to take my vitals. No one said anything about running. After breakfast, I plopped down on the couch, satisfied that Tiffany hadn't told on me. The sound of someone coming down the stairs made me turn around. A small woman with short, mousey-brown hair was making her way into the room. I didn't recognize her but figured she was just another mental health tech.

"Hello, you must be Melissa. My name is Jennie. I'm your nutritionist." Jennie grinned at me and extended her hand to shake mine. I studied her face for a minute before standing up. Her face was square with a sharp jaw line that made it look like she was always clenching her jaw. Jennie was young; she couldn't have been more than thirty-five. The wrinkles that gathered around her mouth and eyes had to be from stress or lack of sleep. Every feature was harsh or sharp looking. Not even Jennie's smile helped to soften her appearance. I followed Jennie up the stairs and into a corner office near the nurse's station. As I glanced around the room, I looked for frames displaying a husband, kids, or even a pet. But the only framed items in the room were various diplomas, each stamped with a different school seal.

"So I see you're from Texas. Is it as hot there as it is here?" I could tell she was making small talk before getting into the real questions. I tried to answer with as flat a voice as possible. I wasn't interested in having a trivial conversation.

"Yea, it's pretty hot in Texas."

"So, how has everything been going so far? Have you been finishing your meals okay?" This question was just as irritating as her previous one. She already knew the answer; my chart was sitting in her hands.

"I don't like cottage cheese."

"Yes, I see that. Is there anything else?"

"When will I be allowed to eat normal food?"

"What do you mean?"

"I mean, when can I stop drinking my meals?"

"Ah, I was just about to mention something about that. Starting with dinner, we will move you to the normal meal plan. You will be able to eat what all the other girls are having with the addition of a few items." At the mention of additional food, I could feel my already clenched fists begin to tighten. Jennie gazed down at my balled fists before beginning again. "Are you nervous?"

"No," I lied.

"Well then, why are your knuckles turning white?" I looked down at my fists, trying to focus on relaxing my grip. Jennie didn't wait for me to reply.

"You have another option if you don't feel capable of supplementing your meals with additional food." Relief flooded over me as I sat back in my chair and dropped both arms to my side. But Jennie's thin-lipped smile was enough to send me right back onto the edge of the chair. I felt like she was laughing at me for being stupid enough to suppose that I could somehow get out of consuming extra calories.

"The other option you have is to get a feeding tube."

A picture flashed in my mind of that skeletal girl I'd seen during my first meal, the one with the feeding tube in her nose that was attached to her cheek with tape. I wasn't that sick; my body wasn't that thin and frail. There was no way I was going to let them put a tube in me.

"A feeding tube would make gaining weight a lot easier. We could put you on a regular meal plan without the additional items. At night, the nurse would just hook you up to a machine that pumps nutrients through the tube while you're asleep. You wouldn't even feel full in the morning." Before Jennie could say anything else, I interrupted.

"How much weight are you going to make me gain?" That same sardonic smile reappeared on her face. It seemed as though the whole conversation was just a game to her; she wanted to keep me in suspense.

"I can't tell you that until family week."

"What's family week?"

"Oh, no one's told you? Family week occurs midway through your stay here. Your parents and siblings will spend time with you and attend therapy sessions. Depending on your level status, there will be certain privileges allotted to you. Some girls choose to go out to eat or spend a night with their families." I stopped listening to Jennie as soon as she started explaining the dynamics of family week. All I could think about was the amount of weight they were going to force me to gain. The change in Jennie's tone made me turn to her again.

"Do you understand?"

"What?"

"I was asking if you understood the conditions of the feeding tube."

I'd forgotten that I hadn't actually expressed my feelings about the tube aloud. "I don't want a feeding tube."

A huffing noise escaped from Jennie's mouth as she jotted something down on a notepad. "All right, that's your decision then. Once you see how hard this is going to be, you might change your mind. Now before we talk about what additional items you are going to be adding, I have one other question. I see that you are a very active person at home. How is that working out for you here? Are you having any trouble with not being able to exercise?"

I felt my stomach jerk at the mention of exercise. Thoughts began to flood my mind. Did she know about the running? Did that girl tell after all? No one else had mentioned anything about the incident to me. I wanted to think Jennie's mention of exercise was just a coincidence and nothing more.

"No, I'm fine." My voice didn't sound right. I coughed once, pretending to clear my throat before speaking again. "Everything is fine." I glanced at the floor for a moment before turning my attention back to Jennie. The smug look on her face told me I had just made a big mistake. The ends of Jennie's lips were curled up in a devious way. Even her eyes seemed to be laughing at me.

"Oh really, so you haven't had any problems with running in place or doing cartwheels in your room?"

Great, now I was really in trouble. The night before, Ally had been showing me how to do a back handspring on the floor in our room. We should have known better than to think we could get away with doing gymnastics moves. No matter where I went, there was always someone watching me, analyzing every move I made. The thought sent a chill up my spine. There was nowhere to go, nowhere to run to just have a moment to myself.

"Melissa, you realize I can't allow you to go off monitoring. By now, we generally allow girls to get dressed and shower without one of the mental health techs. But it seems as though you are not ready for that privilege."

"I'm sorry! I'm sorry! I didn't mean to! I swear I won't do it again. Please don't. . . ." The words escaped before I even realized I was speaking.

"How can I trust you when you just lied to me? If you had told me you were having trouble, or at least not lied about it, I would have considered taking you off monitoring. But you didn't even do that."

Hot tears began to prick my eyes as I tried to formulate some sort of explanation. Jennie began to talk again, but her voice was drowned out by the one in my head. *Why are you so surprised? Screwing up is something you're actually good at. What are you doing sitting in that chair? Get down from there and sit in your rightful place on the floor.* The voice sent a fresh wave of sadness through my body. Melanie was right when she said I belonged in the dirt; the voice was right, too.

"Melissa, can we please talk about your meal plan?" I could tell Jennie was losing patience with me now. She probably thought I was ignoring her on purpose. I bobbed my head in agreement to let her know I was listening. "Okay then, I have the menu for today's dinner. You have two options for the main course. There's either a ham sandwich or spaghetti with meatballs."

"I don't eat meat." I knew I was digging myself into an even bigger hole. "I don't like meat, and I'm not allowed to eat it." When I looked up, I saw that Jennie had a smug look on her face again. It was like this was all a game to her, like she already knew how I would respond to each question.

"Why aren't you allowed to eat meat?"

"I keep kosher."

She smiled again. "Oh, don't worry about that. We already asked your parents if there were any dietary restrictions we should be aware of. They told us you can eat everything." I could feel my face growing hot. Jennie's remark infuriated me, partly because of the game she was playing, and partly because I was being caught at every lie.

Jennie took another thirty minutes to go over the rest of the menu. I decided there was no point in trying to fight her. She could pick out the lies as soon as they tumbled out of my mouth. Instead, I just chose spaghetti and meatballs, and sat there halfheartedly listening to all the additional items I'd be eating at meals and snacks.

At lunch that day I drank down my last liquid meal. The tomato soup was thick and tasted like paste. The thought of never having to gulp down a bowl of soup again was enough to make me finish off the disgusting stuff. After I came back from lunch, another woman I'd never seen approached me. She had a large frame and red shoulder-length hair that was pulled back by a clip. There was a Southern twang to her accent as she introduced herself as Meg. "I'm going to be your therapist for the next few months," she said.

I decided I was going to like Meg when she actually let me walk down the road to her office instead of forcing me to ride in a golf cart. On the way over, Meg asked me trivial questions just as Jennie had done. But this time I didn't mind answering since Meg's voice was jovial and warm, unlike Jennie's.

During my time in New Mexico, sessions with Meg became one of the things I would look forward to during the week. The weekends were always painfully long and dull, but every Monday afternoon I could escape into Meg's office for an hour. We talked about family, school, and horses. I enjoyed Meg's company and learned to trust her for the most part. But there were some things I just couldn't tell her, or anyone else for that matter. I wasn't going to talk to Meg about being sexually molested, or about the Sick Person who demanded control over food and love. I wasn't planning to tell her about my mom or Melanie. Part of me desperately wanted to tell Meg everything, to let the words flow out like water so that I could empty myself of all the pollution that had built up within me. Yet I felt as though someone was clasping a hand against my mouth, forcing me to remain silent.

Two days after my first individual therapy session, Meg scheduled a telephone conference with my parents. When Meg came by to pick me up, Jessie and I were sitting on the floor, attempting to put a puzzle together. Actually, we were sitting on pillows on the floor since it hurt our bony backsides to sit on the carpeted floor without extra cushioning.

"Are you ready, Melissa?" I liked the way Meg said my name in her Southern accent. As we walked over to Meg's office, a cool breeze made me shiver, making me wish I'd brought another sweater with me. I welcomed the warmth that blew over me as Meg opened the door to her little office. "Well, today's the day," she said.

I knew she was talking about the scheduled telephone conference with my parents.

"Yeah, I guess so."

"Is there anything you want to talk about in particular?"

"I don't know." Actually, I knew exactly what I wanted to talk about, but something prevented me from forcing the words out. The conversation I wanted to have was already laid out in my mind and involved only me and my mother. Meg would be in the room, but she wasn't going to take part in the dialogue. I'd tell my mother everything, starting from the very beginning and not stopping until the present. I would tell her all about the pills, the lack of control, the anger, and the guilt. She'd find out about my ravenous hunger for love and the attempts I made to get my fill from Melanie. I'd even tell her about the empty hotel rooms, the pain, and the blood.

But in the end, I never said any of these things. It was as though the words were lodged in a jar with an impenetrable seal and I couldn't, for the life of me, figure out how to loosen the lid.

To get us started, Meg began the conversation in typical therapy fashion by asking each of us how we were feeling. My dad answered in his usual nonchalant manner, chuckling under his breath a little before saying, "Fantastic, never been better." His slightly sardonic tone told me he was lying. The jittery, nervous answer my mother gave was also nothing new: "Oh, Meg, we're just so worried." Her tone of voice rose toward the end of the sentence, putting an extra emphasis on *worried*.

It was easy enough for Meg to identify my dad as the family clown and to tell that my mother played the role of the nervous homemaker, but I still didn't see a point to the game of labeling our roles in the family. Yes, my dad was a clown, but so what? No one ever explained *why* he was a clown. No one pointed out that the reason my dad goofed around so much was that jokes shielded him from actually feeling anything. How could giving each other these names help anyone if all the names did were tell about *what* we were but said nothing about *why* we were the way we were? Without the *why*, the *what* doesn't even make sense! The role I played was the perfectionist, but what good did it do to give me that label if no one understood why I was that way? Of course, *I* knew why I needed to be perfect. If I was perfect, I would finally be good enough for someone to love. More than anything, I wanted to scream at them all for not understanding; I wanted to stand up and yell at the top of my lungs, *Don't you get it? Everything perfect is lovable!*

FACING
MY DEMONS

20

By Friday of my first week at the ranch I was officially moved to green status, meaning that I didn't have to ride in the golf cart anymore. Walking to places felt wonderful. I could stretch my legs out as we walked across the gravel pathways to chapel or art therapy. The only restriction I still had was that I couldn't go anywhere without one of the mental-health techs following me around. Every morning, I hoped to see Mona or Rochelle wandering around the halls or downstairs on one of the couches. The days they worked were the ones I could take a shower, go to the bathroom, and get dressed in private. But after three days without seeing either of them, my scalp was beginning to itch from not being washed. Jane, the nurse, was in charge of following me around on Sunday evening. Usually when she asked me if I wanted to shower I'd tell her no, but after three days I was beginning to feel disgusting. I pulled the blue shower curtain closed, changed out of my clothes, and tossed them into the shower tote I placed just outside the stall. The warm water felt good against my skin, and for a minute, it seemed that Jane was going to let me shower in peace.

"Melissa, I can't let you out of my sight." I could feel my pulse begin to quicken at the sound of her familiar, raspy voice. As I saw her pull the shower curtain to the side, I grabbed onto the curtain without thinking and pulled it back across the stall. "Melissa, let go, please." Jane tried to pull the curtain back again, but my grip was firm. I stood there for a few minutes, trying to hold onto the curtain while simultaneously washing the shampoo out of my hair.

"Melissa, if you don't let go by the count of five . . ." Jane never finished saying what she was going to do once she reached "five." Instead, she just started counting. My heart began to pound as I furiously tried to wash the shampoo out of my hair. As she announced "Five" with finality, she threw the curtain open and I instinctively wrapped both arms across my bare chest.

"Stop it! Get out! Get away from me, Adam!" The words flew out of my mouth like bullets being shot out of a gun. I flung the curtain shut again and grabbed the towel out of my shower tote. I kept my head down low as I walked out of the shower, trying to focus on counting each of the different tiled squares on the floor. Although I knew Jane was probably confused by my sudden outburst, I had no intention of explaining anything to her.

That night, my body wouldn't allow me to get any rest. Every muscle felt rigid, as if each tendon had been stretched so tightly that the slightest movement would cause one to snap. I glared at the ceiling for hours with both hands on top of my stomach. The muscles felt like they were twitching back and forth under the layer of skin. The sensation was odd; stomach tics were not something I'd experienced before. I finally fell asleep about 4:00 AM to the sound of Ally snoring.

"Rise and shine and give God your glory, glory!" By the end of this first week, Rochelle's voice no longer annoyed me as much as it originally did. I welcomed her ebullience because she provided a break from the day's monotony. Usually, I got up as soon as I heard a voice down the hall or a knock at the door, but that morning the lack of sleep made me wish for a few more minutes in bed. When I finally opened my eyes, I noticed that my hands were still on my stomach. The spastic sensation wasn't as intense as it had been the night before, but I could feel some of the muscles in my face contracting. Once in front of the mirror, the familiar sight of shuddering eyelids and flaring nostrils gave me a sinking feeling. I stood there for another five minutes, trying to concentrate on holding everything still, but my unruly body continued to jerk and twist. I wasn't so much surprised by the sudden increase in the frequency and intensity of tics as I was disappointed. Whenever I was under stress, the twitches and grimaces always grew worse; a pattern I had grown accustomed to over the years. Although a large part of me knew they were inevitable, there was still a part of me that prayed the next time would be different and the tics wouldn't get worse. My prayers, though, never seemed to be answered.

Once I was downstairs, even without looking up, I could feel different sets of eyes staring at me. *Get away! Hide your face, cover your body!* The Sick Person's relentless screaming lasted all the way through breakfast. Between bites of toast, my neck jerked to the side, sending me into a coughing fit as I tried to free a piece of bread that had lodged in my throat.

The rest of the morning was painfully slow. During art therapy, I spent most of the first fifteen minutes staring at a bottle of Mod Podge, semilistening to the story Tiffany was telling me about the vacation she took just before being sent to treatment. My attention shifted away from watching the goopy substance drip down the plastic bottle when I heard the sound of the front door open. A tall woman with long, thick, gray hair and brightly painted lips made her way to the front of the classroom.

"Hello everyone! For those of you who don't know me, my name is Pam and I am the art therapist here at the ranch." Pam's voice was loud, yet kind. "Now then, today we are going to be making ED masks. I want each of you to take a moment to think about what your eating disorder looks like. Once you've got a good picture in your head, you can use any of the materials in the room to create your own mask." As Pam walked around the room to hand out white plastic masks, her peasant skirt made swishing noises against the deep-brown leather boots she was wearing.

I took the blank mask in my hands and thought about Pam's idea of personifying ED. I had never thought to give the Sick Person residing within me a real name, much less a face. As the days passed, I was becoming more aware that although the Sick Person resided within me, she was also distinct from me. We were two entities living in one body, like a virus and its host. Occasionally, the Sick Person would gain so much control that the line separating me from her became blurred and distorted so that I could no longer tell if we were two or one.

I flipped the mask around in my hands and looked across the room to see what the other girls were doing. Jessie had a black permanent marker in her hand and was drawing a livid-looking face onto her mask. Caitlin was busily gluing black hair onto her mask, which already had a forlorn expression etched onto it. Sitting back in my chair, I started thinking about the Sick Person and the different tactics she used to control me. I felt real anger as I thought about the Sick Person's incessant screaming and threats, the promises that were made and broken shortly after. How she purred *good girl* when I obeyed and screamed *worthless* and *disgusting* when I didn't. Suddenly, the feeling of anger was replaced by a sickening sensation that seemed to fill my entire body. For the first time, I realized how much the Sick Person resembled Melanie. How could I have mistaken Melanie's desire to control every aspect of my life for love! She wanted me all to herself but for all the wrong reasons. When I obeyed Melanie, she, too, would smile at me and say, *good girl.* If I did something wrong, though, she would turn her back on me, calling me *dirt* instead of *daughter.*

How could I have not seen it? Why had I kept running back to her? Why do I still love her? Thoughts of *how* and *why* clouded my mind, turning my rage into confusion, and then into sadness. I was repulsed by the feelings of love I still had for Melanie. Logically, I could say I hated her, but emotionally, I was still clinging to Melanie's arm, yearning for her love, and fearing I would lose it.

By the end of the art therapy session, my mask was just about finished. When Pam came by the table, I saw a smile spread over her lips as she picked up my mask and said, "Very nice, Melissa, tell me what your mask means to you." I sat back in my chair for a moment before answering.

"One side is the devil and the other is an angel."

"Yes, I see that. Tell me what that means."

I analyzed Pam's face as she spoke, trying to determine if I could trust that she wouldn't laugh at me. Her eyes told me there was nothing cynical or disdainful about her question. The edges of Pam's lips weren't curled up like someone trying to hold back from laughing. Her voice sounded sweet, as though she genuinely cared. Something told me that I could trust her. As I ran my hand around the edge of the mask, I began my first attempt at talking about the Sick Person in my head.

The dining hall was filled with people by the time we arrived for lunch. I already knew that my meal consisted of a grilled cheese sandwich, a bag of pretzels, two small bowls of strawberries, salad with ranch dressing, orange-flavored sherbet, and a glass of apple juice. As I picked up my tray, I thought about Jennie's offer again; maybe a feeding tube would be easier. Eating six times a day was getting harder with the additional items and increased volume. My jaw was sore from the chewing. Sitting at Tonia's table never helped the situation much either. She still placed me in the chair right next to her at every meal.

"Melissa, don't tear off your crust and stop eating your sandwich in circles like that," she admonished. I didn't realize that the bites I was taking were turning the once square-shaped sandwich into an oval. "Bigger bites, mix your food groups, don't eat so slowly. Did I say you could use your napkin?" Tonia's voice rang in my ears, making me want to scream "Shut up!" at the top of my lungs. My stomach felt huge and distended by the end of the meal. The oily grilled cheese sandwich made me feel like my entire body had been doused with grease.

They're all staring at your enormous stomach, staring at that repulsive flesh. The Sick Person's screams only made my tics worse, causing my arms to swing out haphazardly. After the meal was over, I picked up my tray and followed Jessie back to the kitchen, trying to focus on keeping my arms from flailing. Halfway there, though, my left arm flung to the side, sending the tray along with the plates and silverware crashing to the floor. A sinking feeling in my stomach made me keep my eyes down as I rushed to pick up the pieces of broken glass.

"Do you need some help?"

I looked up for a minute, glad to see the familiar Puma tennis shoes Rochelle always wore.

"I'm sorry, I really didn't mean to break everything. I can clean it up." I sounded like a child begging not to be punished for smashing fine china.

"Don't worry about it, silly. I break dishes all the time." Rochelle's singsong voice made me feel slightly better.

After lunch, I sat by the back door of the common room, anxiously waiting to hear Meg's voice. Sitting around without anything to distract my mind was becoming too dangerous. There was too much time to think and feel. Part of me wanted to slip into that state of blissful numbness where nothing really matters. That way, I wouldn't have to think about Melanie or competing. And if no thoughts came to mind, the grief and anger would also stay at bay. My gaze turned to focus on the horses that were grazing peacefully in their paddocks outside. Every time I looked at them, my chest began to ache. I could have very easily looked away; no one was forcing me to watch the horses. Yet something within me welcomed the stinging sensation that rippled through my body, telling me that I not only wanted to feel the pain but that I also needed to. The hurt needed to be unbearable, because only then would I be able to speak up and finally say *I quit*.

After eleven years of horseback riding, I was tired. Willow Wind couldn't be my home anymore because I finally understood that being with Melanie was killing me. As I gazed at a bay gelding swishing flies away with his tail, I tried to think of the last time I actually found riding enjoyable. Competing with Cadence had been somewhat pleasurable, but the type of enjoyment I sought was of a different sort. What I was in search of was that exuberant feeling you get from not having a care in the world, the feeling of being absolutely free. My forehead began to pound as I tried to pinpoint the last time I genuinely enjoyed horses for the sake of horses. By the time I was eleven, riding had already turned into a career instead of a hobby. By age twelve, horses had become machines that were used until they broke and then were disposed of. I adored Cadence, but my love for horses in general had become sickeningly jaded. I despised Melanie for using me, but while staring out the window I began thinking about the similarities between how Melanie treated me and the way I treated Cadence. The thought made me feel especially dirty. I would have sold Cadence if Melanie pushed me hard enough. If her threats of disinterest and abandonment had increased just a little more, I would have traded my machine in for a new one. Horseback riding wasn't my passion; it was my job, and now I was too tired to work.

That afternoon, the walk to Meg's office was spent in silence. I shuffled ahead of her a few paces so that I could pretend not to hear her voice over the blowing wind. Really, I just didn't feel like making small talk. Once I curled up in my usual place on one of the old couches in Meg's office, I just needed to get enough strength to force the words out. The next few minutes were spent with me looking up at Meg, opening my mouth as if to speak, and then shutting it again. I thought about asking for a pencil and paper to write everything down, but then I realized that my parents weren't around to read my writing. I needed to make my words audible so that they could hear me. The only way to force the words out was if I thought about the pain. Melanie's voice began to play in my head like a child's music box: *Your mother doesn't care about you. She wants you to fail. I'm the one who treats you like a daughter; I'm the one who loves you.* The image of Melanie passed through my mind—Melanie mocking me with her piercing blue eyes and twisted smile. I could still hear her words as if they'd just escaped from her lips. Why did I let that woman tell me my mother didn't love me? Even more important, why did I believe her?

"Melissa, are you going to say something?"

I looked up from the weathered, brown chair arm I had been staring at and noticed from the clock on the wall that we only had twenty minutes left to talk.

"I quit."

"What? What do you mean?"

I realized my sentence didn't exactly make much sense taken out of context. "I don't want to horseback ride anymore. I don't want Cadence, and I don't want . . . " I was about to say "And I don't want Melanie's love," but I still couldn't get those words out. I studied Meg's countenance, noticing that her expression was a mixture of happiness and concern. I could tell she was trying to look worried; her lips were pursed, and the inner corners of each eyebrow rose up to form small wrinkles in the middle of her forehead. But Meg's eyes showed a very different emotion: her pupils shone and seemed to be dancing with joy. She was gripping both arms of the chair, which suggested she was trying to resist jumping up and shouting something like *Hallelujah, the girl finally trusts me!* Meg's mixed reactions weren't surprising. I knew she was probably delighted that I was finally beginning to talk about something real.

"When do you want to tell your parents about the horse?"

"I guess I should tell them now."

"Are you sure? We only have about fifteen minutes left for our conference."

I was already bobbing my head before Meg could finish her sentence. There was only a little time left, but if I didn't say something now, I might never be able to. Before dialing the number, Meg let out a soft huffing noise as if she was mentally preparing for a perilous trek through foreign terrain. Once she finished dialing the numbers, Meg pressed the orange speaker button and sank back into her brown leather chair. After two rings, I heard my mother's voice on the other line.

"Hi honey. How are you?"

I sat perplexed for a moment. How did she know I was calling? Our phone call was supposed to be over thirty minutes ago, and we didn't have caller ID.

"I stayed home today because I wanted to wait for you to call." My mother's statement hit me and I felt a pang of sadness. I mouthed each word over and over again, *I wanted to wait for you, I wanted to wait for you.* What my mother had said should have filled me with the warmth that accompanies happiness, but I didn't feel even the slightest inkling of heat. All I could feel was sadness and guilt; the two emotions that overpowered and blocked any and every positive feeling.

"Mrs. Binstock, I believe Melissa has something she wants to tell you." Meg's voice brought me back to the present, making me realize that the time had come; my mother needed to know. There was a momentary silence before I began talking.

"Err . . . um, hi. Sorry my call came kind of late. I've been doing a lot of thinking up here. There is something I need—no, sorry, there is something I want to tell you. I've decided to stop horseback riding. Nothing about it makes me happy anymore." My voice dropped off into silence. I threw a nervous glance at Meg, pleading with my eyes for her to step in and say something.

"Melissa has been really working hard these past few days." Everyone fell quiet for a moment before my mother broke in.

"Is this really what you want, Melissa? You don't want to ride at all?"

"Melissa feels that it would be best for her recovery if she didn't horseback ride right now," Meg said.

I stopped twirling my shoelace and looked across at Meg, trying to tell her thank-you without actually saying anything. "What would you like to do about the horse?" my mother asked. I wanted to know what was going through her head, but her monotone didn't reveal anything.

"Melissa, do you want us to sell the horse?" she pressed. For the first time, I was glad that my mother was referring to Cadence as "the horse." The impersonal approach made it seem like I was asking her to get rid of some strange animal I had no emotional bond with. But the momentary illusion didn't last long as an image of Cadence appeared in my mind—her glistening honey-colored coat and velvety muzzle, the way she always nickered when I walked down the barn aisle. Cadence was a special horse, and we'd been through so much together. At that moment, tears filled my eyes. I hated myself for crying. No one was forcing me to make this decision, and yet here I was bawling and whimpering like a child.

Finally, after taking in a few shallow breaths, I sat up in my chair, leaned over the phone, and answered, "Yes, I can't keep Cadence anymore."

I was glad to hear Meg tell us we'd run out of time. The thought of trying to explain to my mother why I needed to sell Cadence was too overwhelming for the present. That would have to come when I felt ready to tell her about Melanie, the Sick Person, and my incessant hunger for love. There was still so much left unsaid.

CHALLENGES 21

After breakfast on the following Wednesday morning, Tonia called everyone into the back room to announce that we would be having a "snack challenge" that afternoon. "Everyone will have the option of eating their regular snack or taking the challenge. If you decide to take the challenge, you will get to spend more time with your family when they come up for family week. Does everyone understand?" For the remainder of the morning, Ally tried to get different staff members to leak information to us about what kind of food we were going to have to eat, but Tonia only scowled, and Rochelle's response was to pat Ally's head and let out a loud "hahahah."

That afternoon each of us began to mentally weigh the pros and cons of taking the snack challenge. Here we were, nineteen of us sitting at one long table, all with the same solemn expression of fear mixed with grief and frustration impressed on our faces. The mood seemed to lighten a little when everyone saw Rochelle skipping into the room and humming gently to herself. Tonia followed a few steps behind, balancing a large white tray piled high with bowls, plates, and cups. My stomach sank at the sight of the ice cream scoop. Ice cream—they were going to make us eat ice cream. I could feel my palms begin to sweat as Mona walked into the room carrying a tray stacked with tubs of different flavors of ice cream. I looked over the labels and tried to estimate which kind of ice cream had the least amount of calories. Rocky road was automatically out; it was full of nuts and marshmallows. Chocolate chip cookie dough was the equivalent of lard to me. As I looked over each of the different flavors, I realized that every choice was equally evil. Next to the rocky road sat tubs of mint chocolate chip, vanilla fudge ripple, and something I'd never heard of called pralines and cream.

"Why can't you all just let us eat plain old chocolate or vanilla without all this junk?" Cory's exclamation was followed by a series of heads nodding and different voices saying, "Yeah, why not?" The room only fell silent again when Tonia walked in with a platter of chocolate birthday cake. When a plate filled with what seemed like a mountain of cake and ice cream was placed in front of me, my first reaction was to scoot back in my chair so I could get as far away from it as possible.

My head ached as the Sick Person's screams drowned out all the other noises in the room. I felt like someone had injected every vein with a syringe full of anxiety, which was now pulsing through my body and making my heart race. The sensation exacerbated the spastic movements in my face, neck, and arms so that it almost looked like I was having a seizure. The jerking movements in my right arm made me hold back from even touching the plate; I was fearful I'd send it flying across the room. A few of the girls glanced over in my direction and asked me if I was okay. Thankfully, though, most of them were too worried about the snack challenge to notice anything.

"Girls, you have fifteen more minutes."

I forced down the cake and ice cream one excruciating mouthful at a time. By the time I was done, I felt as if my entire body had been dunked in a vat of lard. I was paranoid that there was oil dripping from my skin and clothes. The Sick Person continued to shout in my ear about extending stomachs and unlovable flesh, causing my whole body to feel heavy with sadness. *Hide yourself! Get away! Your body is too disgusting to be seen.* I mouthed the words *please stop* as though imploring the Sick Person to give me peace.

Feeling stuffed to the gills, I had nothing to do until body-image therapy, which didn't start for another hour. I rested in the common area and shut my eyes, hoping that sleep would come and take the rest of the day away. I'd come to treasure the feeling of heavy eyelids. Sleep was a mode of escape from every feeling of guilt and sadness. For a while, I could get away from the tics, obsessive thoughts, and Melanie; for a while, I could even get away from the Sick Person's voice. Forty-five minutes later, I woke up to Ally poking my leg and giggling ecstatically. "Melissa, come on, we're leaving!"

Part of me wanted to stay curled up on the warm couch, but the prospect of walking across the street to the body-image building roused me from my state of semihibernation. With my mind reawakened, the feeling of disgust also returned. My stomach ached, filled with cake and mint chocolate chip ice cream.

Once we reached the building where the body-image class was held, we were greeted by a tall, thin woman with straight, honey-brown hair who was cutting out large pieces of manila-colored butcher paper. "Hello, everyone. My name is Paula. If everyone can grab a pencil and one of these sheets of butcher paper, we are going to be making body tracings today." Paula pointed to the table where there were buckets of sharpened number 2 pencils. After picking up a piece of butcher paper, I sat down at one of the low tables where Tiffany and Ally were already seated.

"Have you done this before?" I asked. "No, have you?" Tiffany sounded nervous.

Our conversation was interrupted by Paula, whose sheet of paper had the outline of a body she had already drawn. "Okay, girls, this is what we're going to be doing today. I need each of you to make a sketch of how you think your body looks in terms of size and proportion. Then what I'm going to do is have you lie down on a new sheet of paper that's the same length as the one you have now. I will trace the outline of your body so that we can see if there's a discrepancy between how you perceive yourself and how you really are. Does anyone have any questions?"

"Do we have to do this?"

"Ally, I think a tracing might help you see yourself, but I won't force anyone to do something that feels uncomfortable."

I didn't like the idea of someone touching me, but the appeal of getting to see the shape of my body was too strong for me to resist. Sitting on the floor with a pencil in hand, I began to sketch out how I saw myself in the mirror. Drawing was something I usually hated doing because nothing I ever drew looked real. But the rational part of my brain told me that the person I saw when gazing into the mirror wasn't real anyway. What I saw was a horrid-looking creature with thick, long limbs and a huge stomach that threatened to sink to the floor. The creature's body jerked in different directions that were dictated by the whims of some invisible puppet master. Now and then, the puppeteer would pull on one of the creature's strings, laughing as she watched the creature's flailing arms and jerking neck.

After I finished my sketch, Paula asked me to lie down on a blank sheet of butcher paper. She used my pencil to trace the outline of my body, beginning with my head and working her way down to the tip of each toe. After fifteen minutes, Paula put down her pencil and rose to her feet again. "There, I'm done now. You can get up."

Part of me was afraid to look down at the outline. I feared being disgusted at the size of the limbs and stomach. At the same time, though, I was desperate to know what my body truly looked like.

Paula hung the two outlines next to each other on the wall. I looked first at my drawing and then at Paula's. I studied the drawings, rubbing a hand against my chin; I must have looked like an appraiser analyzing a piece of art to determine its authenticity. After carefully scrutinizing the two outlines, I could see that the proportions I drew were nearly three times larger than my actual body size. That conclusion provided me with temporary relief. I backed away from the two outlines as Paula began to explain our next task.

"All right, I'm going to hand each of you a piece of string. I need you to take the string and create a circle that shows how large you think your stomach is by guessing the circumference of your waist. But you are not allowed to actually wrap the string around your waist. That's what I'm here for. I'm going to come around to each of you with another string, which I will use to measure the circumference of your waist." Paula walked around the room and handed out small balls of yellow yarn. I held mine in one hand while I unraveled it with the other. When I was satisfied with the length of string, I snipped the end off with a pair of childproof craft scissors. Holding the yarn at an arm's length, I examined the amount; it seemed right. When Paula came around to the table, she handed me a piece of tape, which I used to connect the ends of my string to form a circle.

"Melissa, can you lift your arms over your head for me please?"

Paula pulled out another ball of yellow yarn from her jacket pocket and used it to tie around my waist. Once she'd gotten the string all the way around me, Paula cut the end off, sending the ball falling to the floor.

"Okay, you can put your arms down now."

I looked for the yellow piece of yarn, but Paula had it hidden in her fist. "Before you can see the string, I want to tape the ends together." She walked over to a small brown desk and took out a roll of duct tape. When Paula was done taping the ends together to form a circle, she returned to my table. "All right, let's have a look." She placed the circular shape I had created next to my actual measurements. The vast difference made me blink my eyes a few times before speaking.

"But I was so certain that . . . " My sentence broke off; I was at a loss for words. The circle representing the actual size of my waist couldn't be called anything other than small. The shape I had created from the picture in my mind was four times too big. "Can I keep these?" I asked, while pointing to the two circles of yarn now lying on the table.

"No, I'm sorry. But if you want, I can save everything, and you can come get the strings when you're ready to go home." The mention of home sent a sharp pain through my chest. For a little while, I'd gotten away from reality by focusing on drawings and strings. But now my hour of relief was up; I had to feel again.

Before we went to dinner that night, Terri called the names of people who'd received mail. Mail time was always the highlight of the day, especially when someone got a package. We'd all crowd around the snack table and watch as the lucky recipient rummaged through her package. Of course, one of the mental health techs always had to be around to confiscate any inappropriate gifts. I always found it amusing when people sent things like chocolate bars or caramel candies. When Terri called out my name, I walked up to the counter, eager to pick up a letter or package.

"Here you go, Melissa. I believe Mona is in the back room with someone else so you can open your letter right here." Terri placed a manila envelope face down on the counter. My heart sped up a few beats as I reached out to pick up the envelope. I ran my fingers over the Mickey Mouse stamp before looking down to see if the handwriting looked familiar. I gasped at the sight of the carefully printed letters. I knew exactly whose penmanship that was; for the first time in almost four weeks, Melanie had written me a letter.

"Is everything all right, Melissa? Do you want me to take the letter back?" Terri could see the early sign of tears welling up in my eyes. I turned away from her slightly, making sure my voice was steady before replying.

"No, no, it's fine. I'm fine." As I stood there with my back to Terri, a dialogue began in my head. One side begged me not to read the letter, crying out, *Pain, pain! All you will feel from this is pain!* But the other part of me deeply desired to open up that envelope and dissect every word Melanie had written. *Maybe she's trying to apologize to me. Maybe Melanie still loves me.* The prospect of love was too tempting to resist. I tore open the envelope, eager to find out if Melanie's love was hidden inside.

TIC ATTACK 22

The stationery was familiar; I'd seen it stacked on Melanie's desk at home. In the bottom right-hand corner sat a drawing of a wicker basket full of yellow dandelions and white snapdragons. Weaving vines and greenery lined the edges of the paper, making the card look like a picturesque spring day. I'd always admired Melanie's carefully crafted letters. One time, I'd even tried to copy the way she looped her cursive *m* and dotted her *i*. Slowly, I began to scan the writing:

DEAR MELISSA,

    I JUST WANTED TO LET YOU KNOW THAT CADENCE IS DOING FINE. EMILY IS TAKING WONDERFUL CARE OF HER, AND PAUL HAS BEEN RIDING HER FOR YOU.

    SEE YOU WHENEVER YOU GET BACK,

MT

My heart sank as I got to the last line; there had to be more than that. I must have missed something. She didn't even sign her entire name. Frantically, I turned the letter over to check if she'd written anything on the back, but there was nothing there. After crumpling up the letter, I returned to the couch, waiting for the inevitable flood of emotions to hit. There wasn't much time to work things out in my mind, though, because a few minutes later Mona called us to dinner.

The thought of food made me feel nauseous. I had thirty minutes to consume macaroni and cheese, a bowl of cooked carrots, one piece of greasy garlic toast, a salad with ranch dressing, peach compote, a bag of pretzels, and a full glass of orange juice. Thirty minutes later when Mona called out that the time was up, my plate was still full of food. I knew there would be a huge can of Ensure waiting for me at the house, but I really didn't care. At that moment, all I wanted to do was curl up in my bed and sleep.

My tics got worse when I was stressed out or upset about something; as I began to stand up, my left leg kicked out violently, throwing me off balance. I grasped the edge of the table to steady myself. Once I regained my balance and began to follow Cory out the front door of the dining hall, I tried to concentrate on controlling the tics that seemed to be consuming my entire body. Kicking legs, flailing arms, a twisting neck—all of the excess movements were beginning to make my head spin. My vision began to blur, making me reach out for something to hold on to, yet all I grabbed were fists full of empty air. Losing my balance, I toppled over, hitting the ground with a dull *thud*. When my knees hit the gravel road, I could feel the rocky surface cut into my skin as my entire body began to tremor. Ally's voice rang out from somewhere behind me.

"Oh my God, oh my God!"

"Can you get up? Do you hear me?" I recognized the sound of Mona's voice.

Ally was crying somewhere behind her. "What should I do? Tell me, I want to help!" The desperation in Ally's voice made me want to get up so I could tell her everything was fine. But my body continued to thrash around uncontrollably, making it impossible for me to stand. Every limb felt weighed down, even though I desperately wanted to get up. I could feel Mona wrap her arms around my sides and begin to pick me up. I panicked when I realized she was trying to carry me. I thought my body was too heavy for someone to pick up.

"No, put me down. I want to walk. I can walk," I said. The trek back to the house should have taken no more than five minutes, but it probably took us fifteen. My legs felt like flimsy cardboard and it was difficult to keep myself upright. When we reached the house, Terri placed me in a wheelchair and took me into the same room Tonia always brought me to when I had to drink Ensure. Once inside, my body began to convulse again.

I was mentally well aware of what was going on. I knew my limbs were thrashing around and that there was drool seeping out of my mouth; I could understand the nurses' conversation, and I was agreeing or disagreeing with them in my head. But even though I was in control of my mind, I had absolutely no power to respond to their questions or make my body lie still. My mental acuity didn't last long, though; one of the last things I remember before zoning out was Terri rolling the top portion of my shorts down while Jane stuck me with a needle from behind. I don't know what they injected me with, but whatever filled that syringe caused me to sleep for the rest of that day and a great portion of the next one, too.

I finally woke up the next day to the sound of loud laughter near my bedside. My eyelids felt heavy, and the light in the room seemed five times brighter than usual. When I tried to sit up, a wave of nausea sent me right back down again. In the background a woman's voice was incredibly loud and obnoxious. When the woman saw me trying to get up her voice grew even louder.

"A-ha, I see you're awake at last. Here, would you like something to eat? I saved your breakfast. Look, here you go." She extended a thick arm in my direction. In her hand was a Styrofoam container, which I assumed was full of whatever I was supposed to have for breakfast. I rubbed the sleep from my eyes to see the woman more clearly. She was a heavyset woman with glasses and short, curly, brown hair. Her skin had a reddish hue to it.

"Well, do you want this now or not?"

"Can I get dressed first?" Really, I just wanted a little time before putting food into my queasy stomach.

"Nope, sorry, I can't let you get up without getting the official orders." The woman smiled at me, displaying a mouthful of yellowed teeth. Without saying anything, I lay back down again and shut my eyes, hoping the woman would leave if she thought I was sleeping. When I heard her get up and retreat from the room, I opened my eyes again. Ally's clock radio told me it was 11:45 AM, meaning that lunch was soon. My whole body was sore and tired from the day before. I pulled off the top blankets and noticed that someone had placed Band-Aids on both knees. I wanted to get up and walk around a little, but I feared that the woman would storm back into the room if she knew I was awake. Instead, I sat in bed and tried to piece together everything that had happened before my fall. My mind immediately turned back to the letter. I wanted to think about what Melanie had written, but the fear of losing control of my emotions again held me back. Feeling meant pain and pain always led to more tics.

Don't do this, don't do this, something within me pleaded. Yet another part of me desperately needed to examine each word one more time. I went through the lines again in my mind. Melanie hadn't said anything about missing me or that she hoped I was coming back soon. Her entire letter was completely void of any warmth or love. My eyes welled with tears, but this time I fought to subdue the sadness that threatened to overwhelm me.

A war was going on inside me—the rational part of my brain and the emotional part were fighting for supremacy. The emotional side of me was crying out, *What did I do wrong? What's the matter with me? Why can't I be loved?* But the rational portion of my mind provided an efficient counterattack: *You don't need Melanie. She only used your weakness for her gain. Give up already, it's time now to move on. That woman never loved you, and she never will.* Furiously, I wiped the tears away from my eyes.

"I don't need Melanie." I didn't even realizing I was talking aloud. When the heavyset woman heard the sound of my voice, she made her way back into the room.

"Ah, I see you're up now. How about some breakfast?"

This time, I actually took the container of food in my hands, opened up the lid, and began to eat. As soon as I was allowed to leave my room, Terri wheeled me downstairs. I told her I felt fine, but she said that the wheelchair was just a "precautionary measure." Once we got downstairs, the girls surrounded me, asking if everything was all right.

"Everyone, please sit down. You shouldn't be up anyhow. Melissa is going to be just fine." I grimaced as Terri patted me on the arm; her hands felt cold against my skin. As Terri walked away, an unfamiliar-looking man with tan skin and black hair appeared from behind the nurse's station.

"Excuse me, my name is Dr. Panjar. Do you mind coming with

me?" His accent was thick and sounded Middle Eastern, making it hard for me to understand him. I followed the doctor back to a small office behind the nurse's station. "Please sit down," he instructed. "I just want to ask you a few questions."

I looked around the little office. Dr. Panjar continued, "Tell me, what do you like to do?" I opened my mouth and was about to say "horseback ride," but then I remembered that Cadence wasn't mine anymore.

"I don't know, I don't know what I like to do."

"Really? I don't believe that. You must have something you enjoy doing." I bit down on my lip, trying to come up with something to say, but only images of horses showed up in my mind. When I didn't answer, he moved on to another topic. "Okay then, let's talk about something else, shall we? I read from your file that you have Tourette syndrome, correct?"

"Yeah, I guess."

"What kind of tics do you have?" I stared at him for a moment, annoyed at the question. I was displaying all the tics I had right in front of him. All he had to do was look up at me instead of gazing down at my file.

"My face twitches and sometimes I blink a lot. I have tics in my neck, my arm flings to the side occasionally, oh, and my legs kick."

"Do you feel as though your current medications are helping?"

"No, not really."

"Have you considered taking something different?"

I automatically began shaking my head back and forth. Since being at the ranch, I had agreed to take vitamins and calcium pills. After giving up Cadence, I had even agreed to take Prozac with the hope that the contents of that blue capsule would relieve some of the sadness that weighed heavily on me. Yet, the pills only seemed to make me anxious and fidgety. There was no way I was going to let him prescribe any pills.

"So you are not interested in trying something new?"

"No, I don't want to take any more pills."

Dr. Panjar put the file he was reading facedown onto his desk and turned to face me. "Would you be willing to tell me why you don't want to try a new medication?"

I tried to determine whether or not I was making him agitated by flat out refusing to listen. But Dr. Panjar still had the same serene expression on his face that he'd had when I first met him.

"I just don't like medicine, that's all." Seeing the half smile spread across his lips made me feel a little better about being obstinate. I didn't want to make him angry, but I also didn't plan to heed any of his medication advice.

"Well, just in case you change your mind, there is a new drug that might help you. Here, I printed out this information for you."

He handed me a few sheets of paper that had been stapled together. I glanced over the front page and saw what looked to be a list of the drug's possible side effects. There had to be at least twenty side effects listed: upset stomach, dizziness, insomnia, seizures, hair loss, irregular heartbeat, increase or decrease in appetite, and suicidal thoughts or tendencies. I would gladly take the tics over having to experience any of those possible complications. True, I couldn't control the tics, but at least they didn't cause me to have an irregular heartbeat or suicidal thoughts. I took the information that Dr. Panjar had printed out but only because I didn't want to seem ungrateful. As soon as I was far enough away from his office, the packet was torn up and tossed into the nearest garbage bin.

BUILDING A FORTRESS 23

The only things worse than another session with Jennie were eating food and drinking Ensure. It wasn't that Jennie was unusually cruel; frankly, I just didn't like her because she had confronted me about lying. No one had really ever done that before, and Jennie's office didn't make the visit any more interesting, either. The dull and empty room depressed me; there wasn't even a window to look out. I sat and played with a hangnail while Jennie rummaged through some papers.

"You got weighed this morning." I couldn't tell if she was making a statement or asking a question, so I just nodded. "You lost weight this morning." I pulled the hangnail off and looked up. I was beginning to get nervous.

"I didn't mean to."

"Have you been exercising again?" she asked. Now I could really feel my stomach begin to jump around.

"No, I swear! I didn't do anything this time." There was a frantic quality to my voice, making it sound higher than usual. Jennie searched my face looking for any indication that I was lying.

"All right then, we need to increase what you're eating."

I desperately wanted to ask her if she really believed me, but the mention of adding more food caused every other thought to fade into the background. How could she add onto the amount I was already eating? Six times a day, I had to sit down to a plate of this or a bag of that; my jaw was sore from chewing, for goodness' sake!

"I need you to pick out some level-three snacks please," Jennie said. I could feel the blood drain from my face. There were three levels of snacks, each one larger than the previous. Level three was, of course, the most you could possibly have. I was already eating three level-two snacks, what they called "add-ons" at each meal—three juice drinks and a concoction of vitamin-packed ice cream. The thought of getting a feeding tube passed through my mind again. Everything would be so much easier. I could just get all of my meals pumped into me at night. But I didn't know what the liquid they put into the tube consisted of. At least I knew the nutrition facts for the vitamin ice cream. Usually, the mental health techs covered up the information or blotted it out with a marker, but occasionally they'd forget. The stuff that went into the feeding tube, though, was unfamiliar to me.

Jennie showed me the menu that I'd already filled out for the next day, pointing out what I needed to add at each snack. I read over the options and checked the least threatening ones. After finishing, I scanned my menu one more time before returning it.

The thought of eating so much food terrified me, but there was no point in complaining to Jennie. She wasn't going to change anything. I started to get up to leave but sat back down again at the sound of Jennie's voice. "Before you leave, Melissa, you need to know that for the next couple of days you will be sleeping at the nurse's station."

I could feel the rage boil up inside of me. Turning to look at Jennie, I saw that her lips were twisted up into a sardonic grin. She got a kick out of throwing out these surprises. Why couldn't she just be upfront and tell me from the beginning that I was going to have to move out of my room?

"I just want to have you monitored for a few days. That way, if you have any urges to exercise there will be someone around."

"But I'm not exercising, I don't need to be monitored."

"Great, then you shouldn't have to be watched for very long."

This time, I really wasn't lying. I had tried to make my voice more forceful to convey that to Jennie, but there was nothing I could do.

I used the first fifteen minutes of my weekly session with Meg to complain about Jennie and about having to consume such a large amount of food. "My stomach is going to explode if I have to keep eating like this! No one consumes this much food in one day. I'm sick of being here!" During my rant, Meg only nodded her head at me and tried to appear sympathetic.

"I understand how you feel Melissa."

"No no, you really don't. I can't stand this anymore."

"What do you mean? What is it that you can't stand?"

I was about to rush into a headlong argument about how Jennie wasn't being fair, but Meg's words made me falter. What was it that I couldn't stand? True, the food situation upset me, but was that all? I sat back in my chair and turned to look out the window. Without thinking, I reached up and pressed my hand against the glass pane. Warming my skin against windows had become a habit of mine, because I desperately wanted to heat up my freezing body. Now though, as I sat in Meg's office, it hit me that I didn't need the warmth of the windowpane anymore. I pulled my hand away from the glass as if to test the theory. Slowly, a smile spread over my lips;

I was warm. For the first time in years, my body actually felt warm.

"Melissa, what were you going to say?"

I turned back toward Meg, who probably thought I was going insane. I still hadn't answered her question. "I guess what I can't stand is feeling so empty."

"I thought you said all the food was making you too full?"

"Yeah, all the food does make me feel full, but I'm not talking about that kind of empty. It's hard to explain what I mean. I just feel like there's this gaping hole in me that I keep trying to fill up but never can." Meg's head was tilted to the side; she appeared to be thinking deeply about what I'd said.

"How long have you felt this way?"

I tried to think back to when the empty feeling had first started. "I think it started when I turned eight."

"Do you remember what happened?"

I wasn't sure what Meg was getting at, but I played along anyway. "Well, a lot of things were happening. That was the year my little sister had surgery. It was also when my Tourette syndrome started getting out of control, and the kids at the barn began making fun of me. And that was the year my mother and I started fighting." I tried to read the expression on Meg's face, tried to figure out what she was thinking. Her lips were pursed together, making them appear much thinner than they actually were. The wrinkles gathered around the middle of Meg's forehead looked especially pronounced and her eyes had a glossy sheen to them.

"Do you think the fighting has anything to do with the hole?"

I shifted my gaze away from the floor to look directly into Meg's eyes before replying. "Yes, I think that's what put the hole there in the first place."

For the rest of the day, I sat and thought about the conversation

I'd had with Meg. It was painful to think about the constant arguing that went on between my mother and me. We were always fighting about pills I didn't want to take and doctors I didn't want to see. The constant arguing, yelling, and slamming of doors convinced me that I couldn't be loved by my mother; our relationship was just too damaged. I was starving for love but couldn't get my fill at home. Melanie had been the first person to offer me the love I so desperately wanted. It was like having a do-over of sorts. If I could just perfect myself for Melanie, she would be able to love me. I tried so hard to be flawless for her—God, I tried. I worked so hard at being the ideal daughter that it nearly killed me.

⤳

A week passed before Meg returned to get me for our next session. The cool morning air nipped at my face and gloveless hands as we made our way toward her office. I was looking forward to curling up on a chair in the heated room, but Meg stopped short before we reached the entrance.

"We aren't going to have a session today," Meg said.

"What? What do you mean? Why did you come get me then?" I was annoyed with Meg for pulling me out of the warmth of the house just to tell me we weren't going to be meeting.

"Don't worry; I didn't bring you over here for nothing. I've got something else planned."

We began to walk forward again, and I realized we were heading in the direction of the horse pasture. When I was younger, a warm feeling of joy always washed over my body whenever I caught sight of those gentle giants. Now, though, that soft, sweet warmness was replaced by a dull hollowness. Horses were no longer a part of my life—they were no longer a part of me. I had made the decision to give up Cadence, and with that decision, I had simultaneously given up my identity. For years, I had hidden behind titles like *the horseback rider* or *the equestrian*. Horseback riding was not just something I did; it was who I was. Walking toward the horse pasture suddenly made me feel stripped and barren. *You're nobody now. Worthless girl; what good are you?* The sound of the Sick Person's voice sent a fresh wave of pain across my body. I desperately wanted to ask Meg if we could take another route, but before I could, I noticed an older-looking woman waving at us from one of the center round pens where two horses were quietly chewing on hay. The woman had long, brown hair tucked beneath a cowboy hat that prevented the sun from hitting her already sun-weathered face.

"Okay, Melissa, the reason I brought you out here today is for an equine challenge. Taylor here is going to help us out." I smiled weakly at Meg, trying to mask the pain I was feeling inside. As Meg finished making introductions, Taylor spoke as she leaned over to pick up a pail full of colorful markers and blank nametags.

"Hi there, young lady. As Meg mentioned, my name is Taylor, and I'm going to be explaining the challenge we set up for you. As you can see, I've got some markers, chalk, and name tags here. I've also got some labels on which you are going to write important aspects of your life that your eating disorder took away from you. These labels are going to be placed in each of these feed buckets I'm going to fill with some oats." I still didn't exactly see how the horses connected with the exercise. However, before I could say anything, Taylor extended an arm out to the two horses dozing in the corner.

"Now, Ruby and Black Jack over there are going to represent your eating disorder. You are going to take a piece of red chalk and write some aspects of your eating disorder on the horses' coats. Your mission is to retake those things that your eating disorder took from you. In other words, you have to keep the horses that represent your eating disorder from eating the oats that represent what your eating disorder took away from you. There is a catch, though. You see, Melissa, you aren't going to be allowed to touch either of the horses."

"But, how am I going to keep them from eating the oats if I can't touch them?" The perplexed look on my face made Taylor grin.

"Ah, that's where Meg and I come in. You see, I've got two more name tags. What I would like for you to do is think of two significant people in your life who you could lean on for support in the process of your recovery. Then, I want you to write their names on these tags over here. During your challenge, Meg and I are going to wear the name tags and pose as those people."

I didn't have to think very long to come up with the words I was going to place on the feed buckets. Almost as soon as Taylor had given me the directions, the word *family* popped into my head. The Sick Person led me to believe that my family didn't want me. I was an unwelcomed intruder, an outsider, a pariah. How could they want me when all I ever did was fight with my mother, spend my dad's money, and ignore my sisters? My family life revolved around a cycle of fighting, wanting, and neglecting. Yet, more than anything, the Sick Person's insidious chants and callous remarks convinced me that I was incapable of being loved by my mother—I was just too imperfect, too messed up for her to ever love. After a while, I was so certain that my family didn't want me anymore that I resigned myself to that loss and stopped trying to make our relationships work. Instead, I invested everything I had in Melanie, never realizing I was wasting my investments on empty promises.

The second prerequisite wasn't as easy as the first had been. I didn't know who I could "lean on" or ask for help. I had already said that my eating disorder had taken away my family. Who was left? As I stood there, marker poised in hand, a sharp pain shot through my chest—I was alone. My family was gone, the horses were gone, and now Melanie was gone, too. "Melissa, are you okay?" The concern in Meg's voice brought me back to reality.

"Yeah, I—I just don't know what to write."

"What about writing down Brooke's name or your mom's? I'm sure they would be happy to help you if you only asked." I wanted to believe Meg so badly my heart ached. Yet, I couldn't help but feel she was wrong. Why would my family want to help me after I'd been so horrible to them for so long? In the end, I decided to take Meg's advice and I scribbled "Brooke" and "Mom" on the last two blank name tags.

After writing the names on the tags, I began thinking about which aspects of my eating disorder I was going to write on the horses' coats. How could I narrow down the multifaceted and complicated aspects of my eating disorder to just a few? I thought about just writing down "Sick Person," but wondered if they would even understand what I was talking about. The Sick Person wasn't just an aspect of my eating disorder, she was the catalyst and reinforcer of it. I yearned for the chance to have clearheaded days when I would no longer have to listen to her looped recordings of *fat, fat, fat* or *ugly, stupid girl*, but not really believing that those days would actually come. Part of me wanted to tell Meg more about the Sick Person, but I also feared she wouldn't understand. How could she understand something so crazy? Instead, I decided to write down trivial things I was certain every other patient at the Ranch had written— negative self-talk, body image, exercise, and restrict.

"Okay, are we ready to get started?" Taylor's voice was full of enthusiasm as she clapped her hands together. "I'm going to fill the feed buckets with grain now." At the sound of grain being dropped in the buckets, the two horses lifted their heads and pricked their ears forward. Soon Black Jack, the bay gelding, made his way over to the buckets, followed by a dainty chestnut mare named Ruby. I felt my pulse speed up as Black Jack began dipping his nose into one of the buckets.

"Melissa, what would you like us to do?" The sound of Meg's voice reminded me that I was supposed to give out instructions.

"Um, err . . . I don't know. I guess you both can wave your arms at the horses to shoo them away." As I spoke, Meg began to make *shushing* noises as she flailed her arms in the air. The horses, however, didn't seem in the least bothered by the sight of two people waving their arms around. "No, no—that's not going to work. Meg, why don't you push Black Jack's muzzle out of the feed bucket? Taylor, you could do the same with Ruby."

"Melissa, this isn't working real well. Why don't you tell us to do something else?" Taylor's comment frustrated me. *Of course it isn't working! If they'd just let me do this by myself, I could easily get those horses away from the feed buckets.* Yet, just as the thought crossed my mind, I realized the truth: I couldn't do this exercise by myself, nor could I get better by myself. Was this what Meg wanted me to see? Was this why she gave me this challenge? I had been trying to build a fortress against the Sick Person for years, but to no avail. She was just too strong for me. I needed someone to help me; I needed my family to help me build that fortress. My family, a fortress—that was it! Suddenly, I knew what to do.

"Meg and Taylor, I would like each of you to push the horses' muzzles out of the feed buckets. After that, nudge them away by pressing against their shoulders. As soon as you do that, I want you to make a barrier around the buckets by standing across from one another and grasping hands." As I spoke, Meg and Taylor looked at one another and smiled. Their silent exchange told me that I was doing something right. As the two women grasped hands, Ruby tried to reach for a bite of feed. However, her attempts were in vain as the Meg and Taylor barrier was too strong for her to get through.

That night, I sat in bed thinking about the events of the day. I recognized Meg had used the equine experiential to show me that I needed my family if I really wanted to get better. I knew she was right—I did need them. I needed to feel a part of my family again, I needed to feel like I belonged. More than anything, though, I needed to feel my mother's love. In reality, the equine experiential had been simple and straightforward unlike the complicated web of problems that kept me apart from my family. It was true that I needed their help; I just didn't know what to ask for or how to ask for it.

FAMILY WEEK   24

The next day, I took out the piece of scrap paper I'd been using to keep track of how many days had passed. Now there were forty marks, which meant that I had reached the halfway point of my stay at the ranch. For the past few days, a familiar, anxious feeling crept around my stomach as I thought about what the next seven days had in store for me. Meg had told me a little about what went on during family week, but I was still leery of the whole idea. This week was going to be the first time I would see my family in more than a month. I couldn't help but worry about the therapy sessions that loomed ahead.

There was one part of the week Meg referred to as "truth and loves," where each family member had to apologize for all of the upsetting things they had done in the past. The day before my family arrived, Meg went through the specific phrases we were supposed to use during the truth and loves session. Her voice had a bouncy, excited tone to it as she explained everything to me. "Okay, I'm going to tell you about the outline you are going to use and then I can give you an example to fill in the blanks. Everyone is going to be using statements such as 'When you . . .' 'I feel . . .' and 'I need . . .' statements."

The perplexed look on my face let Meg know that I had no idea what she was talking about. "Don't worry, I'm going to give you an example. Say, for instance, you want to confront your dad about never taking anything seriously. You would turn to him and say, 'Dad, when you turn every situation into a joke, I feel like you don't take the problem seriously. I need you to show emotions outside of happiness.' Do you understand the setup now?" The whole idea seemed strange to me, but I nodded in agreement anyway.

At breakfast the following morning, I had a hard time keeping my nervous hands from shaking. Every few minutes I would gaze at the clock, counting down the hours until my parents arrived. No matter how loud the Sick Person screamed, I pushed myself to eat every last morsel on my plate. I secretly hoped my parents would take me home with them once the week was up, but that would never happen if they found out I was still living off bottles of Ensure. After lunch, Jennie pulled me aside for our last meeting before family week. For the first time, I was actually looking forward to seeing Jennie. She and I were supposed to talk about my weight range. I had gotten so used to seeing that smug look on her face that it didn't even bother me anymore.

"Good afternoon, Melissa. How has your day been so far?" Her voice almost had a hissing sound to it.

"Fine." I wanted to keep my answers as short as possible; otherwise, she might have the chance to psychoanalyze my responses.

"Well, I'm sure you're aware that today is the day I'm going to talk about weight ranges. Are you anxious? Everyone always has some anxiety about weight day." I assumed her question was rhetorical since she never gave me a chance to speak. "Okay then, shall we begin? I'm first going to talk about your weight range. For someone of your height, an appropriate range falls between 122 and 130 pounds." I could feel beads of sweat gathering on my brow. "Now, we would like to get you to the middle of this range, which falls right at 126 pounds. How does that sound?"

I was relieved when Jennie finally stopped talking. Her voice was distracting me from thinking. One twenty-six! The number seemed huge to me. Just as Jennie was about to say something else about my weight range, I interrupted her. "So where am I now?"

Jennie glanced up from the file she was about to read to me and raised one eyebrow as if she was perplexed by my question.

"What do you mean?" The arch in Jennie's brow was getting higher, making the lines on her forehead stand out.

"What's my weight right now? How much more do I need to gain before getting to your range?" I emphasized *your*, trying to indicate I didn't approve of the numbers she'd come up with. But Jennie ignored the extra emphasis and shot me a half smile instead.

"Do you really feel prepared to know?" I couldn't help rolling my eyes at her. Of course, I wanted to know; otherwise the questions wouldn't have been asked! I had an overwhelming urge to yell at Jennie, but I knew she wasn't going to tell me anything if she thought I was acting overly emotional.

"Yes, I would like to know." My voice sounded shaky, but at least it was calm.

"Right now, I actually can't tell you your exact weight, but I can tell you this—you've got a good ways to go."

The rest of the afternoon Jennie's words echoed in my ears: *You've got a good ways to go, a good ways to go.* What did that mean? Was I going to have to gain five, ten, or fifteen more pounds before reaching my weight range? Now I could understand why Ally went around pulling out her hair—these people were driving me insane! My fury grew so intense that I kept breaking the lead points off pencils as I attempted to finish a welcome sign for my parents. When I was done, I sat by the window for nearly an hour until I saw my parents walk up the drive. They weren't late; there was just nothing else for me to do except sit and stare out the small window. My heart began to race when I saw my mother.

For the first time in my life, I was struck by her beauty. Her long auburn hair was swooped back and tucked neatly into a bun. She wore a plain white T-shirt under a soft-brown peacoat. A pang of sadness hit me when I recognized the cream-colored beret she wore; I had borrowed that hat for a few horse shows. The feeling quickly faded as I saw the jubilant look on my mother's face. For the first time, I felt like my mother genuinely missed me. The thought sent me sprinting out the door as fast as my feet could carry me. I didn't give a damn if Tonia made me drink a glass of Ensure later; my mom was here now, and she wanted me.

Being wrapped in my mother's arms filled me with ineffable warmth that only accompanies true happiness. I wanted to stay enfolded in her arms forever. As she let me go, a gasping sound escaped from her lips followed by a flood of tears. I heard myself say "Everything's okay now, you don't have to cry, I'm okay," before giving my teary-eyed dad a hug. As we walked inside, I gripped my mom's hand tightly, fearing I might lose hold of her again. Childishly, I hoped the clocks would stop ticking so that we could spend more than the allotted two hours together. I didn't care to talk much during our first meeting. The fact that my parents were sitting next to me on the couch that I'd sat on alone so many times was enough. To tell you the truth, I don't even remember what words we exchanged during that first meeting. All I cared about was holding onto my mom's hand. Tonia came to get me when our time was up, which caused me to feel angry. How could she just pull me away so soon when my parents just arrived? I could feel my mom's grip begin to slacken as she spoke to me.

"Don't worry, honey, we'll be back tomorrow."

I wanted to cry out to her not to leave me there. The words *take me with you* kept playing in my head as I watched my parents get up from the couch. I could feel the heaviness of my grief as my mom walked out of the room; my whole body seemed to be weighed down by it. Tonia tried to comfort me by patting my back, but I shrugged off her cold hands.

The next afternoon, when the rest of the girls went to art therapy, Caitlin and I stayed behind with Rochelle. Caitlin's mom had also come in the day before, and we were supposed to take the transport van to meet our parents. After a fifteen-minute ride, the van pulled into the parking lot of a building that resembled a country club. As we walked up the gravel pathway, a tall man waved a lanky arm at us and shouted a friendly "Hi y'all."

"Welcome to Blue Fox, girls. My name is Ted, and I'm one of the therapists who's going to be helping y'all out this week. I know you both probably want to see your parents. If you follow me back, I'll show you where they're getting acquainted with each other."

Caitlin and I followed Ted into the front building that led out to a back porch area. My heart sped up at the sight of my parents sitting on one of the gray benches. They were talking to a woman with frizzy brown hair and thick-framed glasses who looked like an older version of Caitlin. After brief introductions were done, Ted guided us back into the building, showing us into a cozy-looking room with couches and colored beanbag chairs. A white dry-erase board was set up in the front of the room with the words "Truth and loves: Let go, let God" written on it.

A few moments later, Caitlin's therapist Mike entered the room along with Meg. They were both holding notebooks and manila-colored files. Meg was the first to speak. "Hello all, I hope everyone is having a nice time so far. As some of you know, my name is Meg. Today we're here to start what we call 'truth and loves.' I know each of you has been informed about how the setup works so we're ready to begin whenever you all are."

Meg's calm composure and reassuring smile were a welcome sight for me. Meg didn't seem at all nervous—but then again, she wasn't the one having to apologize for all the horrible things she'd ever done. I was anxious to get the whole process over with so I could find out whether or not my parents were going to forgive me. But that would have to wait for a while since Caitlin was going first.

During the next two hours, I learned more about Catlin than I had in the past forty days. At first, I was interested to know what led to her illness and if she had the same distinctive voice in her head as I did. For nearly two hours, I listened intently for some deeper meaning behind superficial statements like "I just thought I looked fat." Yet by the end of Caitlin's truth and loves, I still didn't know what was really going on in her mind. She never got down to the core of her problems. Everything was about how her mother didn't let her pursue an acting career and how she didn't get to go to the right schools. All of Caitlin's accusations seemed pretentious, dull, and fake.

When Caitlin and her mother finished hashing it out, they seemed to feel better, although I didn't see how any of their problems could have actually been resolved. Really, all they'd done was bicker at each other. At the end of their session, Caitlin and her mother both stood up and hugged to the enthusiastic clapping of Mike, Ted, and Meg. I was annoyed with the therapists for applauding the superficial resolve.

Meg placed a third chair next to the one put aside for my mom, transforming the setup of chairs into a somewhat circular shape. Anxiety began to gnaw away at the lining of my stomach as I felt different sets of eyes staring at me. I still didn't understand the point of combining families together for the truth and loves process. How were we supposed to talk about personal issues with complete strangers in the room? The whole thing felt like a kind of amusement show where my family was the live act and the therapists were the rowdy audience clapping away and laughing. I could feel my face begin to twitch as Meg approached our circle.

"Okay, so everyone knows how this goes. Who wants to start?" My mom raised her hand while pulling out sheets of notebook paper. Before walking back to her seat, I felt Meg give me a reassuring pat on the back. My mother's voice sounded shaky and hesitant as she began to read from the sheets of paper.

"Melissa, I first want to tell you how proud I am of you. You were so brave to come here. Now, I would like to talk about how your eating disorder has affected my life." My mother looked up at Meg as though seeking her approval. Meg reassured her with a half nod and a smile. "Melissa, your eating disorder has made me feel helpless, sad, and guilty for not knowing how to fix it or make you feel better about yourself. The hardest part for me was when you isolated and hid yourself from us. I miss you being a part of our family." My mother choked back a sob, pretending instead to clear her throat. "You're eating disorder took over your life, and I was afraid for you. I was also very angry when you were unkind to your sisters when they tried to reach out to you."

With each word, I felt as though someone was stabbing me with a knife, quickly pulling the sharp blade out, only to force it back into my flesh once more. The guilt was so overwhelming that I couldn't even lift my head to study my mother's face as she spoke; I was just too ashamed. What she was saying was true, but I knew my mother wasn't revealing everything that had gone wrong between us; it was just too ugly.

"Mrs. Binstock, would you like to tell Melissa what you expect of her when she comes home?" Meg's voice seemed oddly far away as I continued to focus on holding back the tears that were rapidly filling my eyes.

My mom continued on to the next portion of her notes. "Now I want to tell you the expectation I have for your recovery. I expect you to be honest with me and Daddy. I expect you to follow your nutritionist's guidelines and your therapist's plans. When you come home, I expect you to be honest with us, I expect you to share your fear and feelings, and I expect you to be a part of this family and not isolate yourself." She was strong now, no longer showing signs of hesitation or fear.

At that moment, my feelings of guilt began to dissipate and were replaced by anger intermixed with sadness. What good did it do to open up these old wounds? All I could seem to hear from my mother's speech was "I expect, I expect, I expect." My mother was expecting me to rejoin a family I'd never felt a part of in the first place. She was asking me to be open, but didn't she know that that's all I wanted? The problem wasn't that I couldn't talk freely with her; the problem was that I couldn't find the strength to speak at all. How could she demand so much in so little time? Didn't she know about the screaming voice, the pain, and the weight I was trying to carry around? Why couldn't she see how hungry I was for her love and how much I needed to feel her embrace?

In my mind, I replayed the countless times I sat crying in my room after being threatened with pills and hospitalizations. I could still hear the fighting, yelling, and slamming bedroom doors. I could still see my sisters fleeing and hiding themselves in my mother's bedroom, locking the door behind them. The fights always ended the same way: After realizing I wasn't going to take my medicine, my mother would escape into her room to join my sisters. Then I'd be alone in my room, holding the covers over my head. I'd lie there for a while, trying to cry as loudly as my lungs would allow while hoping that I'd hear the sound of a doorknob twisting and the soft *pat, pat, pat* of slippers on the tile floor. But finally my lungs would give out and all would go quiet again. Later, when I'd hear the sound of a door unlatching, I'd sit up and throw the covers off my head. *Maybe she's coming, maybe she still loves me.*

But when my mother entered the room, she'd be carrying a handful of colored pills and a glass of water in her hands. The sight of the medicine would cause me to dive under the blankets again and scream "Get away! Leave me alone!" in a hoarse voice. My mother probably thought I was yelling at her to leave, but actually I was screaming at the pills. She'd leave again, and I'd hear the crashing sound of a glass being thrown into the sink followed by the slamming of doors. Then I'd sob for a while longer, gripping a stuffed animal in my arms while licking the salty tears that dripped down my face. If I had just been able to tell my mother how much I needed her to hold me, maybe we would never have fought at all. But the closest I came to saying anything was the few times I yelled, "It's not about the medicine!" She didn't know that my yells of *get away* really meant *please don't leave me.*

When my mother took a sip of water, I looked up at Meg, trying to tell her with my eyes that I needed a break. All I wanted was a few minutes so I could go away somewhere quiet and lick my wounds before hearing anymore. But Meg was too busy writing on a pad of paper to notice my glances. The next part of my mom's speech wasn't as painful as the first had been. She was trying to make up for the harsh things she said by talking about my love for animals and my good sense of humor. I breathed out a sigh of relief. At least now the stabbing pain was subsiding. Yet the wounds tore open again once I saw my mother's compliments as mere superficial statements, similar to those made by Caitlin and her mom. Yes, I did love animals and I did like to laugh, but just about anyone that talked to me for five minutes could see that. The truth was that neither of us could know the wants or needs of the other person because the two of us were complete strangers. When this realization hit me, I sank back into my chair and sighed. I desperately wanted to be able to tell my mother everything so that maybe we could start again. If I could just get the words out, she would know what went on in my mind—it would be like we were really meeting for the first time as mother and daughter. I gripped the piece of paper I had written my truth and loves on until my knuckles turned white. There was nothing on that piece of paper that really spoke about how I felt. Everything I'd said was sugarcoated and fake because I didn't want to open myself up to a bunch of strangers in the room.

When I heard Meg announce my turn, I unfolded the scrap of paper. Thoughts surged through my mind; *Do I forget about the people here and just speak, or should I read what I wrote and just pull my mom aside later?* The second idea seemed safest. Mentally, I promised myself that my mother and I would talk later in the day. So I began to read my sugarcoated statements just like Caitlin had done with her mom. At the end, I heard the therapists begin to clap and shout "good job." Their enthusiasm was just as phony as the

words I'd spoken. How could they applaud such frivolous statements? All I had said was that I didn't like being forced to take medicine and that I was sorry for being mean to my sisters. Not once
did I mention my hunger for love, my real issues with Melanie, or
the existence of the Sick Person; not once did I mention anything
real. Yet here they were rising to their feet and applauding me.
Afterward, pictures were taken and awards given out to each of us.
I felt like we were all in kindergarten again. The certificates Meg
gave me had a heading that said "Participated in Family Week"
under which sat a big gold star next to my name printed in black
ink. I remembered Ally telling me how much lighter she'd felt after
truth and loves as though someone had released her from the burdens she had been lugging around. I had hoped to experience the
same sensation, but now I knew that I wouldn't feel relief. After the
first day of family week ended, my prediction came true: the weight
of my burdens only seemed to get heavier.

The rest of the week was spent waiting for the perfect moment to
pull my mother aside to tell her the truth. But that moment never
came. My parents left after a few days, and the only things we had
resolved were the superficial "you hurt my feelings" types of problems. I also found out that my homecoming was going to be post-
poned for at least another few months. After finishing my inpatient
treatment, I would be transferred to a "step-down program." For a
while, I fought both my parents and Meg about the decision, but
eventually I gave up when I realized that I had no say in any of it.

MASKING
FEELINGS

25

F ive days before I was to be discharged from the inpatient
program, Meg came by the house to pick me up for one of
our last therapy sessions. As I heard Meg's voice echoing from the
front of the house, my stomach began to do flip-flops. She had told
me the week before that we would do something different during
today's therapy session. "So, are you excited about today?" I tried to
detect something in Meg's voice that would hint at what we were
going to work on.

"Should I be excited?" I asked. Meg merely smiled at my question before telling me to follow her. We passed several buildings
before stopping at the art therapy classroom.

"Okay, so do you remember that mask you made when you first
got here?"

I nodded. Although nearly sixty days had passed, the half angel,
half devil mask I had made at the beginning of my stay wasn't something easily forgotten. Meg continued, "Well, I asked Pam if we
could stop by and pick it up today."

The sight of the half angel, half devil mask made fresh thoughts of Melanie surge through my mind. My mixed feelings about Melanie were an annoyance to me; at one time, I both hated and missed her greatly. After picking up the mask, we headed in the direction of Meg's office when she stopped again. This time, we were standing beside a large wooden cross that had been built across from some of the paddocks.

The day was warm, and I could see some of the horses chewing pieces of yellow hay while they swatted at a few buzzing flies with their tails. My chest ached as I gazed at the pack of old quarter horses. *Why did we have to come out here in the first place, and what was the point of carrying around a stupid mask?* My thoughts were interrupted as I felt Meg taking the mask out of my hands. "Can you tell me about what your mask means?" I let out a small huffing noise and began to recite to Meg what I'd told the art therapist. "It's supposed to represent the voice in my head."

"Elaborate on that a little, will you?" Meg stopped flipping the mask around in her hands and looked at me. I'd forgotten that I hadn't really mentioned much about the Sick Person to Meg, or anyone else for that matter.

"There's this thing in my head, I guess you could call it another person. It's what screams at me when I eat and tells me how I can't be loved."

"Why do you let it control you?"

I looked up at Meg and tried to think about how to answer her question. Why did I listen to the yells? Why couldn't I make them stop?

"I don't know. I guess it's just what I've always done. It yells, I listen."

"But for the most part, you haven't done that while you've been here. Otherwise, you wouldn't have finished any meals."

I turned my gaze over to the small herd of horses trotting around the paddock before I responded. "It's different here. I have to listen to Tonia and Mona because I don't want to drink Ensure."

Meg could tell I was getting distracted by the horses and stepped to the side in an attempt to block my view. "But you could refuse to drink the Ensure," she said.

"I know, but I don't like getting in trouble."

"Because you don't want people to be mad at you, right?"

I began making a hole in the dirt with the toe of my tennis shoe, trying to indicate to Meg that I wasn't interested in talking. "Yeah, I guess."

"Why don't you want people to be mad at you?"

I stopped clearing away the leaves from the hole I was making and looked up. "Who likes being yelled at?" I didn't expect Meg to answer my question.

She got right to the point of the conversation. "Tell me about Melanie."

I felt like someone had just hit me in the stomach, knocking the wind right out of me. Automatically, I wrapped both arms around my stomach as if to block any further attacks. Once I was sure my voice wouldn't fail me, I tried to reply. "She was my old horse trainer."

"I know that, but why did your relationship with her mean so much?"

I knew what Meg was trying to get me to say, and she was right; I did love Melanie. But it was almost as though the word *love* was forbidden for me to speak unless under certain circumstances. The feeling had to be genuine and mutual. When people said *I love you,* they weren't just using regular words like *prefer* or *enjoy;* they were using the term *love,* which to me was the most sacred word next to *God.* There was no way I could admit my love for Melanie aloud because I knew she didn't love me back. Instead, I tried to weave my way around Meg's question.

"Melanie treated me like a daughter. She made me feel special, like I was good enough to be cared about. I guess Melanie kind of took the place of my mom when I thought my mom couldn't love me anymore. But it was just a scam—all Melanie wanted to do was turn me against my mom."

After finishing my sentence, I returned to digging at the dirt with my shoe. I only looked up again when Meg didn't respond. She was staring at the mask while flipping it around in her hands. I tried to read the expression on Meg's face to get an idea of what was going through her mind. She had drawn her eyebrows together, creating a deep set of wrinkles on her forehead. I couldn't see the rosy lip gloss she was wearing because her lips were pursed together so tightly. Everything about Meg's expression told me that she was lost in deep thought. After a few minutes passed, she finally spoke.

"Do you think this mask represents more than just your eating disorder?"

I could feel a smile form on my lips. It was almost as though Meg could read my mind. When I nodded my head, she continued. "Who—who is the mask of?"

I gazed out into the pasture of horses and watched as a few of them swatted at flies with their long tails. "The mask is also of Melanie."

"Do you want to smash it?"

The surprised look on my face made Meg laugh.

"Is that why you took me out here? You want me to smash my mask?"

"Only if you want to." Meg extended her hand and offered the mask to me. I stood there just holding it for another five minutes, trying to decide what to do.

"I worked so hard on it."

"I know. You don't have to smash it if you don't want to."

I turned the mask around in my hands just as I'd seen Meg do. I deliberated for a few more minutes, and then I threw the mask onto the dirt and jumped on it as hard as I could.

"Who's sitting in the dirt now?" The words escaped from my mouth before I even realized what I was saying. Meg gave me a strange look as though she was waiting for some sort of explanation.

"You'll have to explain that statement to me another time," she said. Our time was up. Before leaving, I placed the mask into the hole I'd dug with my tennis shoe, covering it up with layers of dirt and dead leaves.

The last week I spent at the ranch seemed like any other week, except everyone kept asking me if I was excited about leaving. I'd nod my head and smile at them when, in reality, I wasn't in the least bit excited. How could I be excited when I wasn't going home? I was just being shipped off to some new place down the road. Once there, I'd have to get used to sharing a room with unfamiliar girls and put up with new mental health techs. What bothered me the most, though, was that Meg couldn't come with me.

During our last session together, Meg told me that my new therapist's name was Rob. I didn't even need to meet Rob to know that we weren't going to work well together. How was I supposed to talk to Rob about my personal life when I wasn't even comfortable being alone with men? If I had only told Meg about Adam, maybe she would have been able to get the people at the outpatient program to assign me to a different therapist. It was too late now; I wasn't going to bring up that topic during our last meeting.

As I got up to leave our last session together, Meg told me to wait a minute. "I have something for you," she said. Meg's usual ebullience seemed to die away, making her voice sound unfamiliar to me. She handed me what looked like a dark gray stone that had been coated with a shiny glaze. I picked up the rock and turned it around in my hands to examine it.

"What's this?"

"It's a stone I picked out for you. Before every girl leaves, she gets a stone from her therapist. The rock is supposed to be symbolic of your character."

I rubbed the smooth surface with my hand. I wasn't sure how a rock could somehow display the type of person I was. Meg noticed the perplexed look on my face, and she began to elaborate on why she chose this rock for me.

"I picked this stone for you because the dark color represents all that you've had to struggle with. But if you notice, the rock is also shiny. Melissa, I know you have a long way to go before really reaching the point of recovery, but I also know you'll get there one day."

I carried the stone around in my pocket for the next two weeks, holding onto each word Meg had said. *One day, you'll get there; one day, you'll get there.* I wasn't sure where "there" was, but I knew it had something to do with finally feeling good enough to be loved.

THE NEXT STOP 26

The morning I was to be transferred to the outpatient facility went by slowly. I didn't mind, though, because I was in no hurry to go somewhere new and unfamiliar. It was strange to see Mona hoist my pink duffel bag onto Ally's nightstand. I hadn't seen the bag in some time and wondered if my brown shirt was still tucked away inside.

"Are you ready to go, missy?" Mona asked.

Seeing Mona's youthful smile was always a comforting sight. She looked so much like my mom with her slim frame, brown eyes, and upturned lips; I couldn't help but be drawn to her.

"Yeah, I guess so. I think I'll miss this place. . . ." My voice trailed off as a wave of sadness rushed over me. Now I understood why the girl I'd met on my first day at the ranch had cried when she left. I had made so many friends, and now I had to leave them behind.

After I said good-bye to my friends, Tonia ushered everyone out of the house for body-image therapy. I turned to sit on the couch next to the front window so I could look out for the transport van.

Caitlin came downstairs a few minutes later with Rochelle, who was clutching a black rollaway suitcase in her hand. Caitlin's face was jubilant. I couldn't help but feel envious; she was finally getting to go home. While watching Caitlin make her way down the stairs, I tried to think back on what she looked like when I'd first arrived at the ranch. Her brown hair had been lackluster, thin, and brittle. She'd had an unusually gray complexion with deep black rings under her eyes. Caitlin's body had resembled that of a Holocaust survivor, with her jutting hip bones and countable ribs. She, like all the girls at the ranch, had been ravaged by the disease. Now though, as I watched her bouncy step and cheery face, I couldn't believe that this was the same girl.

Everything about Caitlin looked fresh and bright. The light blue polo shirt and khaki pants she wore revealed a woman's figure with breasts and hips instead of her former skeletal and shapeless frame. There was no makeup on Caitlin's face, but now she didn't need to paint her cheeks a rosy hue to hide a wan visage. The signs of health that only come from good food and rest were everywhere, making me wonder if I looked as alive as she did.

When I stood in front of the mirror, it was difficult for me to tell what my body looked like. Even after sixty days of full meals and countless bottles of Ensure, my body still didn't have a shape to it. My frame looked boyish, void of breasts, curves, and all the womanly features that Caitlin now had. I knew that was because my body hadn't gotten proper nourishment for more than eight years. The little fat I consumed was needed to keep me alive; there just wasn't enough to spend on extra things like breasts or curves. My body was so accustomed to the years of malnourishment that even when I ate well, the boyish frame remained.

A van pulled up the driveway, so I gathered my duffel bag and said good-bye to Caitlin. Two older women sat in the backseat. They'd come from the adult facility that was a few blocks away from the adolescent house. One of the women had to be at least forty, while the other looked to be in her midtwenties. Their smiles resembled the joyous grin that Caitlin gave me as we said good-bye. I assumed that both women were also getting to go home. I sat down in the seat behind the blonde woman in her twenties.

"Your name is Melissa, right?" the van driver asked me in a hoarse voice. I nodded my head in assent. "Great, I just had to ask since sometimes the girls here try to sneak away. I'm Sally, by the way. If it's all right with you, we're going to head over to the airport and drop these two young women off. Afterward, I'll take you over to the outpatient facility." The blond-headed girl tried to strike up a conversation with me, but I wasn't in the mood to talk. Instead, I looked out the passenger's window and pretended that I was also being dropped off at the airport to catch a flight home. But my childish game came to an end when we pulled up to the drop-off area and the two women got out, leaving me alone in the van.

I watched as the older woman was met by a man with dark-brown hair who was standing outside the check-in area, holding onto the arm of a little girl who was gripping a stuffed elephant in her small hand. The child couldn't have been more than six years old; as soon as she saw the woman step out of the van, she stretched out her arms. After embracing the little girl, the woman turned to the man with dark-brown hair. I wish I could have seen the happy looks on their faces. In a beautiful gesture, the man wrapped the woman in his arms and kissed the top of her head over and over. At first, I had wondered why they'd come all the way to New Mexico just to fly home again, but after seeing the couple's warm embrace, the answer came to me—the father and daughter made the trip because they loved that woman.

Twenty minutes after we'd left the airport, the van pulled onto what looked like the beginning of a cul-de-sac, with red brick houses lining both sides of the street.

"Here we are. Welcome to the outpatient program," Sally announced. I was too busy inspecting the eerily similar-looking houses to pay much attention to what she said. Once she pulled to a stop, I opened the passenger door and stepped out. Unlike when I arrived at the ranch, no one was here to greet me. Sally continued, "Okay, someone is supposed to meet us at the front office. If you grab your bag, I'll show you where it is."

I followed Sally to an office building that was a few feet away from where she had parallel parked. The building was small with a gray-tiled roof and black-rimmed shutters. Inside, there was a man sleeping on a foldaway couch and a woman standing behind the counter that resembled the reception area of a doctor's office. A heavyset girl with shoulder-length black hair was sitting in a chair beside the foldaway couch, reading a tattered copy of *One Flew Over the Cuckoo's Nest*. When the woman behind the counter saw me, she gathered up a thick manila folder that was lying on top of the wooden desk.

"You must be Melissa. I'm Ruth, and I'll be taking you over to the house." Ruth's hair was brown with honey-colored highlights, which gave her face a warm and friendly look to it. She extended her hand, but I wasn't able to grasp it because the sleeping man was in the way. "Don't worry, you won't wake him up. That's Bryan. He's one of the MHTs here. I think he was up late last night or something." As Ruth spoke, she made her way out from behind the desk and offered to take my duffel bag.

Once outside, I followed her to one of the last two-story houses on the cul-de-sac. I stepped inside and looked around. My eyes caught sight of the kitchen area. I hadn't been around a refrigerator or a pantry full of food in months.

"Are you ready to go upstairs?" Ruth asked. She probably thought I was crazy for standing there gaping at the fridge as if in shock. The carpeted stairway led up to a small hall that branched off into three separate bedrooms. Ruth walked ahead of me and opened the door to the room in the middle. Inside were two closets, a connecting bathroom, and three beds. Two of the beds were bunked on top of each other while the other was a single. "I think the top bunk is open if you're okay with sleeping up there. You can leave your bag in here for now. I think the girls are coming back soon, and you'll probably want to meet everyone."

Soon I heard the front door shutting and the girls coming into the house. I knew one of the girls from the inpatient facility, although she hadn't been my roommate. The other three were either from the house across the street from mine or from the children's facility.

After a few brief introductions, Ruth interrupted, "Okay, guys, those of you who have snacks go ahead and grab them."

Debbie, who looked no older than twelve, grasped my arm. "Come on, I'll show you where everything is." She led me into the kitchen area I had been inspecting earlier. "What level snacks do you eat?"

While Debbie was talking, she pushed her long red hair away from her face and started climbing onto the kitchen counter. I couldn't help but laugh as she clamored around the cabinet, pulling out boxes of animal crackers and granola bars.

"We have lots of things here, and you get to choose whatever you want. Do you like 100-calorie packs?" The mention of *calories* threw me off guard—I almost felt as though Debbie had said a swear word. For the past sixty days, no one had been allowed to speak of things like calories, weight, exercise, or dieting in general.

"Oh, didn't you know? We're allowed to talk about nutrition facts here. They don't really care what we do as long as we behave, eat, and clean the house." I thought maybe Debbie was being overly sarcastic, but soon enough, I learned she wasn't.

At about 4:00 PM, a scraggly man with a shaggy beard and thinning brown hair came in. "Hello, I'm looking for Melissa," he said. I could tell by the crackling sound of his voice that he was a smoker. Ruth pointed me out to him.

"Hi, you're Melissa then. I'm Rob, your therapist." I could feel the anxiety beginning to creep around my stomach, causing my heart to beat faster. "If you would come with me please, I can show you where my office is."

The walk over to Rob's office was made in silence. I already knew we weren't going to work well together, so I had no intention of talking to him. He led me across the street to the office I'd been in earlier. Once inside, we walked to the back of the building and stopped at a small corner room.

"Here we are, home sweet home." Rob chuckled at his own joke, which I didn't find all that amusing. "Come on in and grab a chair."

There was only one chair in the room besides his. I moved it away from the large wooden desk before sitting down. "You're a quiet one, eh?" he continued. "Well, that's all right. Maybe you just need some time to warm up, eh?"

When I didn't say anything, he made a grunting noise and moved on. "Well, why don't you tell me a little about yourself? How old you are, where you are from, and what you like to do."

I knew Rob was just trying to get me to say something since all the answers to his questions were in the folder that was sitting right in front of him. I replied curtly, "Sixteen, Texas, and I don't know."

He made another grunting noise after I responded; he was probably annoyed at my flippant attitude. "All right then, why don't you tell me how you liked the inpatient program and how you feel about being here?" He smiled and sat back in his rolling chair, delighted that he was now making me use more than one word per question.

I twisted around in my chair and found a place on the carpeted floor to stare at. "The inpatient program was fine, but I don't want to be here. They made me come."

At my response, Rob raised one eyebrow and placed a hand on his chin as if in deep thought. "Who is *they*?"

"The therapist I had and my parents." When I mentioned the word *parents,* Rob's face seemed to light up.

"Ah, so you're angry at your parents then?" I glanced up from the brown coffee stain on the carpet and looked at the delighted expression on Rob's face. He thought he'd found the problem, and now he was mentally patting himself on the back.

"No, I'm not mad at my parents. I just don't want to be here."

The smug look on his face began to change into a scowl. "Okay then, why don't you want to be here?"

I was tempted to say that I was tired of eating chocolate and fast food, but something told me that wasn't a good idea. "I'm just tired of being here, that's all."

The rest of our conversation was just as unproductive. Eventually, he figured out that I wasn't going to talk to him and led me back to the house without saying another word.

Two Steps Forward, One Step Back

27

When I got back to the house, some of the girls were sitting around watching TV. When I heard the voices of Matt Lauer and Ann Curry, I stopped dead in my tracks; they were watching the news. I hadn't seen anything other than G-rated Disney movies in more than two months, and now here I was watching newscasters talk about world events. I plopped down next to a girl named Kara who I knew from the inpatient facility, and gaped at the TV screen. It struck me that this was my first real step back into civilization. Twenty minutes later, a stout blonde woman walked into the room.

"All right, girls, it's time for dinner." The woman never looked up; she was too distracted wiping grime off a frying pan with an old dishrag.

"Don't worry, she's always like that." Kara's sarcastic tone made me laugh. As Kara got up, I thought about the first time I'd met her back at the ranch. Rochelle had just brought us back from art therapy when I saw Kara sleeping on one of the couches in the common room. Her cheeks were so puffed up that she resembled a chipmunk with acorns stuffed in its mouth. She was wearing a black jacket with a fur hood, even though the room was warm. When we later spoke, Kara told me that she had only recently left and then returned to the ranch. The shock of being thrown back into a society full of diet ads, overly thin pop stars, and low-fat everything was just too much. Almost as soon as she got home, Kara went back to her cycle of starving, binging, and purging. Even if Kara hadn't told me all this, her swollen cheeks and waiflike frame said enough for me to know what she'd been through. Now that Kara hadn't purged in a few months, her cheeks were no longer swollen. She also wasn't wearing her coat in the house anymore.

It felt strange to sit around a dining room table instead of the usual long gray tables at the ranch. I was shocked to see people reach for their napkins without asking.

"Okay, girls, come and get your plates please," instructed the blonde woman. One by one we got up and wandered into the kitchen where there were plates of steaming vegetables, mashed potatoes, and couscous lined up on the counter. "Whoever has juice, go ahead and pick what you want and measure it out." The woman with blond hair still hadn't introduced herself to me, and I wasn't really sure what she meant by "measure it out." I was about to ask someone when I noticed Debbie pouring orange juice into a plastic measuring cup. I turned to Kara, who was getting a kick out of my reactions.

"Yes, Melissa, we're allowed to actually choose our juice and measure it out ourselves." Her tone was playful, yet something told me she knew exactly how I was feeling. After Debbie handed me the measuring cup, I grabbed one of the empty glasses along with the container of orange juice. Carefully, I measured out a cupful of the pulpy liquid and poured it into the glass.

"Melissa?" I turned around at the sound of my name, almost spilling the juice everywhere. It was the blonde woman; I guess she finally realized she had to fill an additional plate with food. "Here, this is your plate. I'm Sandy, by the way."

I took the plate and walked back into the dining room area. Once everyone was seated, a brief prayer was said and the okay was given to begin. I'd never had couscous before, but it didn't really matter since I had no interest in tasting the food anyway. All I could think about was how long they were going to make me stay there. After dinner was over and the dishes were cleared away, Sandy called my name again.

"I need to explain some of the rules to you real quick. After dinner, everyone has to stay in the living room for thirty minutes so that no one has the opportunity to purge. Once monitoring is over, you can do whatever and go wherever as long as you stay in the house. All right?" I could tell she wanted to go through the rules as quickly as possible. I nodded my head to show her I understood.

"Okay, you can go now." The waving motion she made with her hand made me think of a bored queen sending away the night's entertainment. I was glad to go upstairs after the thirty minutes were up. When I walked into the room, one of my roommates was listening to a CD while the other had the shower running. We said a brief hello before I climbed up on the top bunk to grab my duffel bag.

I didn't sleep much that night. My body couldn't decide if it was cold or hot. I felt like a fifty-year-old woman going through menopause. I had to get up twice to change out of my clothes that had been dampened with sweat. There wasn't a clock in the room, but I had on a glow-in-the dark watch that I checked every so often. At six, I gave up on sleep and decided to get up. After showering and getting dressed, I headed downstairs. The house was eerily silent even though it was almost seven o'clock. I wandered around each room, expecting to see one of the MHTs sitting somewhere. But after going through every room, I realized no one was around. Panic set in as I backtracked through the house.

Something must be wrong, something must be wrong, the words repeated in my head, making me increase my pace as I walked through the house again. I wasn't used to being alone without an adult watching over my shoulder. When I was certain that none of the MHTs were in the house, I decided to walk to the office across the street. Once I was within a few feet of that door, I stopped. None of the lights were on inside and a sign was posted on the door that read, "On rounds. Will be back soon." I turned around and headed back to the house, hoping that someone had showed up while I was gone. Opening the front door, I listened for the sound of people chattering or breakfast dishes clinking. When I realized that the house was still empty, I sat down in the living room and waited.

The silence was making me crazy. Without any noise in the background, there weren't any of the distractions I depended on to keep me from thinking. Now I had nothing to keep the thoughts of food, Melanie, and horses from flooding my mind. *Worthless girl, you disgust me. Can't you see the fat rolling off your body?* The sound of the Sick Person's voice made the panic worse, causing me to roll up the bottom of my shirt and pull at the skin on my stomach.

Flesh, fat, fat, flesh! the voice screamed as I scratched at the skin with my nails. "I hate you!" The words were out of my mouth before I even thought about them. Never before had I actually out-right yelled at the Sick Person, addressing her as a distinct entity separate from myself. "I hate you! Why are you doing this to me?" I said aloud. Tears flowed down my cheeks.

If someone had walked in at that moment, they would have thought I was insane. There I was standing with my shirt halfway rolled up, tearing at my own skin while yelling, "I hate you!" I only stopped scratching when blood began to seep from the wounds. As I rushed into the bathroom to grab a tissue, part of me realized that what I was doing didn't even make sense. I knew my shouts were directed at someone else and yet I was still attacking myself. The whole thing was illogical; I just didn't know what else to do. After wiping away the blood, I flushed the tissues down the toilet and went back to curl up on one of the couches. A few minutes later, a short woman with gray hair meandered into the house. "Oh, you're up early. I'm about to fix breakfast," she said. I eyed the woman for a moment before turning away again without saying a single word to her.

In the afternoon, I had the opportunity to use the phone for the first time. There weren't really any rules about the phone; you just had to get off when someone else wanted to make a call. After dialing my home number, I prayed for someone to pick up. A flood of relief washed over me at the sound of my mom's voice.

"Mommy?" My high-pitched voice sounded childlike.

"Hi, Melissa! How are you? How is the program so far?"

As I began to sob, I realized that my efforts to hold back from crying were futile. "Mommy, I was alone this morning."

"What? What do you mean?"

I realized I probably wasn't making much sense. "There weren't any MHTs in the house, and when I walked across the street, the office was empty." There was silence on the other end, making me fear that we'd been cut off. But then I heard my mom's voice again.

"Are you sure? Hmm, that's not right. Isn't there an eleven-year-old in your house?"

I figured she was talking about Debbie. "Yeah, and one of my roommates is thirteen."

"Well, I'm going to call the office about that. Don't worry, I'm sure it won't happen again. How do you like your therapist?"

I made a face at the mention of Rob. "They gave me a guy therapist, and I don't know why. He's weird. I don't like talking to him."

"Oh." The sound of my mom's voice told me she was disappointed, so I decided to change the subject.

"They're taking us to Target today."

"That's great, honey. Okay, I probably need to go now. The dogs want to go outside. I'll call you tomorrow."

After hanging up, I couldn't help but feel like she was uncomfortable talking to me for very long. I didn't blame her though; we still weren't sure how to speak to each other without horses, Melanie, or yelling involved.

The trip to Target was my first venture out into the real world and away from the safe bubble the treatment centers had provided for the past sixty-three days. Walking into the store felt like culture shock. People of all sizes strolled up and down the aisles, pushing carts, or tugging on the arms of screaming children. The cacophony of voices and screeching carts made me nervous.

"Here, Melissa, do you want a basket?" I was glad to hear Kara's voice. She had gotten comfortable being around crowds of people again. I took the basket in my hands and followed Kara and Jonie around the store. When we passed by a shelf stocked with CDs and books, I stopped to look around. The brightly bound book covers intrigued me. I hadn't been able to read anything but textbooks lately. Since arriving at the step-down program, I had started trying to catch up on the school work I had missed while being in treatment. Although there wasn't much free time, I usually devoted a few hours a day to history and English. I picked up a copy of *Pride and Prejudice* and began leafing through the pages. The prospect of reading made my step feel lighter. Books were wonderful distractions that took me away from myself for a while. Reading made me feel like a child playing a game of make-believe; I could escape into another character and just forget. Yet my happy escape was ephemeral; soon enough I had to put the book down and return to the pain that the Sick Person never failed to provide. Nearby the book section, I found Kara flipping through the pages of a magazine. She began to read aloud when she saw me approaching.

"Lose ten pounds and look great for the summer! What types of clothes hide a full middle? How can I go down a dress size in two weeks?" Kara's playfully sardonic tone made it seem like she was getting a kick out of making fun of the ads. Yet her furrowed brow and pursed lips conveyed an entirely different message. At any moment, I thought Kara might crumple the magazine up and toss it into the nearest garbage bin.

THE BAD EGG 28

I came to understand why all the girls at the treatment center dreaded holidays—with every holiday came more eating. At home, special occasions were always celebrated with a superfluous amount of food and drink. This was also the case in treatment. Unlike at home where we could shun the plates piled high with custards and cakes, while we were in treatment the extra food was unavoidable. Easter was drawing near and the weekend festivities were already planned out. There would be an egg hunt, chapel services, and a big dinner at the end of the day. The mental health techs were trying to give us a "normal" Easter experience.

When I came downstairs on Easter morning, pink and yellow baskets adorned the kitchen counter. Each basket contained chocolate rabbits, bags of M&M's, and plastic eggs filled with jelly beans. Seeing the candies and chocolates made me stop in my tracks. I could feel my pulse begin to increase and the familiar feeling of anxiety clawing my stomach. In the dining room, setting the table was a woman with frizzy black hair whom I assumed was an MHT.

I knew I should probably introduce myself before bombarding her with questions, but my anxiety got the better of me; the painful clawing sensation was just too strong.

"We don't have to eat all of that, do we?" The pitch of my voice was higher than normal. The woman stopped straightening out the tablecloth and looked up at me through a pair of red-rimmed reading glasses that were balanced on the edge of her nose.

"Well hello there. What's your name? I'm Rose." Rose's soft and kind voice made me feel bad for being so boorish, but I had to know.

"Do we have to eat all of that?" I gestured at the baskets lined up on the kitchen counter.

"Hmmm, I'm not sure, dear. I can ask around if you'd like."

I nodded my head and turned to join Jonie and Debbie in the living room. Halfway there, I realized that I still hadn't told Rose my name yet, but she was probably accustomed to that kind of response by now. I'm sure I wasn't the first girl to storm into a room and demand to know something in relation to food or weight.

I had a chance to redeem myself before breakfast began when Rose asked me to retrieve a pitcher of water from the office. I apologized for jumping at her and introduced myself like a civilized person would have done in the first place. Before heading to the office, I looked around the kitchen at the various breakfast foods. A few boxes of cereal were lined up next to milk, bowls, and spoons. On the stove, fragrant bacon sizzled in a pan alongside another pan filled with scrambled eggs. The open stick of butter on the counter told me the eggs had been immersed in it. Piles of toast, a plate of hash browns, stacks of muffins and waffles—it looked like we were stocking up for the winter. The sight of all the food made me feel more than a little queasy. I was going to have to ingest that grease-laden food and live with the voice that yelled obscenities in my head. *Fat, disgusting creature. Get out! Run away! Go hide yourself.* The Sick Person's torments never failed to bring on a fresh wave of pain. Hearing her caustic words made me increase my pace as I walked to the office, halfway believing that if I went fast enough, I might be able to outrun her.

When monitoring ended after breakfast, I stayed curled up on a couch in the living room. The MHTs made us stay awake the entire time they monitored us, which I saw as cruel and unusual punishment. I guess they wanted us to face our feelings and anxiety about food rather than numbing those feelings with sleep, but all I wanted to do was nod off. Jonie had the shower running by the time I got to the room. My other roommate, Veronica, sat on her bed listening to a CD.

"She takes a lot of showers, don't you think?" I was trying to start a conversation with Veronica, and Jonie's idiosyncratic showering habit was the first thing to come to mind.

"Huh? Oh yeah. I guess she does."

I could tell Veronica wasn't in the mood to talk. Instead of trying to push the conversation further, I decided to pull out my copy of *Pride and Prejudice* and began reading. Twenty minutes later, Jonie emerged from the bathroom wearing a white dress and black pumps.

"My mom's coming today," she said. I couldn't tell if she was excited or nervous about the visit, so I just smiled at her. After Jonie left the room, I decided to get ready for lunch. We were supposed to wear nice clothes because some of the staff members were joining us. Before heading into the bathroom, I grabbed a pair of black slacks and a white button-down shirt. I couldn't help but think about how nice it was to get undressed without anyone scrutinizing my body. My pleasant thoughts were interrupted when I stepped into the shower and felt something soft under my bare feet. I finally figured out why Jonie always liked to take long showers—there were still remnants of her vomit on the tile floor.

When lunchtime arrived, Rose led everyone down the street and into what looked like a garage area. Inside, picnic tables were covered with bags of food from different restaurants.

"Okay, girls, go ahead and grab a plate. Everyone will have the opportunity to serve themselves today." Rose unloaded the plates of turkey, mashed potatoes, gravy, spinach, rolls, and some sort of stuffing and placed them on the tables. I took a plastic plate and stood in line behind Debbie. When I got to the plate filled high with turkey, I picked up the large silver serving fork with my shaky hands and took a piece of turkey. It was my first time to actually serve myself food in who knows how long. While eyeing the piece of meat I'd taken, a battle began in my mind between the healthy person and the Sick Person.

You took too much! Cut the meat in half. You have control! No one will notice, and you'll feel so much better afterward. Her cries were countered by a quieter voice, barely audible above the Sick Person's shouts. *No, don't listen! You'll want to restrict more if you start doing this again.* For a moment, I stood poised with serving utensil in hand, debating over which voice to listen to.

Control, control, you'll have control! The Sick Person continued her chant of empty promises that I still wanted so badly to believe. After another minute of deliberation, I picked up my plastic knife and cut the piece of turkey in half.

Good girl, you've done well. You'll thank me for this later, the coy voice hissed in my ear. At the time, I had no idea that taking a half portion of meat was the start of another vicious spiral downward.

After lunch, everyone had to participate in an Easter egg hunt. I couldn't imagine why people liked hunting for plastic eggs and stuffing their mouths full of candy. Even thinking about eating chocolate made me feel like I'd been immersed in cocoa butter. Before beginning the hunt, Rose explained the rules to us.

"Now, girls, we want this to be a fun event for everyone. So turn those frowns upside down and make them into a smile!" I managed to display a weak smile, because I could tell Rose was really trying to cheer us up. Truthfully though, I knew that nothing was going to make us feel better except being told we wouldn't have to eat anymore.

"For those of you who have level one snacks, you'll need to eat a minimum of three eggs. Does anyone have level-two snacks?" Debbie and I were the only two to raise our hands. "Great, you both need to collect five eggs."

"Do we have to eat all the candy inside the eggs?" I don't know why I asked the question since I already knew what the answer would be.

"Yes, dear, this is what people normally do on Easter."

I was about to say that I was Jewish and didn't celebrate Easter, but something told me that whatever I said wasn't going to make a difference.

"All right then, on your mark, get set, and go!" Rose exclaimed. I don't know if Rose was just saying that for effect, or if she really thought we were going to race off to find the best eggs. After Rose shooed us off with her hand, everyone walked away slowly while grumbling about more food and full bellies.

The eggs were stashed in bushes and randomly dispersed on the lawn so they weren't hard to find, especially since some of the MHTs stood by the areas where the eggs were hidden. I found my first egg under a tree a few feet from my house. I placed the "prize" in my basket and went on to look in a bush next to Kara.

"Hey, what did you get?" Kara's voice was barely audible.

"I don't know. I still haven't opened mine." Kara pulled out her egg and poured the contents out—two Hershey's Kisses, a mini-package of Twizzlers, two peppermints, and a box of Nerds. I eyed the candy nervously; it seemed like a lot for just one egg, and they wanted me to eat five.

When I first arrived at the ranch, I was shocked by the amount of junk food we were forced to consume. The typical artery-clogging American diet of pizza, fried foods, ice cream, and cookies was stressed as the "norm" in treatment. Whenever I complained about the type or amount of food we were made to eat, Jennie's retorts were always the same—"Everything in moderation, Melissa, everything in moderation." I knew they were trying to teach us to view food as a source of energy and enjoyment, yet forcing us to eat junk food only made me feel anxious, dirty, and disgusting.

"Come on, open yours." I twisted the top off the lime-colored Easter egg and peered inside. My egg contained the same candies as Kara's except mine had four Hershey's Kisses and no Twizzlers.

"Hey, I'll trade you my peppermints for your chocolate." At first, I was taken aback by Kara's offer and was about to tell her no, but before I could get a word out, the Sick Person began hissing in my ear. *Say yes! Chocolate is the most fattening thing in that egg. Get rid of it!* A coy smile crossed my lips as I pulled out the Hershey's Kisses and handed them to Kara. After the trade-off, we decided to split up in case the MHTs got suspicious, like two children plotting to cheat on a test when the teacher's back was turned. The only thing we cared about was being caught.

The next egg I found was in a bush near the office. When I was sure no one was around, I carefully opened up the baby-blue colored egg and studied the contents—a minibag of M&M's, two Hersey's Kisses, and a few Jolly Ranchers. Again, the Sick Person began to sound off. *Get rid of what you can. Hurry before someone sees!* I picked out the M&M's and the Hersey's Kisses and tossed them into a bush nearby. I did the same thing with the next three eggs. I'd toss a Peppermint Pattie here, a bag of Skittles there, all the while laughing to myself. By the end of the hunt, I was rather satisfied with my half-empty egg containers.

"Girls, when you're done, please come and sit down." Ruth was standing in front of one of the adults' houses, but she managed to project her voice loud enough for everyone to hear. I gripped my basket nervously as paranoid thoughts ran through my mind.

What if she catches me? Will they make me drink Ensure? Yet as I sat down and peered into each of the egg containers, my anxiety began to dissipate. There were more than twice as many girls as MHTs; they weren't going to meticulously examine the contents of each egg. Kara and I sat down on the damp grass and began sorting out our candies. We had successfully deceived the MHTs, and without realizing it, we had successfully deceived ourselves. It never occurred to us that we were already relapsing before even setting foot outside the treatment center.

ART THERAPY 29

The next morning, I woke up to the sound of voices downstairs. It was still dark outside, and I was surprised that someone else was up so early. I headed downstairs but stopped when I was halfway. The center couch had been pulled out into a makeshift bed where an older woman with gray hair sat. The woman's long, thin arms were stretched out in front of her with both palms facing upward. I sucked in a sharp breath of air as I saw inch-long cuts on each of the woman's wrists. I assumed that she must have cut herself during the night because the wounds looked fresh. A moment later, one of the MHTs walked into the room with a few pieces of gauze and some Band-Aids. The surprised look on her face told me I really wasn't supposed to see what was going on. She probably thought everyone was still sleeping, making it safe to dress the woman's wounds out in the open.

"Oh, good morning, you're up early, aren't you? Nancy here was just having some anxiety issues last night. She decided to sleep here since the MHTs don't stay in the adults' house overnight."

I wasn't sure how to respond so I just turned around and ran back up to my room. Later in the day when Rob came to get me, I actually had something to say to him. The way Rob's eyebrows shot up and the edges of his lips curled revealed his surprise that I was initiating a conversation.

"There was a lady in our house this morning. I'm pretty sure she cut herself because her arms looked like they were bleeding." I was about to say something else, but Rob cut me off.

"Those cuts were old. I know because that woman is one of my patients. She had anxiety last night, and that's why she was in your house."

"But I swear her arms looked like they were bleeding."

"You're wrong. Now let's talk about something else." The angry look on Rob's face convinced me to drop the subject. I turned to pulling at a hair band on my wrist and watching it snap back onto the skin. "What did you talk about with your old therapist, err . . . ?"

"Meg?" I finished his sentence for him.

"Yes, yes, Meg, what did you talk about with Meg?"

"Things." I was back to my one-word answers.

"Like what? Can you give me an example?"

"No." I was still pretending to be fascinated by the hair band.

"Why not?" Rob sounded annoyed.

"I don't feel like talking."

"All right then, I'll talk. You realize we have a telephone conference with your parents tomorrow, right?"

I shifted in my chair while nodding my head.

"Is there anything you plan to say to them?"

"Yes." I was actually enjoying watching Rob as he got angrier. I could tell he was trying to remain composed, but there was nothing Rob could do to stop his ears from becoming redder by the minute.

"What do you plan on saying to your parents?"

Before answering, I turned to face Rob, looking him straight in the eye. "I plan to tell them that I hate it here." That was probably the longest sentence I ever said to Rob.

My stay at the outpatient program was supposed to be two months, but I ended up going home much sooner. I wasn't released because Rob thought I was doing well. Actually, he was pretty peeved at my parents for taking me out early. But after I had been left alone, stepped in vomit, saw a woman's slit wrists, and forced to eat chocolate, my parents thought it was about time for me to leave. The decision to take me out early, though, only came after what Kara and I liked to call the cartoon fiasco.

At the outpatient center, art therapy wasn't anything like the sessions we'd had with Pam back at the ranch. Really, I wouldn't consider what they had us do at the outpatient center therapeutic at all. A few days after Easter, Sandy took us to our weekly art therapy session, which was held in a small house across the street. In the main room of the house, three picnic tables had been pushed together to form one long line. On the tables were stacks of construction paper, markers, crayons, and colored pencils arranged in separate tubs. As I settled between Jonie and Kara, two older women walked into the room. One of the women had a large black bag in her hand while the other one was holding a mirror.

"Hello, everyone, I'm Lou Ellen and this is Helen. We're going to be working with you all today. Let me explain what this class is going to be focusing on. First, what we're going to do is learn how to properly apply makeup. Now has anyone here ever been to a makeup class before?"

She looked around the room expectantly but continued talking when no one raised their hands. "Okay, that's great because today you'll have a chance to learn. Now the goal of the first half of this class is to learn about how important it is to take care of your body. That's why we will be learning how to use makeup properly. I'm going to let Helen tell you all about the second part of today's class."

As Lou Ellen stepped back, the other woman bowed ceremoniously and began to speak. "So I think everyone is going to enjoy the next part of this class. I brought in a CD player and a few CDs for us to hear. Everyone can use the resources we have on these tables to draw whatever the music makes you feel." The way Helen began to twirl around the room reminded me of Mary Poppins, except that Helen had to be in her fifties and her moves weren't very graceful. As she spun, her long gray hair flung around, covering her sun-weathered face. Some of the girls were laughing at the crazed-looking woman, but I felt too embarrassed for her to even do that.

I'm still perplexed by the makeup-application class. Everything at the outpatient program seemed so twisted and wrong. Why did they want us to focus on the outer appearance when we just spent the last sixty days learning that only our "inner selves" really mattered? The whole thing seemed narcissistic and dumb to me. A few of the girls went over to the table where Lou Ellen had placed different shades of eye shadow, blush, powder, and lipstick. But I had no interest in joining them. I pulled out a book and tried to read.

"Melissa, you need to take part in the activities." I looked up to see Lou Ellen wagging a finger at me from across the room. I made it look like I was getting ready to stand up, but when she had her back to me again, I sat down and continued reading. Lou Ellen's singsong voice reminded me of Rochelle and how much I missed her. The way Helen kept frolicking around the room resembled someone who had been possessed by Dionysus. Lou Ellen, on the other hand, was busy looking in the mirror and applying a garish shade of green eye shadow onto her wrinkled eyelids. After another twenty minutes of girls patting their cheeks with powder and blush, Helen finally called out that it was time to move on to the next activity. The makeup was cleared off the tables and replaced by a worn-looking CD player.

"Okay, children, we're going to hear some music now. Remember what I said about drawing the way the music moves you!" Before putting in a CD, Helen smiled at us and clasped her hands together as if she was about to break out in prayer. As the music started, I decided to at least try the activity even though the whole thing seemed kind of frivolous to me. The first song was Billy Preston and Syreeta singing "With You I'm Born Again." I heard Kara begin to chuckle at the sappy-sounding love song. How could anyone take this seriously? What meaningful pictures did they want us to draw? I started making an outline of a horse's head but stopped after drawing the ears. A picture of Cadence showed up in my mind, causing a fresh wave of pain. No matter what I did or where I went, there was no way for me to free my thoughts of horses. I had started to draw that horse head without even thinking about it. I tore it into as many pieces as possible.

For the next few minutes I sat poised with pencil in hand, listening to the sappy love songs. I was waiting for some image to appear in my mind so that I could draw the thing and be done with it. A new song started to play. As I listened to the lyrics, I decided they were purposely playing songs to depress us.

I looked over at Kara who was giggling and whispering something to Katrina. When I glanced at Kara's drawing, I couldn't help but laugh. She had sketched two figures with human bodies and frog heads. The frog-humans were kissing each other with their eyes open and making obscene hand gestures. After seeing Kara's drawing, I stopped taking the project so seriously and began drawing a cartoon instead. By the end of art therapy, I had created a lovely sketch of an old man sitting with his dog on the back porch, playing the banjo and smoking a pipe. I thought about putting Rob's name at the top since that's who I modeled the man after. But then I decided that would probably get me into trouble. Rob might psychoanalyze the drawing and tell my parents I was disturbed.

"Okay, is everyone done?" Helen asked. I put down my pencil at the sound of her voice as she continued, "Now before we're through, I want each of you to talk about what your drawing represents." I felt my stomach drop at the thought of showing off my cartoon version of Rob. I considered crumpling up the drawing, but Lou Ellen was two seats away and would likely see me. Kara had no problem explaining her frog people to everyone. I could tell that her satirical tone was making Lou Ellen livid. As Kara continued talking, Lou Ellen's face transformed from a previously serene and relaxed look to an angry scowl. Her bright red cheeks and wrinkled forehead only increased my anxiety, but it was too late to do anything; she'd already gotten to my chair and addressed me.

"And what did you draw, Tiffany?" I resisted telling her that my name wasn't Tiffany and turned my drawing over instead.

"I don't want to show my picture, if that's all right." My voice and hands both shook.

"Now now, don't be a silly head. I want to see what you drew." The color drained out of my face as Lou Ellen turned the piece of paper over. Her reaction told me she was less than pleased. I was expecting her to yell at me, but instead she just picked up the drawing, folded it in half, and continued down the row.

The rest of the class seemed to go by painfully slow. With the exception of Kara and I, everyone else had taken the project seriously. Debbie showed off a picture of a smiling girl standing underneath a rainbow, while another girl named Jackie had drawn pictures of her family members. At the end of the class period, Helen stood up, her eyes glassy as though she was on the verge of tears. She clasped both hands together and began to give what sounded like some sort of a graduation speech. Her exaggerated enthusiasm was nauseating. "Girls, I want to congratulate those of you who completed the project. Thank you for following directions. It warms my heart to see such wonderful portraits!"

As everyone got up and followed the MHT out the door, Lou Ellen called for Kara and me and motioned for us to wait. When the room was clear, the two women approached us with stern looks on their faces. "Now, girls, I would like an apology please. Your drawings were inappropriate." While Lou Ellen was talking, Helen wagged her finger at us as though she was scolding a dog for urinating in the house. I looked over at Kara for some reassuring sign, but she was busy glaring angrily at Lou Ellen. The expression on Kara's face conveyed she was used to this sort of lecturing. As I studied her visage, it struck me how much she resembled a lion. Kara's large brown eyes were halfway closed, giving her a look of invincibility. Her short brown hair, which she always flattened down with gel, contrasted against her honey-colored skin. The way Kara stood there with her broad, square shoulders, pouting lips, and crossed arms was enough to make an onlooker believe she was self-assured and even slightly cocky. Yet her appearance was just a facade, a tough exterior that belied a fragile girl who forced herself to throw up as a form of self-punishment, because she could never seem to do anything quite right. I knew just how she felt.

THE FINAL STRAW

30

Besides being scolded by Lou Ellen and Helen, Kara and I were reported to the MHTs and eventually to our therapist for the drawing incident. Two days after the art class, Rob decided the situation called for an emergency telephone conference with my parents. I'm not sure why he waited two days if he thought it was an emergency. Rob came to get me for the conference right after breakfast; he didn't even wait for the thirty-minute post-breakfast monitoring period to end. As usual, we spent the walk to his office in silence. Once we arrived, Rob quickly picked up the phone and dialed my home number. My dad was the first to pick up. I smiled at the sound of his familiar voice; for once I was glad my dad never took anything seriously. There was no way he was going to get angry over a stupid drawing. Rob didn't waste any time before bringing up the cartoon situation.

"Mr. and Mrs. Binstock, I have some disturbing news for you." I could hear my mom inhale sharply on the other end of the line. "Melissa engaged in some inappropriate behavior during an art therapy session." He paused for a moment for effect. "Now I believe that we shouldn't be angry at Melissa. My gut feeling is that her actions are a cry for help."

I was tempted to yell at Rob to just get to the point. He was purposely weaving his way around the subject to build up my parent's suspense. I let out a huffing noise and shifted in my chair, trying to indicate my irritation with Rob.

Before he could say anything else, my mom interrupted him. "Can you tell us what she did?" I could see Rob's face brighten at my mom's request. He was enjoying making them nervous.

"Yes well, the theme of the art class was self-expression. The girls were asked to listen to a CD and draw what the music made them feel. Now Melissa apparently did not like the topic. She and one other girl proceeded to make inappropriate sketches instead of taking part in the activity."

"What did she draw?" My dad's tone of voice sounded more like he was amused than upset by Rob's graveness.

Instead of letting Rob answer for me, I leaned over the speakerphone and began to explain the drawing. "I think I followed the art therapists' directions just fine. The sappy music inspired me to draw an old man sitting on a porch, playing a banjo, and smoking a pipe. I don't know why everyone made such a big deal out of the picture. It's not like I drew people with guns shooting at each other."

Rob interrupted me before I could say anything else. "Yes, Melissa, but you have to understand that your inability to take the subject seriously is concerning."

"Why? Why does what I drew matter so much?"

Without answering my question, Rob turned away and began talking to my parents again. "Mr. and Mrs. Binstock, do you understand why I'm concerned about Melissa's picture?"

My mom's laughter told me she wasn't getting why Rob had a problem. "Actually, I think what Melissa drew is pretty funny. She gets her sense of humor from her father."

The look on Rob's bright red face made me laugh right along with my mom. He looked like an angry Shih Tzu, with bulging eyes and a set of yellowish teeth. I only stopped laughing long enough to hear Rob recite my punishment.

"The art therapists and I have gotten together and decided what privileges the girls will lose. Melissa will not be allowed to go on this afternoon's outing. I believe they are going to the museum. Also, she will not be allowed to go to cardio this evening." After Rob was done speaking, he leaned back in his chair and crossed both arms. The smug look on his face revealed his pleasure at how visibly upset I was.

"But that's not fair! Haven't we already been punished enough? The art therapists already yelled at us. I already missed another activity by being in here now. Isn't that enough?" Rob's coy smile made me want to scream. My voice escalated with each word.

"I hate it here. When can I come home? Haven't I been gone long enough? The people here are horrible. The first morning I was here there wasn't anyone downstairs. After that I found some lady in our house who was bleeding because she'd slit her wrists; the house is always dirty, but when I try to clean, the MHTs yell at me for moving around too much; my roommate throws up in the shower, and nobody does anything about it; I got in trouble for not wanting to learn how to put on makeup; and now I'm being punished for drawing a stupid cartoon!"

I only stopped when I ran out of breath. Silence fell over the room; I think my parents were shocked by my sudden outburst, while Rob was busy planning a solid-sounding defense.

"Mr. and Mrs. Binstock, I'm sorry for Melissa's little tantrum. I'm sure it won't happen again. Now you must understand that girls with this problem tend to be compulsive liars. I already explained to Melissa that the woman she saw in her house was not bleeding. Those marks on her arm were old; I know because she is my patient. As for the makeup class, I have had many patients tell me that the session was the most beneficial class they'd ever taken. I'm sure that the other issues are being addressed properly, and I'm also certain that Melissa was not left alone the first morning she was here."

I wasn't sure which to be angrier about—the fact that Rob was lying to my parents or that he was calling me a "compulsive liar." Yet, before I could counter Rob's claims, my dad chimed in. "Rob, my wife and I appreciate your concern, but I don't really think Melissa is getting much out of your treatment program." My mother smiled in that forced-polite way that people do when they aren't happy.

"Yes, Rob, my husband and I have been doing a lot of talking lately, and we think Melissa is ready to come home now. She really seems to be doing better, and she's been away for quite a while." Suddenly, all the anger and frustration I felt toward Rob and toward the program in general dissipated and were replaced by glorious feelings of relief and excitement—I was going home! Finally, I was going home.

Rob wasn't very happy about my parent's decision. He made threats, saying things like "If you take her out now, she'll relapse," but after he'd called me a liar, my parents had little faith in Rob's judgment. He was right about one thing though. I was going to relapse, but leaving treatment too soon wasn't the reason.

Actually, my relapse started while I was still in treatment. All of the ice cream and fattening foods provoked the Sick Person's rage, making her hiss and scream until her voice reached an unbearable crescendo. *You've lost control, you disgusting girl. How can you just stand there. Run! Hide yourself!* The incessant shouts felt like needles puncturing my skin, eventually leading me to turn to exercise as an emollient.

No one at the treatment center knew that I'd turned the upstairs closet into my own personal gym. Every morning, I got up extra early to get in a workout before breakfast. I was thankful for the carpeted floor, which made it easy for me to run in place without making much noise. After thirty minutes of running, I switched to sit-ups, shoving my feet under one of the bottom shelves to keep them from coming up. Jumping jacks, push-ups, squats—I did them all, and nobody ever found out. Exercising wasn't my only fallback; I also started to restrict my food intake whenever the opportunity arose. Everyone in the house got a chance to help prepare meals once a week. The MHTs in the outpatient program were nothing like Tonia; they didn't lean over my shoulder as I measured out a tablespoon of peanut butter. When Rose wasn't looking, I'd quickly spoon less than half of the amount we were supposed to have on each sandwich. If she'd ask how much I measured out, I'd lie and say, "Two tablespoons, of course." I guess Rob was right about another thing—when it came to food, as least, I was a compulsive liar.

❧

On my last day at the step-down program, I finally was able to experience the jovial feeling Caitlin had when she left the ranch. For the first time in months, my step felt light and the Sick Person was quiet. When my parents drove up in a gray rental car, I ran out to meet them. While sprinting across the lawn, a smile spread over my face; no one could make me drink Ensure now. As we drove away from the outpatient site, I looked back at the cul-de-sac one last time. "I'm not going to miss this place."

The shock of being back in the real world hit me as soon as we arrived at the airport. We wouldn't get back to Texas until eight at night, so we had to eat dinner. "Melissa, what would you like to get? I don't think we're going to like whatever they serve on the airplane." My mom sounded tired but happy. As I looked around at the multiple restaurants in the terminal, sweat began to gather on my brow; there were so many choices. I finally decided to let my mom pick a restaurant since I couldn't seem to be able to make up my mind. She decided to grab a sandwich at a place near our gate. A glass case displaying different wraps and sandwiches overwhelmed me. When I couldn't decide, I again turned to my mom.

"What are you getting?"

"Well, let's see. The Caesar-salad wrap looks pretty good, doesn't it?" Even though I wasn't sure what was in the wrap, I nodded my head.

"Do you want a bag of pretzels?" I turned away from looking at the big case of sandwiches and saw my mom holding out a bag of pretzel sticks.

"Are you getting a bag?"

"Yeah, I think so, the flight's kind of long."

"Okay, I'll have one," I said. As we walked to our gate, the realization that I was trying to copy my mom sank in. I wanted to do everything my mom did so I could learn who she was and what she liked. I was doing exactly what I'd done with Melanie those first few months after moving to Willow Wind.

During the flight home, the only thing I could think about was trying to be perfect for my mom. The Sick Person who demanded love overcame the one who screamed every time I took a bite of food. *If you're perfect, she will love you; if you're perfect, she will love you.* The words were a chant in my mind. The only thing I had to decide now was what *perfection* meant. For Melanie, I knew that her ideal daughter had to be obedient and absolutely dependent on her for everything. She needed to be willing to obey every command even if it meant betraying friends and family. In other words, Melanie's ideal daughter was her own personal slave. I wasn't sure would make my mom happy, which is why she became my new subject of study. Every move she made was picked apart and analyzed until I could say, *Ah, so that's why she did this,* or *this is why she did that.*

EVERYTHING DIFFERENT, EVERYTHING UNCHANGED

31

Once we were back in Texas, it finally hit me that my parents were really taking me home. While we were in New Mexico, and even on the plane flight back, I had this fear that at any moment my parents were going to turn around and tell me that it was time we headed back to the treatment center. But once the plane landed in Texas, I was certain they weren't going to take me back. It felt odd to be at home again. While I was away, my mom had redecorated my room. She tried to fill the room with vibrant colors, but to me the place looked barren and dull. The ribbons I'd strung along the wall next to my bed were no longer there. My mom had replaced the pictures of Cadence with ones of family members and other pets. As I gazed around the room, I saw that there were no horse posters or trophies; even the stuffed animal ponies that used to sit on my bed were gone. Everything was different, and nothing felt like it belonged to me.

"Melissa! Welcome home!" The sound of Brooke's voice interrupted my thoughts. I was taken aback by the sincerity of her smile and glistening eyes. Before I'd left, our relationship had disintegrated to something almost nonexistent. I wasn't expecting her to really miss having me around since I had never really spent time with her in the first place. After hugging Brooke, I turned to Sam, who was standing next to my mom. Again, I was surprised by the joyful look on Sam's face. She had less reason to miss me than Brooke did. We'd never been close because I was always jealous of the way my mom doted on her. When I still spent time at home, before I was wrapped up in Melanie's web, I'd made Sam's life miserable with my incessant teasing and taunts. She knew very little about who I really was. In the past, all I'd done was torment her or ignore her entirely. In truth, Sam should have hated me—and yet she didn't.

I wanted to feel exuberant joy at Brooke and Sam's genuinely loving reception, but all I felt was the heavy weight of guilt. I tried to displace the sickening feeling by making a silent promise to myself that I would be a good sister from here on out. The guilt was so overwhelming, though—I didn't see how I could possibly make up for my past behavior.

Before I went to bed that night, I planned out my breakfast for the following morning. My mom had stocked the fridge and pantry with all the foods I had come to like while at the ranch. There was an abundant supply of granola, oatmeal, whole wheat bread, peanut butter, yogurt, and fruits of all kinds. While lying in bed, I decided I was going to get up early the next morning and make everyone breakfast. I felt a warm glow inside as I thought about how happy my mom would be when she saw the table set and the food already prepared.

The next morning, I rose at 5:30 AM and quietly walked into the kitchen to begin setting the table. By 6:30 AM, when my mom and sisters walked in, I had breakfast prepared and displayed on the table. The praise I received from everyone filled me up with a sense of warmth that I hadn't experienced in a long time, the kind that only accompanies happiness. I wanted to show my mom I was useful and no longer the selfish girl she'd known before.

I'd set four places since my dad never ate breakfast. It felt strange to sit down at the table with my mom and sisters. While chewing on a piece of toast, I tried to determine the last time we'd eaten together.

"Melissa, you can put your napkin on your lap if you want to," my mom offered. My thoughts were interrupted by the sight of my mom holding out a napkin in front of me. I still wasn't used to being allowed to place a napkin on my lap. A few minutes later, everyone was done eating except me.

"I need to go to school now, Mel. We'll talk more this afternoon." Brooke scooted her chair back from the table and grabbed her book bag before heading out the front door. Sam and my mom remained at the table, but I could tell they were just there to keep me company. After another ten minutes, I'd finished scraping up the last morsel of food on my plate.

"Good job! You ate it all!" My mom looked like she was about to start clapping at my outstanding eating performance. The whole thing rather annoyed me; I wasn't a circus animal, and eating was not some sort of talent. When I got up to clear the table, I looked around at everyone's bowls. It was distressing for me to see that no one else had finished their meal. The treatment center hadn't really prepared me for the shock of being thrown back into a society where people talked about dieting and didn't always finish what was on their plate.

My mom gave me the option of staying home for a few weeks before returning to school, but I wanted to go back that first morning after arriving home. There was nothing for me to do at home, and I was afraid that all the free time would allow me to think too much. I needed something to occupy my mind, and school was the perfect distraction. After breakfast was cleared away, I returned to my room to pick out my clothes for the day. As I sorted through shirts, I felt my chest tighten with anxiety. I was certain all the teachers knew I'd been treated for an eating disorder. I could imagine their hushed whispers now that I'd returned. Would I still be Melissa to them? Or, would I be the anorexic? After twenty minutes of debating what to wear, I finally pulled out a black T-shirt and a pair of faded jeans. *Good yes, wear black. The color will mask your enormous stomach*, the Sick Person hissed in my ear.

Everything at school looked the same—the dimly lit hallways and old brown carpets, the locker room where the broken snack machine sat next to a sink. The desks in the study hall were still covered with swear words and a few obscene pictures carefully sketched in black marker. The only difference was the sanguine and extremely obese study hall monitor. I couldn't help surveying the copious amount of food on the woman's desk: a bag of miniature oranges, two sandwiches, beef jerky, a few cookies, and a plate of carrot sticks.

"You must be Melissa. Hi, I'm Ms. Fullen. I have your schedule here if you'd like to pick it up." I walked over to the obese woman's desk and took the piece of paper she handed to me. My schedule was the same as before I had left. At nine, I was supposed to go to history, then geometry, English, and chemistry. After getting my schedule, I walked down the hall to say hello to Mrs. Tiltman. At first, I was excited to see my favorite teacher and return to the sunlight room where I'd spent so many quiet afternoons. As I began talking to Mrs. Tiltman, though, my excitement quickly waned. I felt as though she was more interested in examining me to determine how much weight I'd gained than in listening to what I was saying. Her stares reminded me of Terri scrutinizing my body back at the ranch, and frankly, I was tired of being stared at.

The school year ended shortly after I returned from treatment. I was able to keep up with some of my studies while at the step-down program, but not geometry and chemistry, which I would have to complete in summer school.

By the time summer school began, I'd already lost about ten pounds. I had internists and nutritionists monitoring me, but they weren't like Jennie; no one questioned what I said I ate. If I told them I'd eaten a cheeseburger, fries, and an ice cream sundae, they believed me despite my ever-decreasing weight and withering frame. At first, the weight loss was unintentional—going to school and walking around more was enough to cause me to lose. As my nutritionist continued to tell me I'd gone down in weight from the previous week, the Sick Person slowly regained control. Restricting was no longer just a form of control or self-punishment; restricting had become my entire life. Not eating became especially easy because my depression took away all the hunger pangs.

The overwhelming sense of sadness was like nothing I'd experienced before. It was a different sort of sadness from what I'd felt each time Melanie rejected me. This new sensation was one of complete emptiness, making me feel as though I'd been locked in a pitch-black closet with no place for light to shine through and no hope of ever escaping. I was stuck there without a plan or place to go. Now that the horses were gone, I had no idea who I was or what I liked to do. The pain was omnipresent because everywhere I went and everything I did somehow reminded me of horses. On my way to school in the morning, I'd drive by an open lot and say to myself, "That'd be a good place to go trail riding." At noon and again at

5:00 PM, I'd think, "It's time for Cadence to eat." I couldn't stand to watch horses on TV or even hear people talking about them.

Covering up my depression became almost as important to me as hiding my restricting of food. I tried to always appear happy and content, especially around my mom. How could she love me if I wasn't pleasant to be around? Instead, I hid every emotion, stuffing and suppressing each one until I couldn't contain my sadness any longer. The sensation of sadness had filled me so completely that it began to overwhelm me, like water rushing out of a burst levy.

A week after summer school started, my mom planned for us to spend a day at the annual international festival that was being held downtown. I was already having a bad morning, even before leaving the house. My body was beginning to feel weak and achy again from lack of proper nourishment. Even though I wasn't restricting myself to just apples and soy crackers, I'd returned to the familiar routine of eating the same thing every day. No one said anything because my parents had been instructed by my therapists to not be the "food police."

As we piled into the car that morning, I put on a thick pair of black sunglasses to cover up my watering eyes. Really, I wanted nothing more than to go back home and crawl into my bed. Thoughts of horses swirled through my mind; even the skyscrapers downtown made me think of horses. When we got to the festival, the sight of a police officer on a chestnut-colored gelding made me feel like someone was thrusting a knife in my side. I cried out as if in pain, no longer able to subdue my sadness. The tears that filled my eyes ran freely.

"Melissa, what's wrong?" My mom seemed surprised by my sudden outburst. I tried to answer but choked on my tears. Instead, I just pointed at the horse and continued sobbing.

Rehab Redux   32

Once school started again in the fall, I began seeing Dr. Lancaster on a twice a week basis. With my weight steadily decreasing, she wanted to monitor me more closely. Dr. Lancaster came with high recommendations from the ranch, but I wasn't comfortable with her. I found it particularly odd that an obese doctor specialized in the treatment of anorexia.

Going in to be weighed was never a fun experience, and Dr. Lancaster's staff certainly didn't make it any better. Whenever a nurse weighed me, I'd purposely stand on the scale backward so I wouldn't have to see the numbers. But as soon as I got off, the nurse would shout out my weight anyway. In addition, I couldn't help but feel uncomfortable about the cartoon drawing that hung above the scale. It depicted a girl standing on the scale crying while another girl stood behind her patting her on the shoulder. *How was this an encouraging illustration*, I wondered.

When my weight didn't improve with Dr. Lancaster, my parents decided to send me to a new internist with the hope that maybe she'd be able to help me. During my first visit with her, I couldn't help but notice how much the clinic resembled the ranch. I had to once again change into a frumpy hospital gown while a nurse watched. After I'd changed, the nurse asked me if I had anything else on. I'm not sure why she bothered to ask since even when I said no, she patted me down anyway just to make sure I wasn't hiding anything in my underwear. After a few hours of waiting in an exam room, a young woman with long brown hair strolled into the room. She was wearing a gray pants suit with a colorful ascot tied around her neck. After introducing herself as Dr. Anderson and shaking my hand, she proceeded to ask me the same questions I'd answered so many times before.

"So why don't you tell me a little about yourself?"

I concentrated on staring at the floor. Open-ended questions always left me feeling slightly agitated. I wish she'd just be specific and tell me what she wanted.

"What would you like to know?"

"Why don't you tell me why you're here?"

"My parents wanted me to come."

"Okay then, why don't you hop up onto the table so I can take a look at you."

As I sat down on the examining table, Dr. Anderson's focus immediately turned to my legs. "Are your legs always purple like that?"

"Sometimes, I guess." In reality, the purple hue of my skin was fairly new, but I really didn't think about it all that much. I flinched as Dr. Anderson placed two fingers on the top part of my calf and began running her hand down my leg. She stopped just above my ankle before turning to me.

"Here, take your hand and feel this part of your leg."

I moved my hand down to just above my ankle, feeling the cold skin against my fingertips.

"Your heart isn't strong enough to pump blood all the way down your legs and arms. That's why you're purple, and that's why your skin is so cold."

I think she was expecting some sort of reaction from me, but I just sat there with my hand pressed against the chilled skin. After Dr. Anderson finished her examination, she sent me home with a set of instructions that read, "Melissa needs to add at least three hundred calories to her meal plan." While walking out of the clinic, I balled the piece of paper up and tossed it into the nearest trash can.

The Sick Person was slowly regaining control of my mind and body, her voice becoming so loud that every other noise sounded muffled against her cries. Slowly but surely, I began cutting foods out of my diet until I was living off steamed vegetables and fat-free yogurt. When Dr. Anderson threaten to put me in the hospital, I didn't really care. Every week she made the same threats, but in the end she always gave me another chance if I promised to "do better the next time." After a while, I just stopped taking her seriously. I never tried to add anything to my diet because, frankly, I didn't give a damn. When I didn't eat, the Sick Person was quiet and that's all that mattered.

Two more weeks passed before Dr. Anderson finally took action. I still didn't believe her when she told me she was admitting me into the hospital that day. It wasn't until my mom showed up with a suitcase full of clothes that I started to take Dr. Anderson's threat seriously. When I saw my mom standing next to the doctor, I attempted to get up to make a run for the door, but a wave of nausea hit me, sending me back into the chair.

The doctor's office was located in the hospital so all we had to do was wait for a room to open up and fill out some paper work. I was too enraged to answer any of the doctors' questions or sign the forms they laid out on the table. When the doctors realized I wasn't going to answer them, they stopped trying to get me to talk and worked on taking my vitals instead.

"Her blood pressure is sixty over forty, and her heart rate is forty." I knew a normal heart rate was somewhere around sixty, but nothing the doctors said had an effect on me. "All right, Melissa, we'll come get you when a room opens up."

I have no idea what those two doctors looked like, because my eyes never left the floor. As I waited in the examination room, I started to feel more chilled. I couldn't understand why nobody else was cold but me. My limbs had turned purple, and I tried to roll up in a ball to get warm. No matter what I did, my body still shivered. By the time a room was ready, all my fingers and toes were numb and bright purple.

I don't remember how I got to my room. Maybe they brought a wheelchair downstairs or I might have walked. My mind was too weak to pay much attention to what was going on around me. All I wanted to do was wrap myself up in warm blankets and go to sleep. As soon as we got to the room, I climbed into the bed and dove under the covers. The material felt scratchy against my skin, but I was too cold to care. Even under multiple layers of blankets, I was still freezing.

A few minutes later I heard my mom talking to a man outside the door. "We need some more blankets. She's shaking and her skin is purple." When the man returned, he had more blankets in his hands along with two cans of Ensure.

"No! I don't want those." I must have sounded like a whiny child who didn't want to eat broccoli. But the man wasn't paying much attention to me. Instead, he calmly turned to my mom.

"We need her to drink these please." While he spoke, my mom took the cans from him and placed them next to me on the night table. But before she could say anything to me, I jumped out of the bed and began pulling my clothes out of the drawers she'd placed them in. As I tossed some shirts back into my suitcase, my mom began to yell.

"Melissa! Stop it! Where are you going to go? How are you going to get home? You can't just leave. What, are you planning to take the train?" Her volume increased with every word, until I thought the whole floor could hear her. Her yelling caught me off guard; she hadn't screamed like that since before I'd left for the ranch. I dropped the jeans I was holding and turned around. Mom's face looked wan and tired. The desperate look in her eyes made me want to reach out and tell her everything was going to be okay. Not once during this whole ordeal had I thought about anyone other than myself, and now here was my mom standing at the foot of the bed, begging me with her eyes to give in and eat. Without another word, I returned to my bed, picked up a can of Ensure, and began to drink.

Waking up in the morning to the sound of a beeping portable blood pressure machine down the hall made me feel like I was back at the ranch again. A knock sounded at the door; a nurse wheeled in the machine along with a portable scale. The routine was exactly the same. I had to get two sets of vital signs, one lying down and another after standing up. Then I had to change into a blue and white pinstriped hospital gown and go to the bathroom while the nurse watched. She didn't have to tell me to step on the scale backward. I knew to do it so I wouldn't see my weight and obsess about it. I was a pro at all this by now. After being weighed, the nurse watched me get dressed before rolling the blood pressure machine and scale out the door again.

A few minutes later, there was another knock at the door. I watched as a short woman whose name tag read *Maria* entered the room with a wheelchair. She had an annoyed look on her face, as though she really didn't appreciate having to wheel me around. She pushed me across the hall to a room that resembled a kitchen.

I was happy to see that my breakfast wasn't composed of watered-down oatmeal. The night before, I had actually gotten to choose what I wanted to eat. One of the nurses explained the system to me, which was a lot like the points system people on Weight Watchers use. Every food was allotted a different number of points, and I had to have a certain number of points at each meal. For breakfast, I chose to have Cheerios, an apple, and a carton of fat-free milk.

"Can I use my napkin here?" I guess Maria thought my question was funny because she began laughing. When she realized I wasn't kidding, her face went serious again.

"Yea, you can use your napkin. Okay, you all have thirty minutes." One of the other girls was eating so fast that I thought she might choke on her bagel. I only had to eat eighteen points during the day, but she was up to forty-two. I prayed they wouldn't raise my points that high. After breakfast was over, Maria wheeled me into a room that was connected to the kitchen. Inside were a large TV screen, two chairs, and a couch.

"Hey, my name's Rachel. Did you get here yesterday?" I turned to the girl who was talking to me. Her long, black hair was pulled back tightly in a braid, making her already pronounced cheekbones stand out even more.

"Yeah," I said. I guess Rachel understood that my terse words and disinterested tone indicated I didn't feel much like talking, because she didn't ask me anything else, and directed her next question at the others.

"What do you guys want to watch?" Rachel was tossing a pillow from one hand to the other.

"I don't care. How about the news?" This time a girl with shoulder-length brown hair named Lea answered.

"*Argg*, do we have to watch the news? It's so depressing. Can't we watch Regis and Kelly instead?" Helen had draped her arm dramatically across her forehead, making it seem as though she would positively die if we had to watch the news. The sight of Helen's theatrical performance made me smile for the first time in days.

Of the three girls, Lea was by far the sickest. She had the same pallid countenance that so many girls at the ranch had, and her frame was so frail and thin that I was surprised the nurses were even letting her walk around. When Lea stood up to turn the TV on, her body looked almost concave.

After monitoring time was up, Maria wheeled me back into my room. Before leaving, she turned to me and wagged a finger in the air. "I'm not going to sit here with you, but be aware that a camera is installed on the back wall. We have a station down the hall and there's always someone there watching you." With that, the stout woman left the room. Glancing in the direction Maria had pointed, I saw a video camera strategically hung in the uppermost corner of the room so that no one would be able to reach it.

Scowling at the camera, I began to hear the Sick Person scream about food, fat, and flesh. *Shut up, shut up, shut up!* I didn't care that I was shouting the words aloud; I just wanted the voice to go away. I tried to distract myself from the Sick Person's cries by reading the latest Harry Potter book. It was nice to escape into another world for a while, and I was slightly annoyed to hear someone knock on the door half an hour later. As I looked up from the book, I saw a woman with bright orange hair standing next to a younger man whom I learned was a medical student.

"Good morning, Melissa. My name is Dr. Wilkerson, and I'll be filling in while Dr. Anderson is out of town. How was your first night?" By the time the doctor finished speaking, she was standing so close to the bedside that I thought she was going to hop onto the bed with me.

"When does Dr. Anderson come back?" I didn't like the fact that my doctor skipped town right after admitting me.

"Oh, she'll be back next weekend, I believe. Don't worry though. She did leave me with some instructions. I read from your chart that you have hepatitis. How long have you had it?"

"I don't know. Dr. Anderson took my blood about a month ago and that's when she told me."

"Now you know that this isn't the type of hepatitis people get from dirty needles, right? Hepatitis just means inflammation of the liver."

I nodded my head to indicate to her that I already knew all that. My body was so starved of fat that my liver wasn't functioning properly anymore. After the doctors left the room, I leaned back against the railing of my bed and began thinking about everything I'd put my body through. The years of starving and purging were catching up to me. My liver was failing, I had open cuts and sores that wouldn't heal, my skin was so dry it broke open and bled, my heart rate was low, I had to cut my hair because so much of it had fallen out, and that was only the half of it. Even lying in bed had become painful because there wasn't enough fat on my body to pad my bones.

I was sick and miserable, and yet I still didn't know how to block out the voice. I desperately wanted to be relieved of the Sick Person, and I thought that by appeasing her, I could make her omnipresent cries stop. In fact, after I obeyed her demands, the Sick Person would hush for a little while. Yet I had no idea that my efforts to gain control over the Sick Person—by giving into her demands—were equivalent to hacking off the head of a hydra, only to watch two more grow back again shortly thereafter.

ENSURE-ANCE   33

The mealtime routine at the hospital reminded me of my experience at the ranch. The rules were a little more lax, so no one minded if I didn't mix my food groups or if I ate my sandwich in a circle. Really, the only thing the monitors cared about was that I finished eating on time. Just like at the ranch, if you didn't eat your meal within the allotted thirty minutes, a big can of Ensure would be set aside just for you.

My hatred for Ensure peaked about two weeks into my hospital stay. It happened during dinner after the MHT called out that we'd run out of time. As I glanced across from me, I saw that Rachel still had half a container of applesauce and some mashed potatoes left on her plate. The MHT that night was a woman with tightly braided black hair and a nose reminiscent of a pig's snout. I never learned her name because she didn't tell me and I didn't ask. After everyone had cleared away from the table, the woman pulled out two bottles of Ensure from an overhead cabinet. I guess Rachel wasn't used to drinking Ensure because the potent stuff made her sick. The rest of us turned away as projectile vomit covered the table and floor. Each time Rachel threw up, the livid MHT handed her another bottle to drink.

"Can we go to another room?" Lea was holding her nose and trying not to watch as Rachel continued to throw up.

"Nope, sorry, there's no one else to watch you all. Dang it, girl, I'm *gonna* get this into your stomach even if I have to put a tube in ya!" The battle lasted for another ten minutes; Rachel would drink a small amount of Ensure, throw it back up, and wait as the MHT gave her another bottle to down. I tried to turn my head away, but no matter what I did, the smell of vomit still infiltrated my nostrils.

My mom showed up a few minutes later. When I saw her through the glass window, I frantically motioned for her to come in the room.

"Excuse me, ma'am, but you can't be in here right now. We're still in monitoring time."

"Can I take Melissa?" my mom asked. Nervously, I watched the expression on the MHTs face, trying to determine if she was going to let me go. She began shaking her head back and forth, but before saying anything, my mom broke in. "She's my daughter, I'm her mother; and I think I'm capable of watching her." At that moment, I wanted to jump up and cry for joy. My mom's voice was so forceful. There was no way the MHT could say no.

"Fine, you can take her. Just make sure she *don't do nothin'.*" I breathed a sigh of relief and left the putrid-smelling room with my mom. That night before going to bed, I thought about what my mom had said. *She's my daughter, I'm her mother.* The words sounded so sweet to my ears. At one time Melanie had said something very similar, except she only called me her daughter because she wanted to use me. Melanie's words were purely business-oriented; if she could trick me into believing she loved me, I'd work harder at convincing my parents that they needed to buy another horse, pay for more lessons, or send me to another show. Every word Melanie had said was empty and meaningless; everything she did was completely void of love.

The days at the hospital started to go by faster once I got used to the routine. Actually, after a while I even started to enjoy myself. After breakfast I'd go back to my room, pull out a copy of *Anna Karenina,* and spend the rest of the morning reading. As long as my mind was occupied, everything was okay. Sometimes I'd read aloud as a way to drown out the Sick Person's voice. On good days, my efforts were successful, but then there were those days that no matter what I did, the voice would somehow overpower me.

Weak girl, disgusting, lazy girl, all you do is eat! Your body has gone soft. Go look in the mirror! See the drooping flesh? Take it off! Get rid of it! The Sick Person's cries filled my mind so completely that I couldn't concentrate enough to read. Running to the bathroom, I obeyed the Sick Person's demands and quickly pulled off my shirt. *Look! Look at your stomach. Turn to the side, what happened to the ribs? You've lost control, you've lost control!* Giving into her commands once more, I turned to the side and ran a hand down my rib area, trying to count the indents between each bone.

Can you count them? Are the bones still visible? No, they've been covered by fatty flesh and disgusting lard. How can anyone ever love you now? The Sick Person's incessant screams moved me into a fury. "Shut up! Shut the hell up!" I yelled aloud. My words helped silence the Sick Person for a few moments, but then she returned with a vengeance.

What's the point of your life? What good are you, you unlovable girl. You still want to live? Well then, get rid of the flesh. Hurry, get rid of it! Run! Before even putting my shirt back on, I began to run in place. I ran and ran and would have kept going if one of the nurses hadn't knocked on the door to my room. Hurriedly, I threw my shirt back on and jumped in bed. As the nurse rolled the blood pressure machine in, I concentrated on keeping my breathing steady and slowing my heart rate down.

"Hun, you're sweating and your face is red. Do you feel okay?" the nurse asked. I had the thermometer under my tongue so I didn't say anything. When the thermometer beeped she looked at the numbers. "Hmmm, ninety-six point nine degrees. You don't have a fever, but it is somewhat warm in here. Do you want me to make it cooler for you?"

"Yeah, I was sleeping under a lot of blankets, so maybe that's why I'm sweating." The nurse patted my arm before leaving the room again. A smile spread over my face when the door shut. I didn't care about lying to the nurse. The Sick Person was quiet now and that's all that mattered.

After Dr. Anderson released me from the hospital, the length of time I stayed well was significantly longer than when I left the out-patient program in New Mexico. I realized that I had been in the midst of a relapse before even leaving the ranch. Dr. Anderson was the best doctor I'd had so far, and the well part of me wanted to trust her. I liked the fact that she allowed me to stay at a weight under the range that Jennie had prescribed. She was honest with me, and for the most part I appreciated that. Yet it was precisely this honesty that triggered yet another downward spiral.

Before my release, Dr. Anderson and I had agreed on a set weight range I would need to stay within if I was to avoid being readmitted. The top of the weight range was 118 pounds, and Dr. Anderson promised to tell me if I ever went above that. For some reason, 118 seemed like a safe number to me. It was under the weight Jennie had prescribed, which satisfied the Sick Person and made her believe she was getting her way. As long as I stayed at 118 pounds or less, the Sick Person remained quiet, allowing me to follow Dr. Anderson's meal plan without worrying about negative repercussions. I began to construct a mental barrier to block the Sick Person from entering and to repel her noxious cries. The taunts became softer until all I heard were whispers that I blocked out as much as I could.

Everything worked out well for a few weeks. I followed Dr. Anderson's plan diligently—almost to a tee. In the back of my mind, though, I knew something was bound to come along and destroy the peace I was experiencing; the Sick Person couldn't be quieted for long.

My inclination was right: one month and two days after getting out of the hospital, Dr. Anderson told me I'd gone slightly above my self-imposed maximum weight. Dr. Anderson's news came at a time when my barrier was still weak and penetrable, allowing the Sick Person to barge through and take control once more. The knowledge that I was above my weight range reinvigorated the Sick Person and just about tripled her strength over me. I grew weaker as she grew stronger, and eventually I couldn't ward off her screams and cries any longer. I began restricting and cutting out food groups once again. Two weeks after being told I had gone above my weight range, I had tossed Dr. Anderson's meal plan by the wayside.

❧

The school year drew to a close, graduation followed, and in the fall I headed off to college. I had dreamed for years of going to a school in Connecticut that was well-known for its psychology program, but I never applied because my parents had told me right off the bat that they weren't going to allow me to go out-of-town for undergraduate school. Although my parents' decision disappointed me, I never argued with them. In the back of my mind, I knew it would be impossible for me to go to college far away. The Sick Person's hold on me was just too strong, and I knew I couldn't trust myself to stay well. Having my parents close by was comforting, In the end, I decided to apply to a small liberal arts school in town.

I was looking forward to a fresh start. There no one would know anything about me, and I wouldn't feel like people were constantly analyzing my body. The thought of being able to walk around campus without someone telling me to eat some chocolate or ask about doctor's appointments was so nice. The only thing I needed to worry about was controlling my tics and hiding my eating disorder from my roommate. Luckily, the girl I ended up rooming with thought my habit of filling the fridge with fat-free yogurts and sugar free Jell-O was pretty comical. No one suspected anything, and since I was away from home there wasn't anyone to force me to eat. The first few weeks of class went pretty well. As the weeks carried on, though, I began to feel more like a circus performer than a college student. Around other people, I put on a magnificent show with fake smiles and false laughter. No one knew about the Sick Person or her whispers of weakness and inevitable failure.

When it came to food, the Sick Person's incessant cries plagued my mind and controlled my body, making me a slave to her every whim. At meal times, I could hear the healthy person within me begging for nourishment—a piece of bread, a cup of fruit, anything! I would go to the cafeteria and pick up the package of bread used to make sandwiches, only to set it back down again once I caught sight of the nutrition facts. *Not for you, you can't have any!* The Sick Person's cries made me feel as though I was walking around in someone else's body and had to obey the dictates of that person. I had become an intruder, a stranger unto myself. As the weeks carried on, the Sick Person endeavored to extend her reign over my mind entirely by gaining control over my intellect, the one thing I had left.

Walking to class in the morning, I began to feel as though I was stepping to the beat of *fail, fail, fail* as the Sick Person sneered at me for thinking I could do well on a test or quiz. Yet the healthy person within me desperately wanted to fight back, refusing to surrender the one thing still in my control.

Shut up, shut up! You don't know what I can do! I'll show you. I will not fail. You just wait and see. The healthy part of me fought back by striving to get good grades so I could prove the Sick Person wrong. Grades became more than just letters on a sheet of paper; they became reflections of the battle to regain ownership of my body. Getting anything less than an A would send a rush of panic through my limbs.

You're losing! You stupid girl. What were you thinking? You'll never succeed. I fought back by studying even harder, memorizing passage after passage from textbooks and spending weeks perfecting my papers. I had to succeed, because if I didn't I would be giving up another portion of myself to the Sick Person. Spending so much time on my work left little time to eat, much less socialize with friends. After a while, I stopped leaving my dorm room except to go to class, the gym, or the grocery store to buy more sugar-free Jell-O.

NOURISHMENT AT LAST

34

I somehow managed to complete an entire semester running on nothing but Diet Coke, sugar-free Jell-O, and fat-free yogurt. Really, I'm not sure how I was able to go on so long without collapsing. By the time Christmas vacation came, I had lost a total of ten pounds along with a good amount of hair. I was afraid to wash, brush, or even touch my hair—even running my hands through the thin strands caused clumps to fall out. I dreaded going home for the Christmas break, fearing my parents would make me eat again or that they'd notice how much weight I'd lost. Not once during the semester had I missed anyone from home. My mind was too full of the Sick Person's screams and schoolwork to think about the love I'd longed for only a short time before. I had no idea that Christmas break would change all that. As I drove up to my house, I could feel anxiety beginning to gnaw at the lining of my stomach.

Leave! Get away! Hide! They're going to make you eat! They're going to make you huge! The Sick Person's shouts filled my mind as I pulled into the driveway. Before getting out of the car, I grabbed my pink duffel bag full of clothes and containers of yogurt. As I hoisted the bag onto my shoulder, I heard the sound of the front door opening. I looked over to see my mom standing in the doorway, smiling at me. The Sick Person's cries began to dissipate as new thoughts started running through my mind. *Did she miss me? Am I good enough to be missed? Could someone care for me enough to actually miss having me around?*

At dinner that night, my mom kept placing her hand on my arm or running her fingers through my hair. I didn't even care that my hair was probably coming out with each touch. The Sick Person's jeers of *Unlovable girl* became inaudible as a voice called out, *She loves me! I'm loved! She missed me, and I'm loved!* The soft pats and displays of affection served as an unequivocal testament of my mother's love, the love I couldn't accept for years, because the Sick person convinced me that I had damaged our relationship beyond repair.

When I returned to college after Christmas vacation, I experienced terrible homesickness, beyond anything I had experienced before. The wave of sadness that rushed over my body made me feel as though I was grieving a beloved friend's death. Finally, I had the love I'd been trying to grasp onto for so many years. I thought that leaving my mom for the dorms would only make me lose my grip. Two days after being back on campus, I couldn't take it anymore. I had grown use to the pain that came from hunger and the Sick Person's shouts, but adding homesickness into the dreadful mix was just too much for my greatly weakened body and mind to bear. I was so tired and just wanted something to ameliorate the pain so I could rest. After a long day of classes, I returned to my empty dorm room, overwhelmed by a sickening sensation of weakness, hunger, and loneliness. I picked my cell phone up from the desk next to my bed and stared at the numbers for a minute before calling Brooke. Silently, I prayed she would pick up and after three rings, I heard the familiar-sounding *hello* of my sister's voice.

"Brooke, I'm sad." My declaration sounded dumb, but I didn't know what else to say.

"What's wrong, Mel? Did something happen at school?" Brooke's voice was so full of love and compassion that it made the tears I was trying to hold back spill onto my cheeks.

"No—I mean—I don't know. I'm just really sad. I miss being at home." My voice sounded strange and childlike.

"Do you want me to come visit you? I can miss school. Boston isn't too far from Texas, and I've saved up some money. . . ."

"No, I don't want you to get behind or something. I'm just sick of feeling like I have to always go around wearing a mask on my face that has a smile plastered onto it. I feel like I'm lugging around this horrible weight that I can't carry by myself anymore."

"Do you have someone at school you can talk to? I'm sure there's a guidance counselor or a professor you could talk to."

"No, I can't do that. I like all of my professors, but I don't want them to know anything about me. They'll think of me differently; they'll think I'm a freak. I just don't want to do this anymore."

"Do what?"

Deep down, I was well aware of the fact that Brooke knew exactly what I meant; she just wanted to hear me say it aloud.

"I mean, I just hate feeling this way. I'm sick of being sick. I don't want to be in pain anymore; the day shouldn't be painful."

"Have you called Mommy?" The mention of my mom sent a fresh wave of sadness coursing through my body.

"I miss Mom, I miss her a lot." I felt like a child, crying to Brooke that I missed being at home with my mom. As I wiped away my tears, I glanced at the radio alarm clock sitting on my shelf.

"Brooke, I have to go now. I need to study."

"All right. Call me when you're done studying. Oh, and Melissa, your dorm is only twenty minutes away from the house. You can leave anytime you want to."

Brooke's advice was simple and true; the dorms were only a short distance from home. Really, I could go home anytime I wanted to. But I was a college student, not a child. I wasn't supposed to be living with my parents anymore. For once, I was doing something normal and going home now would disturb that. After hanging up the phone, I curled up in my bed and slept for the rest of the day.

My continual weight loss prompted Dr. Anderson to recommend another hospitalization. But now that I was over eighteen, I simply dismissed her suggestion. The only reason I went to appointments was to keep my parents happy. Before a weigh-in, I'd down as much water as possible to add water weight, sometimes even drinking a bottle while going up the elevator to her office. I didn't think anyone would notice my withering frame.

At school, my first exams of the spring term were approaching and I wanted nothing more than to sit in the quiet of my room, study, and not eat. A few days before my first test, I stayed up later than usual reading Cicero's *Laws* for the third time, trying to memorize the different arguments. It seemed like no matter how many times I reread a paragraph, I still couldn't absorb any of the information. As I glanced up at the clock sitting on my desk, I saw that it was three in the morning.

Maybe I'm just tired and need to sleep. I'll be able to understand this stuff in the morning, I told myself. Part of me wanted to believe that my lack of concentration was due to fatigue, but in truth, I knew it was because my mind had been deprived of nourishment for too long. Before going to bed, I decided to put some of my laundry away. As I walked back and forth from the hamper to my dressers, the feeling of nausea brought me to a sudden halt. When I tried to take a step forward, a sea of blackness rose up before my eyes just before my body collapsed onto the floor. Through all the years of starvation, I'd never passed out. True, I had a few dizzy spells and had fallen over once when carrying a saddle. But, I had never lost consciousness before. The fear I felt is indescribable. My body was damp with sweat, and yet I was still freezing; my heart was racing, and yet my pulse felt weak; I took in deep breaths, and yet I felt like I couldn't get in any air. And then I heard a small, frightened voice in my head begin to cry out, *I'm going to die. This is it, my time's up.* I stayed on the floor for a while before pulling myself onto my mattress. I avoided sleep although my eyelids were heavy and my mind was overwhelmingly tired. I used every ounce of energy left to fight against the urge to drift off to sleep, fearing I might not wake up again.

At some point during the night I did fall asleep, only to wake up a few hours later to the beeping sound of my alarm clock. My head felt heavy, and all my limbs ached. But I had to get up; missing class was not an option. I went into the bathroom to layer my cheeks with brightly colored blush to hide a wan expression. It wasn't very cold outside, but I dressed in multiple layers to hide my skeletal frame and purple skin. The walk to class always felt extra long in the morning, so I called my mom on the way. I had no idea our conversation would lead beyond the usual dialogue of "How are you?" and "I miss you." Of course, our phone call started out that way, but then my mom moved to the subject I wanted to avoid the most.

"How did your doctor's appointment go yesterday?" The question wasn't particularly unusual, but it startled me because I'd decided to skip my visit with Dr. Anderson. My mind began to race. *Should I tell her I couldn't make the appointment, or do I say everything went fine? The latter, choose the latter!* The Sick Person cooed in my ear. "Everything went well. I'm maintaining my weight."

"Oh, that's good, Melissa, I think I'm going to give Dr. Anderson a call this afternoon. I just want to check in." The drop in my mom's tone told me she knew I was lying. Panic set in as I processed her disappointment. *You filthy liar. How is it that someone can destroy absolutely everything she touches? No one can love you, because all you do is screw up.* The formation of tears made me stop walking. If I was going to cry, I needed somewhere safe to go where no one would see me.

"Melissa, are you still there?"

I didn't even realization that I'd stopped talking. "Yeah, I need go, though, class is starting soon." Another lie—I always left the dorms at least thirty minutes before lecture to read or work on papers. Once we hung up, I resumed walking and almost made it into the lecture hall before stopping again. *She's going to call the doctor and find out I didn't make the appointment.* A fresh wave of grief rushed over me as I thought about my mom's disappointment. Although hiding the truth awarded me praise from the Sick Person, lately the feelings of guilt and distain were worse than the accolades. The battle that often took place within the confines of my mind between two distinct voices took on new force.

Lie! Don't tell! You know how hard it is to get in touch with that doctor. Keep quiet, and no one will make you eat. You'll have control!

No! You've had enough! These lies, this starving; it's no way to live. Speak up and get help.

The warring voices made me feel as though there were two people residing within my body. The battle went on with each persona trying to convince me why I should join her side.

Who could love something as disgusting as you? You who are covered in thick layers of fatty flesh, how can you let the world see something so grotesque? Call and you'll be sorry. That doctor only wants to add layers onto the flesh.

Then I'd hear the well person work to allay and soothe my fears, countering the Sick Person's wretched words with her forceful cries of *No! Don't give in, close your ears! Haven't you lived this way long enough? Haven't you been in enough pain? Nourishment! For God's sake, I need nourishment!* The pain of being jerked to one side and then the other became unbearable.

If the choice between the Sick Person and the well one had been simple, I would've chosen to dismiss the Sick Person long ago and spared myself the years of pain and starvation. When the Sick Person first started making demands when I was only eight, perhaps I could have chosen to ignore her. Yet when my body was plagued by tics and my mind unable to make sense of words, the Sick Person's promises of control made her look like a dear friend. At the time, I had no idea that a mere desire for control would be the catalyst of a long downward spiral. After almost twelve years of denying food to my body, I no longer had the option of simply choosing to be healthy or sick. Starving was the only thing I knew how to do. I'd forgotten what it was like to eat a piece of bread and not worry about calories, fat, and sugar. Living without the sick person was uncharted territory for me, which is why the treatment centers and hospitalizations could only help my body but not my mind. The fact that I could actually hear a second voice in my mind crying out for nourishment was something strange and new to me. Why did all this occur after a phone call? Maybe I heard the healthy person because my tics finally subsided at the beginning of college, and I felt in control of my body again; perhaps I heard her because the lack of nutrients threatened my school performance, or maybe I heard her because I was just sick of being sick. Truly though, I believe it was a combination of everything.

Instead of going to class, I decided to call home again. My mother picked up on the second ring.

"Mommy, I lied to you. I didn't go to my appointment."

A moment of silence passed as a wave of panic rushed through my body. *She's disappointed. I've disappointed her again.* As the words ran through my mind, tears began to flow down my face. I didn't try to wipe them away and could have cared less if people were staring at me. The only thing I was thinking about was losing hold of my mom's love again. My thoughts were interrupted by the sound of my mom's voice.

"Oh, Melissa, we all know you're sick. All we want to do is help you. Please just tell me how we can help you." The sadness and desperation in my mom's voice made my vision blur with tears that continued to flow freely.

"Do you think I could come home for a while?" I sounded like a child but I really didn't care.

"Of course you can. All your dad and I want is for you to be happy. I love you, Melissa. You know that don't you? I love you." The flood of tears began to slow as I took in my mom's words. The sound of her voice was so firm, yet caring, as though she was trying to express the seriousness of her love for me. At that moment, a multitude of thoughts raced through my mind. *She loves me! She does! Can't you see that now? For God's sake, can't you see that now?* The depth of my mom's love made me feel as though I was stepping outside for the first time after being liberated from a long captivity. When I spoke again, my words were no longer hollow lies but the truest words I had ever said aloud.

"I know you love me. I love you, too, Mommy."

AFTERWORD:
COPING WITH MY DISORDERS

When I first began writing a conclusion to this book, I thought I wrote about reaching a break-even point in my recovery, about how I was neither sick nor flourishing. It's been over a year now since I had that idea, though, and many things have changed. Today, I can confidently tell you that I am no longer the same shy girl who said little and walked around campus with shrugged shoulders and eyes to the ground. I am no longer Tourette syndrome, anorexia, or dyslexia—I am Melissa. Reclaiming my identity as a person has been a large part of my recovery. As you read, I used to personify Tourette syndrome, dyslexia, anorexia, and OCD—as though they were malevolent forces that were taking over my body and mind. My disorders became intertwined with me as a person, like vines slowly wrapping around the walls of a home. And eventually, I could no longer distinguish myself from the tics, inabilities, fears, and compulsions.

This process of becoming the creator of my own identity has been arduous and anxiety-provoking, making me feel as though I had been assigned to paint an enormous blank canvas with a single, tiny brush. At the same time, though, the thought of being able to shape and mold my life cannot be described as anything other than awesome. When I was sick, I would often lie in bed at night and wonder what it would be like to live. Yes, I was alive in the technical sense of the word, but I wasn't *living*. I would dream elaborate plans about what I would do when I was better, only half-heartedly believing that the plans would ever be carried out. I had difficulty envisioning a time when I wouldn't be sick, because sickness was all I knew. I lived in a state of a seesawing ambivalence for years, but that began to change during my sophomore year of college. What prompted me to begin to change? I got hungry.

I'm not talking about hunger in the physical sense of stomach rumbling, although that may have been true, too. No, this was a different kind of hunger. It was a hunger so strong and undeniable that it pulled me toward health—it was a hunger for life. I yearned for that supreme feeling of being alive—to touch, to taste, to feel, to smell. For so many years, I had been living in a world of fear, suppression, and self-induced numbness, and now I wanted out.

My own recovery has been a slow process. It was important for me to feel in charge of it, so I needed to go at my own pace. I can still recall the mixed feelings of fear, relief, and anticipation the morning I first added a tablespoon of peanut butter to my diet—the shaking hands as I scooped the peanut butter out of the jar, the queasy feeling in my stomach as I lifted the spoon to my mouth, and the blissful taste of that rich substance as it hit my tongue. After eating that small dollop of peanut butter, I waited for the Sick Person to sound an alarm. Naturally, she did . . . but, this time I was ready. After years of allowing her to run my life, I was ready to take it back. I countered her insidious chants of *fat, fat, fat* with a statement I still use today: "I want nourishment." Over time, as I continued challenging the Sick Person, I noticed the obsessive thoughts about weight and food began to dissipate. That's not to say I didn't have slipups or setbacks—I've had my fair share of those. Yet, my hunger for life was too strong to deny. I was sick of achy joints and foggy thoughts; I was sick of the depression, anxiety, and emptiness. More than anything, though, I was just sick of being sick. It's been over a year now since I added that tablespoon of peanut butter, and I can honestly tell you that it was well worth it.

What is my life like today? I'm a pretty typical college student. It's still sort of strange to think of myself as "normal" but, for the most part, I am, although I still have to cope with my disorders. Recovering from an eating disorder is an ongoing and continual process. I have created a stringent plan for myself to stay on the path to recovery. Part of this plan entails only allowing myself to exercise for a set number of minutes and not allow myself to ever skip a meal or snack. My recovery has been very goal-oriented. Some of these goals are more immediate, such as being able to think clearly during my counseling and psychotherapy class. But, I also have long-term goals, such as going to graduate school, and my goals keep pushing me forward as I continue on that winding, wild road of recovery.

Learning to live with Tourette syndrome is more about acceptance than action, although I have found some techniques that have helped me cope. Humor is a wonderful coping mechanism I tend to use often. Over the years, I have come to accept the fact that I have tics. Although I may not always be able to control them, I do have some power over other things in life, such as my class schedule at school. I avoid taking night classes; evenings tend to be harder for me and I have more difficulty subduing my tics—I don't think my classmates appreciate listening to a lecture accompanied by the sound of barking in the background! My barking, I suppose, makes me sound like the stereotypical case of Tourette syndrome as portrayed by the media. Actually, whenever someone first learns I have Tourette syndrome, one of the first questions is almost always *So what swear words do you say?* Personally, I have never shouted out swear words. The question never fails to leave me feeling slightly annoyed, since in reality, swearing is a relatively rare tic. So I try to control what I can and accept what I cannot, a basic skill we all have to develop in life.

In a similar vein, I also do what I can to cope with my learning disabilities. I order textbooks prior to the beginning of the term, start assignments early, and study small chunks of information every day after lecture. A big part of coping with a learning disability is being proactive. Over the years, I've figured out what works best for me, and I have also discovered that there really *is* no such thing as a stupid question. Having a learning disorder does not mean you are dumb, slow, or inadequate—it just means you are different, and that's okay. Besides, if everyone was the same, this world would be one heck of a dull place!

Although learning to live and cope with neurological and psychological disorders can be an arduous task, I have learned over the years that it is vital for me to be able to let loose during the day. For a long time, I wasn't sure where to find an outlet because my relationship with horses had become so tarnished. I couldn't enjoy the gentle giants I used to love, because every time I went riding, I would become overwhelmed by feelings of anxiety and tension. Yet, with patience, time, and the help of a dear friend, I learned to calm my anxiety so riding could once again be fun. Horses now provide me with that same outlet I had when I was younger—an outlet that has proven to be an essential part of my recovery.

At times, recovery has felt a bit like an experiment: I have tested out different techniques and strategies to determine what works and what doesn't. Although this trial and error effort seems taxing at times, it has been vital to my recovery. Most important, my experience has taught me that although I may have multiple diagnoses, nothing will ever prevent me from being fully nourished.

APPENDIX

Melissa's Diagnoses:

1. Tourette syndrome—A neurological disorder characterized by repetitive, involuntary movements and vocalizations.
2. Dyslexia—An inability to attain language skills commensurate with intellectual ability. Affects reading, spelling, writing, memory, and concentration.
3. Obsessive compulsive disorder (OCD)—Individuals are plagued by persistent, recurring thoughts (obsessions) that reflect exaggerated anxiety or fears.
4. Attention deficit disorder (ADD)—A neurological condition characterized by behavior and/or learning disorders that is often evident from childhood. May cause restlessness, disorganization, hyperactivity, distractibility, and mood swings.
5. Anorexia nervosa—A psychophysiological disorder characterized by an abnormal fear of becoming obese, and therefore a distorted self-image. This results in an unwillingness to eat and often to an obsession with exercise, which leads to malnutrition and extreme weight loss.
6. Learning disorder (LD) not otherwise specified (working memory)—A working memory deficit that affects the brain's ability to receive and process information. Information is lost as it is being processed.
7. Generalized anxiety disorder (GAD)—Characterized by chronic and exaggerated worry and tension, even when there is little or nothing to provoke it. Anxiety can be so extreme that it takes a physical toll and interferes with an individual's ability to function.

Melissa's Medications:

The following is a list of the generic names of medications that were prescribed to me throughout my childhood and adolescence. Brand names are included in parentheses for easier identification.

1. Amphetamine-dextroamphetamine: a central nervous system stimulant that affects chemicals in the brain and nerves that contribute to hyperactivity (Adderall)
2. Bupropion: atypical antidepressant (Wellbutrin)
3. Clomipramine: tricyclic antidepressant (Anafranil)
4. Clonidine: antihypertensive agent used to treat high blood pressure and Tourette syndrome (Catapres)
5. Diazepam: used as a tranquilizer and to treat anxiety disorders (Valium)
6. Fluoxetine: antidepressant (Prozac)
7. Fluphenazine: antipsychotic (Prolixin)
8. Fluvoxamine: antidepressant (Luvox)
9. Haloperidol: tranquilizer for psychotic disorders (Haldol)
10. Imipramine: tricyclic antidepressant with antiobsessional properties (Janimine, Tofranil)
11. Methylphenidate: a central nervous system stimulant that affects chemicals in the brain and nerves that contribute to hyperactivity and impulse control (Ritalin)
12. Olanazapine: atypical antipsychotic (Zyprexa)
13. Quetiapine: antipsychotic (Seroquel)
14. Resperidone: antipsychotic (Risperdal)
15. Sertraline: SSRI antidepressant (Zoloft)
16. Tetrabenazine: dopamine reducer (Xenazine)
17. Valproic acid: mood stabilizer (Depakote)

ACKNOWLEDGMENTS

Writing this book has been an incredible journey, and I have many people to thank. This book would have been impossible if not for every one of you.

My family: Cathy and Bob Binstock, I couldn't ask for better parents. Your constant love and support, even through my darkest days, have been a blessing, a gift, and a treasure worth more than anyone will ever know. Brooke and Samantha Binstock, you are not just my sisters—you are my best friends as well. You both have been there through all the highs and lows of this roller coaster we call life. We have cried and rejoiced, fought and loved. I love you both with all my heart, and I thank you both for all you have done for me through the years.

Joseph Ademek: Thank you for your unconditional acceptance, support, and love. I never thought I could feel as close to a person as I do to you. Thank you for helping me accept and love myself. I cherish our relationship.

John Jurica: Your friendship means the world to me. You have been there for me through both the good and the bad. I entered college weary of people, and you not only taught me how to trust again but you taught me the meaning of friendship as well. I feel blessed to have you as my colleague, friend, and confidante.

Meg Pringle: Without you I would not have had the strength to overcome my anxiety and find my love of horses again. Thank you for your patience, support, and friendship.

My friends: Marla Morris, thank you for your encouragement. Mike Siegal, thank you for your unceasing support and for bringing my story to the attention of my publisher. Nicole Walker, you are a source of undying inspiration, vitality, and strength. My recovery would not have been possible without you and your friendship.

My teachers: George and Judy Tenney, I found safety, solace, and unequivocal support at your school. You prepared me for college, yet more than anything, you prepared me for life. Denise Siegal, first my teacher and now a dear friend as well, your impact on my life is too immense for words to describe. Krista George, you helped open up the world of words that I hold so dear. I will forever be grateful to all of you.

My doctors: Dr. Don Shaffer, thank you for your loving care. You were always there when my family and I needed you. Dr. George Glass, thank you for always listening. I owe a good deal of my success to you. Dr. Amy Middleman, you are one of the primary reasons I am here today. Without you, my recovery would not have been possible. Dr. Michael Winters, I will forever be grateful for your support and care. Dr. Elizabeth Dybell, you are a mentor and a dear friend as well. I will be forever grateful for your support and guidance.

My wonderful professors at the University of St. Thomas: I have found a home at UST, and that is largely due to your support and encouragement. Special thanks to Drs. Elizabeth Maynard, Terry Hall, John Hittinger, Maia Larios-Sanz, Rosie Rosell, and Jo Meier-Marquis.

Everyone at Newman Communications and at HCI Books: Thank you for helping me to share my story with so many who might benefit from it. Special thanks to my editor, Candace Johnson, for her guidance, support, and expertise.

ABOUT THE AUTHOR

Melissa Binstock is an honors student and a junior at the University of St. Thomas in Houston, Texas, where she majors in psychology with a double minor in English and theology.

In her youth Melissa was diagnosed with obsessive-compulsive disorder (OCD), Tourette syndrome, attention deficit/hyperactivity disorder (ADHD), anorexia nervosa, generalized anxiety disorder, dyslexia, and a learning disorder not otherwise specified (working memory). Her desire to make sense of the chaos in her mind led her to search for books by others who shared her disorders, but she found none; her desire to offer hope and understanding to fellow sufferers led her write about her own experiences.

Melissa was honored for her work in the mental health field by Mental Health America of Greater Houston as a recipient of their 2010 Mental Health Makes a Difference Award, and was the keynote speaker at the 2010 Tourette Syndrome Foundation's annual gala. She has been profiled in multiple media including the *Houston Chronicle* and the *Dan Patrick Show*. In 2005, Melissa was awarded the Gold Key Award by the Alliance for Young Artists and Writers for excerpts of *Nourishment*.

Melissa plans to attend graduate school to obtain a doctorate in clinical psychology with a special focus on Tourette syndrome, learning disabilities, and eating disorder prevention. Learn more at www.nourishmentthebook.com.